SPEAK
AND GROW
Rich

Dottie Walters • Lilly Walters

PRENTICE HALL
Paramus, New Jersey 07652

Library of Congress Cataloging in Publication Data

Walters, Dottie.
   Speak and grow rich / Dottie and Lilly Walters.—[2nd, rev. and
expanded ed.]
     p. cm.
   Includes index.
   ISBN 0-13-490400-1
   1. Public speaking—Handbooks, manuals, etc. 2. Oral
communication—Handbooks, manuals, etc. I. Walters, Lillet.
II. Title.
PN4098.W35   1997
808.5'1—dc21   97-21559
                                             CIP

Printed in the United States of America

10 9 8 7 6 5 4 3

ISBN 0-13-490400-1

ATTENTION: CORPORATIONS AND SCHOOLS

Prentice Hall books are available at quantity discounts with bulk purchase for educational, business, or sales promotional use. For information, please write to:
Prentice Hall Special Sales, 240 Frisch Court, Paramus, New Jersey 07652. Please
supply: title of book, ISBN, quantity, how the book will be used, date needed.

PRENTICE HALL
Paramus, NJ 07652

On the World Wide Web at http://www.phdirect.com

PRENTICE-HALL INTERNATIONAL (UK) LIMITED, LONDON
PRENTICE-HALL OF AUSTRALIA PTY. LIMITED, SYDNEY
PRENTICE-HALL CANADA INC., TORONTO
PRENTICE-HALL HISPANOAMERICANA, S.A., MEXICO
PRENTICE-HALL OF INDIA PRIVATE LIMITED, NEW DELHI
PRENTICE-HALL OF JAPAN, INC., TOKYO
PEARSON EDUCATION ASIA PTE. LTD., SINGAPORE
EDITORA PRENTICE-HALL DO BRASIL, LTDA., RIO DE JANEIRO

Dedicated to:

"Cowboy" Bob Walters, the best father and husband God ever created.

The one we have 'grown rich' for, and who makes it all possible.

Acknowledgments

Some very good friends took our many pages of manuscript and trudged their way through with suggestions and insights! Thank you: Rick Butts, Dr. Joe K. Clema, Patrick D'Acre, Jeff Dewar, J. Greg Gimba, Daniel Janal, Deborah Lilly, Scott McKain, Tom Marcoux, Leonard Laskowski, and Carlos Rangel.

Foreword
by Earl Nightingale

Dottie Walters just doesn't quit. She has never quit, even back in the early days when she was pushing a baby stroller with two babies in it, cardboard in her shoes, extra cardboard in her purse for replacements. Dottie was determined to earn the money to make her house payment by selling advertising in her shopper's column. One of the stroller wheels kept coming off. Dottie would watch the wheel and when it was in danger of slipping off the axle, she'd kick it back on again, but she didn't slow down, and I hope to God she never does. We need her.

This is a first-class book for budding speakers. It is also a first-class book for professional speakers who want to know more about the industry, and want to see if they're on track when it comes to fees and such.

A speaker is a strange creature. Kipling told the story of a band of primitive Stone Age men huddled around a campfire. They had engaged in a tremendous battle that day with a woolly mammoth or a sabre-toothed tiger, or perhaps both. Suddenly, one of their number leaped to his feet and began walking up and down, gesticulating and talking, making sounds so graphic everyone around the campfire "saw" the battle all over again. He told them the story of what they had done, and they were filled with awe and frightened all over again, for there was magic in his words. So they took him away and killed him.

Today they would have paid him a fee.

I recall flying home one night after a speech. It was late, I was tired, and it was a long flight. The woman sitting next to me suddenly asked, "Do you mind if I ask you what you do?"

"Not at all," I replied, smiling. "I'm a postprandial ululator," I said.

Her eyes widened. "You don't say!" she exclaimed "My! That must be very interesting."

"Yes, it is."

It ended the conversation, and I could imagine her telling the members of her family about sitting on the airplane next to "one of those postprandial ululators!" I could hear the gasps.

Postprandial means after a meal. An ululator, since the word comes from the howling of monkeys, is one who howls. The words simply came to me at the moment and I couldn't resist. But I was wrong when I told the woman that was what I did. I'm a writer/broadcaster who is regularly sought out as a speaker. Last Saturday I was in Boston. In a week or so, I'll be in Winston-Salem, then Texas, then Chicago. In about a month I'll be speaking in Munich; last October it was a speaking tour of Australia's principal cities; before that, Guam and Hawaii.

Yes, a speaker does some traveling. A speaker does a lot of waking up in motels with a view of the parking lot, eating restaurant food, and putting up with airlines' plastic lunches and late arrivals.

But most of the time, I do what I'm doing now—sitting at my computer making little marks on the screen, because writing's my work. A speaker, in my opinion, should have real, honest-to-God work in the world in addition to speaking. Dottie Walters calls this being a "real person" who speaks from personal experience.

Now a trainer is something else. That's his or her business. Trainers are experts at training people to be better at what they do, and because they're so good at it, they're asked back to the same companies and organizations again and again, year after year. They earn large incomes and deserve every dollar they earn. It's hard, demanding, cerebral work. After a couple of hours in front of several hundred people, they're as tired as they would be after working for eight hours with a pick and shovel. They're good at what they do, they meet an important need, and they work hard. They are also an important aspect of this book.

A speaker is asked to speak because of something he or she does surpassingly well. As Lee Iacocca is asked to speak on management, Dottie Walters is asked to speak on what she does. She has that special talent of putting her thoughts into words so that the words go out and move people. She is an expert with words, and if you have the urge to be a postprandial ululator, you will need to be an expert with words, too. You'll need to know everything that's in this marvelous, delightful book. This book is as important to a budding speaker as *Chapman's Small Boat Handling* is to the new small boat owner. It's very, very important. For in addition to being a world-class expert at what she does, Dottie Walters is a kind, loving, helpful person who has never for a moment lost her human touch.

By all means read *Speak and Grow Rich* by Dottie and her daughter, Lilly Walters. You'll get to know these remarkable women in the process. They are in every paragraph, and the love comes shining through, clear, and bright. I cannot recommend this book too highly. I hope it sells a million copies every year.

Earl Nightingale has been inducted into the International Speaker's Hall of Fame and the Radio Hall of Fame. He holds the Napoleon Hill Foundation Gold Medal Award for Literary Excellence. He and his late partner, Lloyd Conant, pioneered the audio-publishing industry, forming the Nightingale-Conant Corp. of Chicago. Earl's famous "The Strangest Secret" has exceeded sales of a million copies and has earned him the only gold record ever achieved for speaking. His "Our Changing World" radio show was currently carried in all 50 states, Mexico, Canada, a dozen countries overseas, and on Armed Forces Radio Network. Earl wrote the foreword for Dottie Walters' first book, *Never Underestimate the Selling Power of a Woman,* published by Prentice Hall.

Introduction from Dottie

As much as any other business, professional speaking takes drive, vision, imagination, determination, inspiration, and hard work. In addition, as the actress Rosalind Russell once said, "If you have a little talent, that's nice."

Speak and Grow Rich shows you how to achieve success in the lucrative world of professional speaking, writing, creating products, consulting, and selling the ancillary rights to your special knowledge over and over again.

Our book highlights and reveals top speakers' techniques, shortcuts, and methods to jump-start your speaking career and keep it moving steadily upward. We show you how, step-by-step. We draw upon our own extensive experience in the professional speaking business to give you clear road maps that can help you see the myriad routes to your golden destination. We'll show you how to become an expert in a topic that will open the door to highly paid bookings. We tell you how to identify your markets and set fees for your work, and we show you how to offer a smorgasbord of services so that your clients will buy several of them at one time.

Being a professional speaker will lead you in many different and exciting directions. As the world of professional speaking expands at a rapid rate, opportunities for all kinds of speaking, training, teaching, writing, and related products are accelerating. Because Lilly and I are professional speakers, authors, and consultants and run a large international speakers' bureau, we speak from personal experience.

Speak and Grow Rich is your handbook for the forms you will need, as well as tips on how to work with many speakers' bureaus, book yourself, negotiate contracts, work smoothly with meeting planners, create your own five-figure seminars, and design products that will double—even triple—your income while they instruct, inform, and inspire your audiences. We reveal secrets of publicity, promotion, and advertising, so that you can become the impresario of your own speaking, writing, and consulting career.

Most important of all is the rich reward you will receive from your audiences. People will write, call, and visit you from around the world, and say you have changed their lives, inspired them and helped them. In our speakers' bureau, we know thousands of successful speakers. Many share this thought: "I love the business so much, I will never retire. I would do this even if I were not paid a cent." This book shows you how to enter this marvelous, exciting world and be paid more money than you have ever dreamed possible. You will *Speak and Grow Rich*.

Introduction from Lilly

Will you *Speak and Grow Rich*? Those who grow rich in this industry have one factor in common: They first *enrich* the lives of their audience. All of the tips, strategies, facts, and figures we will share with you here will not help you to "grow rich" if your focus is not first on bringing enrichment to your audience.

We are thrilled and flattered that our first edition of *Speak and Grow Rich* is today considered the handbook of the professional speaking business. It was a best seller, and continues to do well. But it came out in 1988. The most advanced technological thing we said (more or less) was, "Gosh, you really need a fax machine!"

As a marketing resource tool for speakers, consultants, and business experts, we recognize your need for information on how to use the World Wide Web, fax-on-demand, E-mail, videoconferencing, mailbot, virtual seminars, E-mail newsletters, and much more in your speaker business. The challenge was that we didn't want to tell you, "Go get a website . . ." if we hadn't walked the walk on the old cyber-highway ourselves. So, we created a website, used fax broadcasting, used fax campaigning from our own office, and interviewed literally hundreds and hundreds of speakers to gather their results in using the same tools.

Added to this second edition are the results of exclusive surveys of over 1500 professional speakers, seminar leaders, and trainers on a variety of topics.

You will find the results from these survey questions throughout this book. We wish you the passion, compassion, and purpose you will need to enrich others and grow rich.

Endorsements

Standing Ovations

". . . my first full year as a paid speaker during which I made a whopping $40,000. Keep in mind that I left a corporate job making $120,000 plus a company car, plus expenses. In *Speak and Grow Rich* you made mention that public speakers make in excess of $225,000 per year and I remember thinking to myself 'Yeah, right.' . . . My wife in all of her infinite wisdom said, 'Why don't you do exactly what the book suggests?' I did. In 1995 my gross bookings were in excess of $700,000."—**Tony Parinello,** author and speaker.

"As we move into the next millennium, Dottie and Lilly are there to navigate us through the maze of new technology that will affect us all—from marketing on the Web to virtual seminars. Their role is to make our journey easier, more enjoyable, and always more profitable as they invite us to share their insights and combined experience and propel us to even greater heights as we do what we do best—speak from our lips with the messages bursting forth from our souls."—**Les Brown,** CPAE, author of *Live Your Dreams* and *It's Not Over Until You Win,* radio talk show host, and president of Les Brown Enterprises.

"*Speak and Grow Rich* contains the crown jewels for professional speaking. The value of the information inside cannot be calculated. I hope that none of my rivals in the UK *ever* gets to see a copy!"—**Graham Davies,** British humorist.

"Dottie and Lilly Walters have done it again! They are masters of the game (business) of Professional Speaking. This is the road map to success that every beginning and veteran speaker is looking for. Own this book, and shorten your learning curve by five years."—**Bob Burg,** Author of *ENDLESS REFERRALS: Network Your Everyday Contacts into Sales* (McGraw-Hill).

"As a professional speaker for 25 years I still see this book as an 'absolute must' for the beginning, developing, or master speaker."—**Naomi Rhode**, Past President National Speakers Association.

"As a professional speaker who has spoken in all 50 states and major world capitols, I have observed speakers and bureaus worldwide. Dottie and Lilly Walters know 'where it's at' in the business of professional speaking. They are truly in touch with the industry."—**Somers White,** CPAE, Former Arizona State Senator.

"Dottie and Lilly are tigers! What a wonderful book. Filled with the real, honest information and wisdom of all their years in the professional speaking business. Well done, good friends!" **John Hammond,** Past President, National Speakers' Association.

"Dottie and Lilly Walters have shared ideas that have polished many a speaker's mind. Their nurturing, knowledgeable counsel has been the catalyst for a remarkable number of successful professional speaking careers."—**Rudy R. Wright,** CMP; Past President, Meeting Professionals International. (MPI)

"Dottie Walters has been one of the most valuable people in America in helping speakers to learn the 'ropes' of the business of speaking. Her newsmagazine, *Sharing Ideas,* seminars, and consultations have helped thousands of speakers to find direction. I commend Lilly and Dottie Walters."—**Mike Frank,** Past President, National Speakers Association; Speakers Unlimited Bureau.

"Lilly and Dottie, I only wish I had read this book 30 years ago. I would be a billionaire now."—**Irwin Zucker,** Founder, Southern California Book Publicists Association.

"The lecture industry existed for 100 years with many factions and infighting. Then Dottie had the dream of an Association of Speakers' Bureaus. Her dream became the reality of IGAB. She pulled the industry together, overcame 100 years of dissent, and started a new era of cooperation."—**Ed Larkin,** President, International Group of Agents and Bureaus; Speakers' Guild Speakers' Bureau.

"This book is a great help to both beginners and full-timers in the speaking business. Dottie and Lilly have written about many subjects that need to be addressed. It will help everyone in or thinking about professional, paid speaking. This book should be on every speaker's desk."—**John Palmer,** First President, International Group of Agents and Bureaus; National Speakers' Bureau Inc.

"By using this book you can learn to speak and not only you but your audience can grow rich."—**W. Mitchell,** CPAE, host of TV's "Finding Common Ground," speaker, and author of *It's Not What Happens to You, It's What You Do About It.*

"Dottie and Lilly Walters bring a true and unique voice to our professional speaking arena. From the enviable perspective of their own first-hand experience as polished professional speakers, they have clearly demonstrated how to 'walk the talk.' Whether you're the newest novice or the seasoned star of professional speaking, you'll grow rich in a variety of ways. Here's your chance to really learn from two of the 'pros' in our business."—**Edward Scannell,** CMP, CSP, author of the *Games Trainers Play* book series.

"Each night before I fall asleep and every morning when I awake, I spend time with two books: the Bible and *Speak and Grow Rich.* My copy is dog-eared, highlighted, underlined, and filled with notes. It is because of your book of instructions, support, and valuable information, that in one very short year, I am a recognized national professional speaker."—**Pegine Echevarria,** international expert on family issues, MSW, former Directory of Family Dynamics.

"I have addressed more than a million people in 21 countries and I have studied the business of professional speaking in great depth. I can therefore say that this is the finest book ever written on the subject. I recommend it to every single person who has any interest whatever in speaking for fun or profit."—**Brian Tracy,** author and professional speaker.

"I love this book! *Speak and Grow Rich* will cut ten years from your professional speaking learning curve. I love the authors, Dottie and Lilly Walters. We are proud to feature their stories in our

Chicken Soup for the Soul books."—**Jack Canfield,** coauthor, *Chicken Soup for the Soul* series

"Like many other Aussie speakers I have benefited enormously from your book, *Speak and Grow Rich*. Your expertise, your own speaking skills and your willingness to share ideas are greatly appreciated by us all 'down under.' Good luck, good life, good fun . . . and tons more success."—**Max Hitchins,** Australian President, National Speakers Association.

"*Speak and Grow Rich* is a great blueprint for anyone looking for success in this exciting business. Read it! I give it a 10!"—**Peter Vidmar,** Olympic Gold Medalist in Gymnastics.

"*Speak and Grow Rich* is a must read for anyone who seriously wants to be a professional speaker. Had this book been available to me 20 years ago when I started, I'd be twice as far along."—**Mark Victor Hansen,** coauthor, *Chicken Soup for the Soul* series.

"*Speak and Grow Rich* is must reading for anyone who works as a professional speaker or is considering a career in speaking. I keep a copy on my bookshelf for ready reference because it is the best book on the business of professional speaking that I have ever read."—**Michale LeBoeuf.**

"The best guide available on how to build your business by speaking."—**Paul and Sarah Edwards,** authors of *Working from Home*.

"The speaking field is growing unbelievably. So is the sage advice on the subject by Lilly and Dottie."—**Art Linkletter.**

"This book is a treasure. Those who follow its teachings will find the pot of gold."—**Gerald C. Meyers,** former chairman of the board of American Motors.

"Very seldom do you read a book that truly delivers what the title promises. *Speak and Grow Rich* is one such book. The ideas in this book were the foundation for helping me to build my speaking business. I can say without hesitation that Dottie and Lilly Walters have made me a lot of money! Read this book and they'll do the same for you."—**Jeff Slutsky,** CSP, Street Fighter Marketing.

"When seeking information on becoming a professional speaker, there are no universities to go to or degrees to earn. Most of us have done it by trial and error, over a long period of time. However, in *Speak and Grow Rich,* Lilly and Dottie Walters offer an education available nowhere else. Not only do they present the skills needed, but the business savvy as well. Through their tutoring you truly can *Speak and Grow Rich!*"—**Florence Littauer,** CSP, CPAE.

"Whether you want to be a pro, promote a cause or product that needs exposure, or are just a business executive that needs to know more about how to utilize the speakers' platform as a communication tool, reading *Speak and Grow Rich* is a must. I have recommended it as a 'must read' to all of my members and as a coach of speakers and consultants insist that anyone who is serious read Dottie and Lilly Walters' *Speak and Grow Rich.*"—**Bernard Hale Zick,** CEO, International Society of Speakers, Authors and Consultants; Author of *The Negotiating Paradox.*

"Who knows more about growing a seven-figure speaking business than the Walters family? This is the Bible for speakers and future ones as well!"—**Danielle Kennedy.**

Contents

Welcome to the World of Professional Speaking

"Being on the rope is everything. All else is waiting to perform."

—*Karl Wallenda,*
circus tightrope performer

Professional speakers feel the same way about the thrilling business of appearing before audiences and delivering useful information in an entertaining and beneficial way. Being before the audience—speaking—is everything. All else is waiting (and preparing!) to speak.

You, too, can follow this powerful calling. You can educate, inspire, and lead people to take action and make important changes in their lives. By becoming a professional speaker, you can prosper at levels you may never have dreamed were possible in your life. Based on your own ever-growing body of knowledge you can also write books, create other useful products, become a professional consultant, and add many more valuable "accessories" to your speaking career. If you have the drive and the dream and can follow our plan, you literally can *Speak and Grow Rich*.

Speaking—speaking *well*—is like a great dance involving your audiences, your customers and the great minds of all the ages. You coordinate the many intricate steps of this dance: the gathering of knowledge, the marketing, learning to better touch hearts and minds. As you take each step, *Speak and Grow Rich* will act as your instruction manual, your source of information, and your inspiration.

1

At first you will struggle to hear the music that is meant for you. Soon, you will discover your market and your strengths; then you will enter the dance with confidence!

Who Called to Your Heart from the Platform?

Many professional speakers say that they were inspired to begin their careers while they sat in an audience, watching and listening to a great performer. Speakers influence, encourage, motivate, and communicate with the spirit. If your heart has been filled with longing to become a speaker as you listened to a wonderful performance, you have felt that mighty call. Suddenly, you are certain.

"I can speak like that!" you tell yourself. "Someday, I will be up on that platform. I will touch every heart in the auditorium."

Every speaker we have known tells a similar story of hearing this call.

So, who was it for you? Was it Tony Robbins, Brian Tracy, Jack Canfield, Mark Victor Hansen, Lady Margaret Thatcher, John Gray? Or perhaps you heard the gruff and practical Red Motley of *Parade Magazine,* or leaped to your feet in a standing ovation for Dr. Norman Vincent Peale, Jim Rohn, Les Brown, Barbara de Angeles, Zig Ziglar, Earl Nightingale, Rev. Robert Schuller, Mother Teresa, or Bill Gove. The speaker who inspires you becomes your own personal hero, a source of lifelong inspiration. It has always been so. Every generation has its William Jennings Bryans, Jack Kennedys, and Winston Churchills.

Perhaps you were in one of Dottie or Lilly Walters' audiences when you felt the call. We hope so.

The Call: "You are the one I came for."

Kenneth McFarland, famous former spokesperson for General Motors, told us a story about his mother. She saved her money for two years to purchase a Victrola and a record of William Jennings Bryan's famous "Cross of Gold" speech. Little Ken listened to that record over and over again. Then, one day, the orator, William Jennings Bryan himself, arrived in their town. Ken ran down to the railroad station in his "summer ensemble"—overalls and bare feet—to meet the great man in person. Bryan touched the little boy's shoulder. "What will you be when you grow up?" he asked. "I want to speak like you!" young Ken answered, confident in his vision of his own future.

Lilly Walters, as you can imagine, heard the call through years of hearing and watching Dottie inspire audiences. For Dottie Walters the call came when she heard Bruce Barton speak at an Advertising Association meeting. "I was twenty-one, just starting in the advertising business," she recalls. "It was the first big meeting I ever attended. I remember thinking as he spoke that I really could handle the advertising business I was struggling so hard to build. I had the talent. I had the power. Mr. Barton confirmed my ability.

"I was so enthralled with his message that I stayed after his speech and waited until everyone else had left the room. Then I went up to him, wanting to tell him how his message had helped me. I shook his hand and said, 'Everyone else came today to listen. But I heard you in my heart.' Bruce Barton put his other hand over mine and said, 'You are the one I came for.'"

After every great speech you will see a number of audience members pressing around the speaker. People with teary eyes come up to speakers to say, "You have changed my life," or "After hearing you the last time, your message turned my life around."

Who of those looking at you after a presentation are "the ones?" Who is ready to hear? Who will be so inspired that one day they too will use their words and expertise to change lives?

The Nine Skills of Successful Professional Speakers

When you sit in an audience and watch and listen to a star keynote speaker, or take part in a fact-filled, smoothly flowing seminar presented by a professional, the business of speaking looks easy, like a circus trapeze artist performing flawlessly.

The trapeze artist, however, has spent many months outside of the public eye, practicing and perfecting daring flights above a safety net. Before they can succeed, professional speakers must also perfect their speaking skills. Great speakers constantly work on ways to improve their performances. Speakers like Harvey Mackay, a very successful celebrity business speaker, hire speech and drama coaches so they can continue to hone their skills. They never stop learning or creating new products.

But there are several other skills that are just as important as speaking skills. *Professional* speakers must perfect all nine of these skills—*if they wish to be paid for their craft*!

As you go through the list, compare your own background and knowledge against the requirements for each skill. This process will enable you to see where you stand now and which of the skills must be strengthened to support your career. Our book will show you the steps you must take to master all nine skills. Study them; you will see these principles used throughout this book.

Please note that we put "a greater speaker" last. Without the other skills, it will not matter how well you speak. You may be the most brilliant speaker in the world, but if you don't sell the program, you will never be a paid speaker! If you don't become a business person with great service, you won't get asked back a second time!

As you progress in setting up these nine pillars, you will continually keep working on them, shoring them up and making them stronger, throughout your professional speaking career. The business of gathering and trying new material, learning, improving, rehearsing, and marketing never stops.

The Booming World Market for Speakers

Videoconferencing, business television seminars, video training sessions, "virtual" on-line classes: Every day technology seems to find a new way to keep us talkin' to each other electronically, rather than in "face time." We look at these wonders and can't help but ponder, "Will there be a need for speakers in the future? Real-time speakers in front of a live, real-time audience? Will computers eventually put speakers out of business?"

There are two strong reasons why technology will never drive speakers to the sidelines. **One:** Speakers learn to use the latest technology to reach audiences in new ways. People need to learn more, yet they have less time available in which to learn it. As they turn to the new technologies, *so will you* simply learn the steps needed to be one of those speaking **on** the information highway, with these new tools.

Figure 1:1. The Nine Essential Skills of the Successful Professional Speaker

Speaker must be . . .	How?	Why?
1 . . . **a passionate expert on a topic.**	List the business subjects you know and approach with enthusiasm. You must develop expertise in your chosen topic and constantly keep working to improve your knowledge to stay on. (See Chapter 5: Become the Expert and Leading Authority.)	People are willing to pay to hear experts. Passion will drive you to become that expert and it also will give you enthusiasm and zest on stage that compel. Brilliant speakers do not say, "I could speak on 100 topics," or even worse "I can speak on anything." Our speakers bureau has never had a meeting planner ask us to find a speaker who speaks on "anything."
2 . . . **compassionate toward the audience.**	Love the audience you speak to. Research will show you the aspects of each audience for which you will be able to feel empathy. Speak to several members of your audience before the presentation; then you will hold a conversation, not give a "talk." (See *Secrets of Successful Speakers - How You Can Motivate, Captivate and Persuade* by Lilly Walters, McGraw-Hill, 1993)	Cavett Robert, founder of the National Speakers Association (NSA), says, "They don't care how much you know, until they know how much you care."

Figure 1:1. (continued)

Speaker must be . . .	How?	Why?
3 . . . a target-specific marketer.	From the topics you are passionate about, ask yourself, which of these subjects will audiences pay to learn more about? Find the appropriate and specific market. (See Chapter 3: Targeting Marketable Topics and Titles.)	Audiences believe that a "jack of all trades is a master at none." They want experts who can offer practical solutions to their specific problems.
4 . . . able to customize the topic to a particular audience within the market.	Carefully research the problems of this specific audience. Hold personal interviews with former and current attendees before the presentation. (See *Secrets of Successful Speakers - How You Can Motivate, Captivate and Persuade* by Lilly Walters, McGraw-Hill, 1993)	Even an expert on a specific topic and a specific market can use that extra magic touch—knowing and understanding the actual group in front of them. Customization can often be an extra fee item and can be lucrative.
5 . . . a creator of marketing tools.	Create presentation folders, content one-sheets, demo tapes (audio or video), business cards and letterhead. (See Chapter 7: Marketing Tools for the Speaking Trade.)	A professional must have these tools. Without them, it will be almost impossible to book you.

6 . . . a salesperson.

You must learn to sell yourself and your products to buyers and speakers' bureaus. Follow the ideas and suggestions in this book, a compilation of many successful speakers' great ideas, to give full measure and value-packed deals to clients. (See Chapter 4: From Free to Shining Fee.)

"Nothing happens until somebody sells something." If you wait for someone else to sell you, you may never be bought!

7 . . . a serviceperson.

Cultivate a "you" (not "me") attitude. Make everything you produce serve your clients' needs, wants, and potential problem situations. Make it easy for them to buy you.

Sales skill gets them the first time, service brings them back. The market is very competitive, there are thousands of brilliant professionals out there working to attract the same buyers you are. Often the victor is simply the one who offers ease and pleasure in the purchase.

8 . . . a businessperson.

Follow up all booking leads and sales in an immediate, businesslike, concerned, friendly, and consistent manner. Let professionalism surround everything concerned with you: your letterhead, the people who answer your phone, etc. (See Chapter 7: Marketing Tools for the Speaking Trade.)

There is nothing that turns a buyer off faster than not being able to reach the speaker. Time is of great importance.

Figure 1:1. (continued)

Speaker must be . . .	How?	Why?
9 . . . a great speaker.	Practice, practice, practice. Then constantly strive to be even better by improving delivery, content, and knowledge. Speak with a sincere, eloquent speaking style. As you speak, keep your eyes on the audience, talk to them as if they were one person. Tape yourself speaking, and listen carefully. Always practice out loud. (For more tips, see *Secrets of Successful Speakers—How You Can Motivate, Captivate and Persuade* by Lilly Walters, McGraw-Hill, 1993.)	Pope Pius II said, "A mighty thing is eloquence . . . nothing so much rules the world." Benjamin Disraeli said, "Eloquence is the child of knowledge."

Technology is affecting everything we do, and association meetings are not immune. Members are demanding more opportunities for distance learning—through CD-ROM, on-line, video, and audio conferencing. Does this suggest a downturn in face-to-face meetings? We don't think so.

In fact, in a recent trend analysis survey, 41% of our members reported that they expect to hold more meetings in 1996, and 47% said they will hold about the same number.

But we are looking for more sophisticated use of technology connected to those meetings—members want to register on-line, exhibitors want modem hookups and cellular phone service, members want their training time to be available "on-demand," and more.

—Elissa Matulis Myers, CAE, Publisher,
Vice President, American Society of Association Executives

Two: Humans need the magic of sharing laughter and tears face-to-face to create *esprit de corps*. There will always be a need for real-time speakers, with a real-time audience. No movie or television program can compare with hearing and seeing a speaker in person. As more interaction is done electronically, we feel the need for great speakers will increase and they will be at an even greater premium than they are today.

Even in this age of instant electronic communication, the world loves speakers. Perhaps it is because the speaker's human spirit is magnified on the stage and because most members of an audience fantasize about mesmerizing people with their own words, thoughts, and ideas. In addition, audiences often want to ask questions, shake hands, and have pictures taken with the speaker face-to-face.

Today's market for professional speakers is a thriving, expanding, international business. Convention centers, conference facilities, hotels, and resorts of all kinds are being built from Beijing to Kansas City to Paris. Meeting rooms and auditoriums are booked around the clock to accommodate the burgeoning meeting industry, literally all over the world, on ships at sea, and with virtual meeting hookups in most of them. Theaters are being connected with each other so audiences can hear speakers from a distant site.

Meeting expenditures soared from $19.5 billion in 1983 to $27.5 billion in 1995. Corporations held about 797,100 meetings in 1995 and associations, 175,600. The majority of corporate meetings are sales meetings, management meetings, training seminars, and professional/technical meetings[1]—all of which use professional speakers!

When are conventions held? Figure 1:2 provides the answer, according to the 1996 Meetings Market Report, commissioned by *M&C Magazine* (Meetings and Conventions).

Figure 1:2. M&C 1996 Meeting Market Report on When Conventions are Held

17%	October
11%	September
10%	November
9%	May
9%	June
8%	March
7%	August
7%	January
7%	April
7%	July
6%	February
2%	December

We sorted the above list to show you the busiest months for speakers first. As you can see, September to November tend to be busier and December is usually very slow.

Cruise ship companies, which once focused their business only on pleasure passengers, now recognize the popularity and enormity of the meeting business and are going after a greater share of it. Many huge new vessels are under construction with special decks and facilities to accommodate conventions on board.

---

[1]The 1996 Meetings Market Report, commissioned by *M&C Magazine* (Meetings and Conventions), reports on the health of the meetings industry. This report uses responses from over 1,000 corporate and association meeting planners.

Conventions may use as many as one hundred paid, professional speakers during three to four days of sessions. For example, there may be meal-function speakers, whose programs are humorous and entertaining. Then there are the keynoters, who are inspirational headliners. A convention may also have speakers known as "grand-opening mixers," who help attendees get acquainted, plus health and exercise session leaders, speakers for children's programs, speakers for workshops and seminars in which expert techniques are taught (often for career credits), plus summarizers and specialists of other kinds. A myriad of speakers, all experts in their various fields, fill the slots at conventions, retreats, and many other types of meetings.

Colleges present star speakers in their auditoriums and offer long lists of seminars through their continuing education divisions. Many colleges and universities also have conference facilities that can be rented by business users. Churches, hospitals, Chambers of Commerce, and art galleries are other sources of seminars and programs that require professional speakers.

The local meeting business is also booming. Banquets, training sessions, and special-interest groups of all kinds are housed in local conference centers, hotels, and restaurants. The Kiwanis, Soroptimists, Rotary Club, Chambers of Commerce, and many other service clubs meet as often as once a week for regular meetings, and also hold large annual banquets and training sessions.

Seminar companies and independent seminar producers are constantly on the move, bringing new seminars into the major cities of the world. There are also private business colleges that hold special programs in hotels and other meeting places. The number of these private learning places is increasing rapidly.

A growing trend today is for companies such as banks and hospitals to hold seminars for their customers and prospects. They hire speakers to present these programs in order to attract new business. We see many companies such as office supply firms holding seminars and programs in their stores to attract those who plan to start a business, or who already operate one. Usually, the store hires the speakers, advertises the programs, and gains business. Paul and Sarah Edward, authors of *Working from Home,* have spoken across the nation for Sears and many other large companies.

AT&T does seminars via telephone! They hire speakers to present, from a telephone, to the attendees who are in their offices listening on their own phones!

The Internet has opened up another whole realm of possibilities. Presenters at home, E-mail class instruction to their students. The students E-mail back their work. Sometimes students gather together for a live interactive "chat" through the Internet. Just amazing!

We will talk about all these areas and how you can best profit from them as we progress through this book. (See more on all the ways speakers earn income in Chapter 2: Sources of Income for Professional Speakers.)

Time and Money: How Much Should You Invest in Your Professional Speaking Career?

At our *Speak and Grow Rich* seminars, this is a frequent question: "How much time and money should a novice invest to begin a professional speaking business?"

The answer is to invest a *little* money and an *enormous* amount of your own burning desire, determination, and enthusiasm on a *consistent* basis. These three characteristics are far more important than cash and cannot be purchased from anyone else. Our passionate purpose in this book is to show you how to begin, step by step, so that you can purchase the materials that cost money as you earn, and thus constantly improve on a pay-as-you-go basis. Most speakers start their careers as a part-time operation. You will develop your materials, marketing, and expertise as you progress.

We advise you to invest in yourself by taking as many speaking classes, seminars, and coaching sessions as you can. If you do not have the money for these, you might offer to help a speaker with back-of-the-room product sales or do office work in trade for the training you need. If you can work in the office of a successful speaker or speakers' bureau, you can learn a great deal about the business in a short time.

Purchase books, cassettes, and video albums, and tickets to hear the best speakers you can find. Use a notebook. Watch and listen as a great football coach would watch a game. Ask yourself, "What is this speaker doing right? How would I improve on what this speaker is doing?" Ask the personal coach in your own head how you could do it better. Concentrate on it.

As Sir Isaac Newton said in his old age, "I have stood on the shores of time picking up a beautiful seashell here and there, while all before me lies the great sea of life, undiscovered." Never stop learning. Never stop getting better or thinking of ways to give more to your audiences.

The Path Will Not Always Be Easy

So many of the very best speakers have had tough times. Six-foot-seven Tony Robbins slept in his Volkswagen when he began his tiny business; today his seminar events bring in millions of dollars! Brian Tracy was homeless at one time; today his expertise is sought in books, speeches, and audio programs around the world. Young Mark Victor Hansen slept on the floor of his tiny first office because he could not afford an apartment. Today Mark is not only a brilliant motivational speaker, but his extraordinary book series, *Chicken Soup for the Soul* (coauthored with Jack Canfield) has made history by holding the #1, #2, and #3 spots on *The New York Times* Best Seller List *at the same time!* Many speakers began their seminars in their own living rooms, such as Jean Nidetch, who created Weight Watchers, and Barbara DeAngelis, the famous author, speaker, and TV personality.

Our ultimate goal in *Speak and Grow Rich* is to give your speaking career a head start if you are a beginner, and a quantum leap upward if you yearn to move higher in the world of paid, professional speaking.

Sources of Income for Professional Speakers

Professional speaking is like a mansion with many rooms. You will find room after room of opportunities opening before you as you explore products, consulting, and many other "accessories" discussed in this book. You are not limited to the spoken word on the platform, but only by the value of the ideas, information, and inspiration you offer.

There are many avenues of opportunity available from which speakers can earn income through their expertise.

- Speeches
- Entertainment
- Panels
- Master of Ceremonies
- Infomercial host
- Commercials
- Spokesperson
- Expert Witness
- Consulting, Coaching, Troubleshooting, and Professional Advice
- Writing Educational Articles
- Training, In-House Seminars, and Workshops
- Moderator/Facilitator

- Seminars to Promote a Client
- Public Seminars
- Virtual Seminars
- Speaker Products

By including all of the areas in which you are available to participate on your Fee Schedule/Menu of Services, you are able to gently remind the people organizing meetings that these concepts can add value to their event. The planners also benefit because they pay for only one sleeping room and one plane fare, which makes them much happier. You add additional income sources to your contract, which of course makes you happy!

Later in this chapter we will take the above list and go over each entry in more detail. Several items on the list are self-explanatory, like Master of Ceremonies, and we have only included a brief paragraph. Others, like public seminars, virtual lectures, and products are very involved. We have included entire chapters on those later.

When you are booked by a client, all fees are on the contract you submit. The client expects to pay all travel and hotel expenses, either as an additional bill after the event, or as part of the original all-inclusive fee you quote up front. Often additional fees are paid to the presenter for educational materials, consulting, books, audio cassettes, or other educational materials produced by the speaker and purchased in advance by the client for each attendee.

Speeches

Keynotes and General Sessions

At a meeting, some sessions are attended by everyone, in comparison to breakout sessions where the participants break into groups and several meetings go on at the same time. The full assembly may be called the general assembly, plenary session, opening or closing session, or by the name of the meal functions that the general assembly is attending, e.g., luncheon session/program, dinner/banquet session. These general session speeches can be as short as 15 minutes or as long as two hours, but are generally about an hour. Meal programs are usually the shortest time slots, running 20 to 45 minutes.

When most people think of a "speaker," they think of the "keynoter," the person who delivers the main address to the entire gathering. A "keynote" originally meant the fundamental point of a speech. Today the term refers to the main speech at a meeting, or one of the featured spots at an event. The keynote sets the tone and carries out the theme of a meeting. Convention keynote session speakers have the highest visibility of all presenters because they appear before the entire assemblage. Often a celebrity speaker is used to keynote a meeting, someone of renown to this particular audience, for instance, the president of the organization.

Usually, general session speakers are more motivational and entertaining than specialized speakers. But the ones most in demand and able to command the highest fees provide educational value that is specific to challenges facing the audience at hand. An outside keynoter is often paid the highest fee of all the speakers involved in a convention.

Breakout Sessions

Breakout sessions involve splitting the main group of attendees at a convention or meeting into smaller groups. Attendees are divided into several concurrent sessions to hear special material on differing special interest topics. Breakout programs go on throughout the convention. Breakout presentations may be repeated several times in the day to different groups of attendees, so the speaker may present the same workshop four times, stretched out over several days. Alternately, you could present three or four different topics at these breakout sessions.

These programs are actually mini-seminars on specific subjects. Sometimes the attendees receive credit toward a degree or certificate by attending these learning sessions. Seminar and workshop breakout speakers educate as well as entertain. You are paid per performance, plus workbooks or other materials, although many presenters offer a reduced rate for making additional presentations at the same event.

Partner and Youth Programs

Speakers may put on special programs for the significant others, guests, or children of the convention registrants. In 1996, nearly 43 percent of those planning meetings were including some kind of activities for guests, and 13 percent were planning activities for children.[1]

Since women now hold 35 percent of the 12.6 million executive, administrative, and managerial jobs in the U.S., the days of convention programs on "How to Tie Scarves" are long past. At a recent large convention, for example, four buses were reserved to take the spouses on a shopping trip. The spouses, however, refused to leave. The buses stood empty while the spouses crowded in to hear the main luncheon business speaker. Today, if there are sessions for spouses, they are often tagged "Partner Programs" and may feature computer techniques, managerial skills, or other technical information. Programs for the children of attendees are also beginning to gain popularity. Often the same speaker on the main platform will deliver a special program to the spouses or children of the attendees for an additional fee.

Entertainment and Humorists

Within this industry, entertainment refers to a non-message presentation, such as a comedian. A humorist usually has a message of some type. We say usually because there are always exceptions to the rule. Whoopie Goldberg and Robin Williams are comedians, yet they rarely deliver a performance without a message of some type woven in.

Many speakers present serious topics, then list on their fee schedule their ability to also perform a humorous or entertaining program. These programs are ideal for luncheons and banquets.

Panels

Many programs include a panel or two on topics that fit the theme and concerns of the audience. These can occur at conventions, retreats, or any sort of meeting when having experts discuss an issue is valuable. You and other speakers may each be booked to present ten-minute speeches on a panel. Sometimes a Q & A session is offered so that the audience can ask the panelists questions.

---

[1]The 1996 Meetings Market Report, commissioned by *M&C Magazine* (Meetings and Conventions).

Set your fee for being a panel participant at less than what you charge for being a panel moderator.

Master of Ceremonies

A Master of Ceremonies acts as a moderator and connects the separate sessions of a meeting together. An M.C. might also act as the Introducer for the other presenters. This person might also be thought of as the Toastmaster/mistress, and preside at the banquet, announce the toasts, call upon the various speakers, etc. A warm, outgoing personality is usually what is required. Being good at customized fun and humor is a definite selling point.

Infomercial Host

An infomercial might be a lucrative addition to your speaking income, and make you famous as well. Many speakers, such as Anthony Robbins and Barbara DeAngelis, have done very well in the infomercial world. As infomercial host, you are paid a fee or a percentage of sales of the product or service. Sometimes your own book may be part of what is sold on the infomercial. A good example of this is Cherie Calbom who wrote the book *Juicing for Life* and appeared on the "Juice Man" infomercials.

Commercials

Many speakers are featured in commercials for the clients for whom they present programs. Sometimes speakers trade their speaking skills with media in return for commercials for themselves. An example is a sales speaker who trains a radio sales staff in return for radio time in which the speaker sells tickets to his self-produced seminar.

Spokesperson

Companies often look for speakers who can act as spokespersons for their products, services, or public image. The speaker may travel to many areas, present speeches and seminars, and participate in media interviews or personal appearances to promote the sponsoring organization's products, services, or image. If you are an expert in a special field, consider contacting all of the large corporations or organizations in your area that relate to and need your topic. You have seen athletes who are spokespersons for national firms. This same idea is at work when a speaker represents a client, and speaks to the client's customers.

The American Floral Service hires many florists whom they train to speak on a variety of subjects such as floral arrangements, the history and meaning of flowers, appropriate flowers to deliver a certain message, etc. They sponsor these presenters to speak at conventions and meetings of all kinds where AFS clients and potential clients are gathered.

The great Dr. Kenneth McFarland, who was often referred to as the "dean of public speaking," began exactly this way with General Motors. Bill Gove, the first president of the National Speakers Association, represented Minnesota Mining and Manufacturing (3M). Ira Hays began the same way with National Cash Register. Judith Briles is the spokesperson for Clairol products. The Canon Home Copier company hired Paul and Sarah Edwards, speakers and experts in the area of home business, to speak on television across the nation to promote Canon's products. This proved to be a perfect tie-in with their famous series of books on working from home. While the Edwards' promoted the Canon copier, they promoted themselves and their seminars as well. This sort of sponsorship creates winning situations for everyone.

A sponsor company may be interested in using a speaker on a fee-basis, per-head or per-seminar. When you approach a sponsor, keep in mind that only a part of their agenda is to make donations to the community; a larger objective is to receive publicity value back in return.

Expert Witness

There are several good directories of Spokespersons and Expert Witnesses. Check with the reference librarian at the public library. If you are an expert in your field, list yourself in these directories. You will be called to appear on television and radio shows, by the print media for an expert comment on a situation, or even to appear as an expert in court cases. These can all be lucrative and add to your prestige as an expert in your field.

Consulting, Coaching, Troubleshooting, and Professional Advice

Often companies need special help with a problem. They don't want a preestablished training course, but look instead for an expert, a consultant from the outside, to evaluate their problems and offer concrete customized suggestions for improvement. Consulting might mean going out in the field with the client's salespeople or monitoring incoming calls, then preparing a presentation.

Speaker Bob Popyk, for example, does this type of consulting work. He calls hundreds of car dealers by phone, acting the part of a buyer who wants to purchase a new car. The dealers' responses are recorded. His programs for those same dealers use the recorded phone calls as examples of how to, and how not to, handle buyer inquires.

Many speakers have been invited to become members of large client companies' boards of directors, so they can provide continual consulting and professional advice. In this case, part of the payment may be in company stock.

Writing Educational Articles

If you are an expert you can also become in demand as a journalist. Many speakers earn a substantial amount of their total income from the articles they produce for various publications. It is also the best passive market strategy available to you. In the 1996 Walters Speaker Services Exclusive Industry-Wide Survey of Professional Speakers, we asked the question, "What is your best passive marketing tip, that will work without you, while you are working with your clients and do not have time to actively market yourself?" "Exposure through the press and writing articles" was the answer most often cited.

Training, In-House Seminars, and Workshops

Once a company or association has used you as a speaker, you have an excellent opportunity to be hired again for consulting, writing workbooks, or conducting training sessions. Training can be delivered to large groups, or one-on-one. You might actually go out with the sales crew to their customers, or sit in with telephone sales groups inside a company.

The training field is one of the largest areas of opportunity for professional speakers. Training seminars made up the largest number of meetings planned in 1995 by corporations, a total of 216,300.[2] Many companies buy the services of a professional trainer or seminar leader for a few hours a week rather than keep one trainer on staff full-time. Trainers and seminar leaders also develop books and audio and video materials. These may be custom products created for a particular client or generic ones that can be used by any client. Training can be at one location within the client's facility, or at different locations. A training session can be booked for one day, several days, a month, or whatever length of time the client needs. The astute speaker seeking a training booking will ask the potential client well-focused questions about needs, set a consultation time, and then offer a proposal to fill those needs.

The largest organization for trainers is the American Society for Training and Development (ASTD). The society provides excellent opportunities for advancing your training skills.

Moderator/Facilitator

Many presenters are paid to simply moderate discussions. They might have the group do an interactive exercise, then simply listen and direct the conversation after it, or debrief the group. Some moderators are paid to direct problem-solving sessions.

Seminars to Promote a Client

We believe this type of speaking is one of the most exciting of the new opportunities in the speaking world. Retailers such as Price/Costco, Staples, Sears, and Nordstrom advertise and promote seminars for their customers, usually held in their stores. They hire speakers who are experts to present seminars to these customers. Paul and Sara Edwards, who are experts on the topic of working from home, have spoken internationally for their clients. Sometimes

---

[2]The 1996 Meetings Market Report, commissioned by *M&C Magazine* (Meetings and Conventions).

the sponsors are retailers, and sometimes manufacturers of products, such as computer disks.

Often speakers present programs at schools, which are paid for by clients instead of the schools themselves. Providers of sporting goods, shoes, etc. are often sponsoring organizations.

Public Seminars

A public seminar is open to the public, rather than held for a specific group. Tickets are sold to individuals rather than the costs being paid by one overall group. This subject is so lucrative and extensive we have devoted an entire chapter to it. (See Chapter 7: High-Profit Public Seminars.)

Virtual Seminars

The "virtual seminar" is the next wave in speaking industry trends. The Internet, satellites, and computers are changing what a "meeting room" looks like. Often presenters don't go to a meeting room, but to a "virtual" meeting room conducted through mail, phones, and the Internet for a tele- or videoconference. (See Chapter 8: Virtual Seminars: Correspondence School to Net Classrooms.)

Speaker Products

Much of the information you use in your speeches can be sold in standard versions, and also in customized programs which you will create especially for individual companies and associations. You can create videos, audio albums, workbooks, consulting sessions, CD-ROM disks, training materials, reports, calendars, posters, magazine articles, screen savers, software programs, T-shirts, hats, and even toys based on your expertise. These are the valuable ancillary products of the body of knowledge in your speeches. (See Chapter 9: Speaker Products: Triple Your Income.)

Listen to your customers, and hear what they say they want. Many, many years ago, Dottie was told by a furniture store owner who advertised in her Shopper's Column, "I don't want you charging me more than double your regular rate to be the first paragraph in your Shopper's Column each week!" Although he said this in a cross voice, she realized he had just given her a great idea. She had not thought of charging extra for this position until then, nor had she thought of the "each week" idea of continuous contracts. Listen to your customers when they say, "I wish . . ." even when they sound angry or upset about it at the time! There are seeds of new business opportunities everywhere.

By increasing your abilities so that you are able to include many different services on your Fee Schedule and Menu of Services, you:

- Gently remind the person organizing the meeting that these concepts just might add something special to the event
- Help organizers save on expenses
- Add additional income sources to your bill of fare

Targeting Marketable Topics and Titles

To profit from speaking, you must be able to attract paid bookings. To obtain speaking engagements that pay, you must offer attention-grabbing topics that meet a need in a specified marketplace. The steps are:

1. target your market/s;
2. then pick topics that will help solve problems in the market/s;
3. create title/s for your topics that will grab the attention of your audience and buyers immediately.

This chapter focuses on how to do those three things.

Who Is Your Market?

We groan when speakers send us an inquiry and say, "I was wondering if you are interested in a speaker who specializes in the corporate and association markets." Right. Those are not the markets we are talking about. All speaking will fall into those two categories, and a bit into the college market. You need to decide which industries within those broad categories are your market: health care, insurance, plumbers, doctors, contractors, etc., etc., etc.

Who Will Pay? Individuals or Businesses?

Speakers often come to us for help in finding markets for their subjects. Frequently their subjects are similar to these: "How to Predict

Your Love Life through Numerology," or "How to Dress to Attract the Opposite Sex." These presenters ask us to help them obtain bookings within the corporate, or association markets in which our speakers bureau specializes. They have heard that these markets pay the highest fees, which they do.

Imagine for a moment the awards banquet for a large corporation. Now look at the titles above. If our speakers' bureau suggested these titles to the corporate buyer we would be thought either insane or incompetent. No matter how important these topics may seem to the presenters, they are not the sort a business would suggest that their employees enjoy for an awards banquet.

Ask yourself, **Who will pay** for people to attend my presentation? Who will benefit most from it? The individual or a sponsoring company?

Visualize a fork in the road, with two paths leading away from it: Selling to individuals lies in one direction and business presentations lie in the other.

If you are selling to the individual, public seminars are the path for you. Also, some associations that are specific to entrepreneurs might be interested in these topics. The people in these audiences usually buy their own "tickets." For example, a seminar topic such as *How to Find Your Ideal Mate* belongs on this route, as do many topics involving personal improvement.(See Chapter 7: High-Profit Public Seminars.)

The second fork leads to the business market. On this path, the business or business/professional association pays for the seminar or speech. You reach the business market by going directly to businesses, or to associations that serve businesses. Topics here benefit the "business," rather than just the individual. A business owner will want topics such as customer service, telephone sales techniques, building a great business team, etc. Topics on this route help the employees and managers do a better job so that the business prospers. You will find meetings for these people at corporate conventions, conferences, and some association meetings that cater to these same people.

It is possible to adapt a personal interest topic so that it can be brought into the business world. For example, "Dressing to Attract the Opposite Sex" could be converted to "Dressing to Look More Professional and Close More Insurance Sales." Instead of, "How to

Find and Marry Your Ideal Mate," the business side of the coin would be, "How to Find, Hire, and Keep Great Salespeople" (or telemarketers, office workers, computer operators, etc.).

Both the individual and the business route offer profit for speakers, but each requires specific targeted topics and titles if you wish your marketing efforts to be successful. Some speakers offer both kinds of topics. Their fee schedule might include a retreat for which they sell themselves, and several fee-paid programs for corporations and business conventions. Different titles and material must be prepared for each type of audience.

Building a Strong Foundation

Always begin your search for a topic with who you are and what you know. You cannot find an audience that needs your topic until you identify your specialty. Your own background, business experience, or perhaps military experience, youth leadership (such as the Boy Scouts or Girl Scouts), family, education (either in the academic or business world), form the foundation on which you stand as a speaker. All booking, marketing, advertising, and promotion begin with this foundation.

For some reason, most people who come to us for advice on being paid to speak ignore this simple question: What industry did you "grow up" in? These beginners want to do something "new" so they create a mental block about where they came from. For example, one person consulting with Lilly was marketing himself as an expert on customer service. A good, marketable topic, as many successful speakers such as Ken Blanchard and Harvey Mackay can tell you. But the market is flooded with presenters on customer service. Lilly asked him, "In which industry did you gain your expertise?"

"Well, telecommunications."

"And how many years were you in that industry?"

"Fifteen."

Lilly told him the same thing we tell many who consult with us. "Why compete with the half million who present general programs on customer service? Why not compete with the 100 who speak on "customer service for the telecommunications industry?" That's a huge, specialized market with many opportunities for lateral marketing to similar industries after you become successful.

Dottie Walters began all of her businesses from her own foundation, which in the beginning seemed minimal indeed. She created her first opportunity by using the foundation she had gained from working on her high school newspaper as feature editor and advertising manager. She went to a small county newspaper when she was desperate for work and asked for a job. They were curt and rejected her. She felt at that moment a light came on in her mind. She realized she needed to start with all the experience she had gained from own her base. "Ah, I'm so sorry, I said that poorly. I am here to buy space." Immediately she was treated with respect! She began a tiny advertising business by buying that space at wholesale from the local weekly newspaper and reselling at retail to local businesses, adding her own special comments and insights in a shoppers' column.

She began speaking to service clubs to promote her sales in this column. Her subject was "What Does Your Customer Really Want?" What did she have that these business people wanted? She sold her expertise as "Your Customer," which was the moniker with which she billed herself. As someone who lived in the community and was the customer of the businesses, she saw what their problems really were! She believed that if customers who read her column and visited her advertisers on her advice were treated coldly or curtly, they would not make a purchase. She was able to show the advertisers how to reach and sell the local customers by using her own "expertise."

The column grew, and her customer base grew. She built her small Baldwin Park advertising business into 4 offices, 285 employees, and 4,000 continuous contract advertising accounts using no-fee speeches as her method of promotion.

What is your base? Start with the experiences and industries you already know.

Specialize in an Industry

Pamela Yellen's foundation was sales, so she chose sales as the topic for her programs. She started out earning $250 per program. Then she decided to focus on the insurance industry. She made a no-fee presentation for a local insurance company in return for a critique and recommendations to other insurance audiences. Soon she was giving 20 presentations a month in the insurance market. Her expertise and information geared to their specific needs grew at a much faster rate than someone who is a generalist in sales. Very quickly, she was netting $20,000 a month. These figures were only the beginning of her career. Pamela now speaks worldwide for the vast insurance field. Starting with her background in sales, she applied it to a huge specific market, constantly learning and studying how her experience could be applied to a specialized field. (See Chapter 5: Become the Expert and Leading Authority.)

Customize Your Topic Laterally

Market to your best bets first. As Benjamin Franklin once said, "Go first to those you are sure will buy." Once you are successful with your topic in one market, you can customize it to suit a smaller or related group. Then take your materials to those whom you think might buy and show it to them. They will very likely become buyers, too, if the material is aimed at their particular needs. For example, two New York actors successfully offered a seminar on "Broadway Stage Tricks for the Courtroom" to large law corporations and to Bar Associations. This topic might be equally adaptable for any group who need to make business presentations.

Take a big piece of paper and write "Who Cares" at the top. Now list your areas of expertise. If your best experience and knowledge is "How to Get Along with Difficult People," you might change it without lessening the impact to how to get along with difficult neighbors, employees, salespeople, customers, clients, patients, doctors, retired people, foreign-born employees, managers, nurses, spouses, bosses, computer operators, suppliers, and so forth. As you can see, each of these opens a huge new market.

List the specific businesses or organizations that need help in these specific fields. Your "Difficult People" topic is an umbrella that can be customized to assist dentists with difficult patients, banks with difficult customers, managers with difficult employees. Whatever else any business does, it also deals with people. Topics that address specifics on how to manage people and their problems will evoke immediate interest and response.

Jim and Naomi Rhode, of Phoenix, Arizona, have specialized in the world of seminars and products for dentists. They are so successful that they are now replicating and customizing these programs and products for seven other major professional markets.

How to Pick Marketable Topics

Here are the rules for picking the best topics and creating great titles:

- Prepare material for those that have meetings.
- Listen to what the market is asking for.
- Use surveys to target topics and titles.
- Pull through an idea from the marketplace.
- Check the best-selling lists.
- Profit from the flip side of topics.
- Always look for new topic ideas.

We will cover all of these in this section.

Prepare Material for Those That Have Meetings!

Don't spend time preparing a subject that is only appropriate for people who do not gather together in meetings. Find the associations and corporations that need and want your topic.

It is vital to all aspects of your professional speaking career that when you prepare your material, you keep in mind the key words, "target group." A target group is one which will naturally be interested in your topic. Focus on your primary marketing targets. These are the people for whom you prepare your material. Get to know them well.

Listen to Your Buyers!

Listen to what the marketplace is asking for. Get in tune with the problems your target group is facing. If the programs you offer are only marginally relevant to the real demands of their jobs or the business, they are not going to be interested in using you.

Frances Kyper designed a new way to decorate cakes, reproducing color photographs in the cake frosting. She made cakes for weddings and other events, and thus developed a small business.

One day she was invited to a wedding where the cake she had made was the focal point of the wedding reception. Another guest said, "Oh, how I wish I could learn to create pictures in icing the way you do!!"

Some might have answered, "That is my secret process, I will never reveal it to you!"

Not Frances! She heard opportunity knocking at her door. She replied, "What a coincidence! I am starting cake decorating classes in my own kitchen starting next Saturday. Give me your name and phone and I will call you and tell you how to get there, and the price for the lessons.

Thus began her career as "The International Cake Lady." She designed special tools for the purpose, wrote books, and created videos, which are carried in catalogs and at gourmet cooking shops. Frances has spoken and demonstrated her technique to associations of chefs, bakers, and people who love to cook all over the world. She has been featured on the top television shows.

Please realize the reason for her success: She heard opportunity knocking *and opened the door* instead of bolting it.

Use Surveys to Target Topics and Titles

If there is one most valuable piece of information that you gain from this book, it should be: *Take a survey.*

Sound simple? In fact, it is! Go directly to the industry you want to speak for and conduct a survey. Try for a cross section of management and workers. Ask them your questions orally or in a written survey. If you are doing the survey by phone, buy a tape recorder that will record phone conversations.

Surveys can be taken by mail, in person, by phone, by fax, and/or E-mail. This book contains results of many surveys we took. We did ours via fax and E-mail.

Benefits of Surveys

If you ask a cross-section of 50 people in your target market these questions, you will:

- understand the industry better than most people within it,
- more quickly become the leading expert in the field,
- create a list of their problems by importance,

- be in the best position to create and discover ideas about how to solve those problems,

- make friends in the very group at which you are aiming, and

- quickly and easily do your research and have enough material for speeches, workshops, seminars, products, and magazine articles.

You will experience a great leap of the mind when you begin to immerse yourself in your chosen industry. Suddenly you will think of new ways to solve their problems based on your own area of expertise. Often people are just too close to their own problems to see the answers. Taking a survey also lets you know in which areas you will need to target your research.

We get the most responses by asking only two or three questions that require simple, direct answers. If we need more information, we repeat the process a few weeks later. Even when our target list is small (about 300 names) we get a minimum of 50 responses back within 3 days. Doing it via E-mail is wonderful! It's much faster (and cheaper!) than faxing or mail. Also, the responses are already typeset for you when they come in on E-mail. Very nice!

From Survey to Marketable Presentations

Once you have compiled the results of your survey, you are on the road to becoming a "leading expert" on your topic. As the conductor of your market research survey, you gain prestige. Napoleon Hill, John Nesbitt, Tom Peters, and Faith Popcorn all became famous speakers through the use of surveys.

Give your audience what they want to hear by using the survey information to focus your topic. Make up charts and graphs of your target group's problems, along with your *solutions.*

Before taking a survey, Lee Boyan spoke on sales topics in general. Then he took a survey of the salespeople in his audiences. He asked them, "What bothers you most about your work?" There were a number of answers, but the majority replied that they hated knocking on new doors, the rejection of "cold calls." Although it is no great secret that most salespeople hate cold calling, the survey helped Lee focus on "what hurts?" He decided to zero in on how salespeople can find new customers without rejection. When Lee changed his topic title to "Conquer the Cold Call," it was a hit. He has since written books and prepared videos, and even has other people offering his seminars all across the country.

Lee's secret was to focus his topic. But first, he created a survey to show him what his audiences wanted and desperately needed.

It can be a bit of a balancing act to be a specialist, yet speak with broad enough interest so your topic is appealing to a large enough population that you will earn an income. If you choose an obscure subject that no association or corporation is asking for, you will waste your time and money trying to find buyers.

Ask yourself these questions when picking out a topic:

1. Do people want to spend money on this subject?
2. Does your target market need the content of your program?
3. Is your background such that an audience will be eager to listen to you speak on this topic?

Find Topics in the Best-Seller Lists

To find out what is selling in the marketplace, note which books are selling. The self-help best-seller list will show you what topics are most appropriate for public seminars. The business book best-seller list will show you what the business market is looking for. Here's a sample of what was selling in the summer of 1996.

The New York Times *best-selling paperbacks from the self-help category for August 4, 1996*

1. *Chicken Soup for the Soul,* compiled by Jack Canfield and Mark Victor Hansen. (Health Communications). Stories meant to "open the heart and rekindle the spirit."
2. *Dr. Atkins' New Diet Revolution,* by Robert C. Atkins. (M. Evans). Ways to lose weight and achieve a healthy body.
3. *A 3rd Serving of Chicken Soup for the Soul,* compiled by Jack Canfield and Mark Victor Hansen. (Health Communications). Inspirational stories.
4. *The Seven Habits of Highly Effective People,* by Stephen R. Covey. (Fireside/S&S). Principles for success.

Profit from the Flip Side of Topics

Many successful seminars have been presented on assertiveness during the past twenty years. The other side of the coin of assertiveness is the plight of those who are stressed by the assertiveness of others. "How to Handle Cranky Customers" and "Calming the Exploding Phone Caller" are examples of how some speakers have taken advantage of the flip side. There are even management seminars on "How to Handle Employees So They Will Not Quit When They Must Cope with Assertive Customers!"

Many speakers can turn their topics around and create a new market. One speaker, who teaches seminars to people employed by the government and large companies, attended our *Speak and Grow Rich* seminar. His seminar title was: "How to Be Successful at Interviews Pertaining to Job Raises and Promotions." The attendees at his seminars are the interviewees, who pay for his course themselves.

When we spoke of the other side of the coin, he got a great idea. He began another series of seminars for those on the other side of the table, the interviewers. In many companies, the interviewers have no special training on "How to Conduct Job Raise and Promotion Interviews."

He found an even larger and more lucrative market waiting for him with these interviewers. Companies pay for his expert training because he's already proven himself to be an expert in his field.

Ways to Get New Topic Ideas

Topics for speeches are all around you. Here are five more ways to get new topic ideas.

- Listen to people when they say "I need . . ."; "I have a problem . . ."; and "I wish I could find. . . ." Try replying with Dottie Walters' famous four magic words: "Tell me about it!"
- Take notes when people talk. You may hear the seed of a seminar or speech topic.
- Be alert when you are conducting question-and-answer sessions in your programs.

- Attend meetings related to your field and listen for topic ideas. Ask those you are seated next to their opinions of the program, and what they wished had been included. Ask them what helped them most. You can take a mini-survey from the two people seated on each side of you.

Creating Titles That Grab Attention

Like it or not, people often buy books by their covers, or at least they are attracted to take a closer look at the book's content because the cover has caught their attention. Comparatively, speakers often are ignored because of their speech titles. One speaker had a long and slightly obscure title on her promotional material. Then she heard a corporate employer say, "If only I could get an honest day's work for an honest day's pay." This comment inspired her to add the words "How to" at the front of this phrase and create her new title: "How Employers Can Get an Honest Day's Work for an Honest Day's Pay." Her programs are now selling briskly to business associations.

Title Formula: How It Can Work for You

Your material and speaking performance must both deliver what your title promises. They must be first rate, of course, or you will never be booked again. However, if your title doesn't attract the buyer's attention, you will not have the opportunity to show what you can do.

Titles are like headlines in newspapers and magazines. You buy the publication because the headline promises information you need or are interested in.

Titles are very important. Publishers have purchased titles without a book. Movie producers have done the same with scripts.

A great title attracts the attention of the buyers, because it features something of interest to them. Have you ever seen the title of a book or a movie that "grabbed" you? You say to the person next to you, "That is what I need! I have to have that."

The title of your presentations must have this same sense of urgency—make the public or the corporation or association want it *now*. The best way to accomplish this effect is to highlight the buyers' benefits in the title of your topic.

Use Dottie Walters' Magic Topic Title Formula. No matter what your title, it should say, plainly and simply, the following:

"HOW TO _____ SO THAT YOU CAN _____."

The title points out the problem and implies that your material contains the answers that the audience members can't find, or don't have the time to find, for themselves. This is called a "benefit title."

Target the Title to the Market

Your topic title must be of interest and offer help to the one who pays your fee. Dottie recalls that her Scottish grandfather often said "He who pays the piper calls the tune." Your title and topic must benefit those who pay you. They "call the tune."

A gentleman called our office for a consultation with Dottie on why his mailings to various Chambers of Commerce had generated no response. "What topic did you offer them?" she asked. He very proudly told Dottie his topic title was, "How to Take This Job and Shove It. Get into Business for Yourself!"

No wonder he had no response! Chambers of Commerce members are composed of business owners. What employer would want to sponsor a seminar for employees that gave them advice on how to quit?

Once you have a pithy, interesting title, target it to the exact audience you wish to reach. If you are a sales expert and you wish to speak to the auto industry, use titles for that specialized audience like "How Automobile Salespeople Can Close Contracts Time After Time," "Telephone Qualifying for Greater Insurance Sales," etc.

Twelve Tips for Producing "Grabber" Titles

Think of your topic as a movie marquee or the jacket of a book.

- Start with, "How to _____, so you can _____." Use this as the basis for creating something quick and pithy.

- Write out the entire title, then take away all the unnecessary words. Pare the title down to the very essence of the idea.

- Avoid titles that are long or obscure.

- Use simple, easy-to-understand words that will intrigue people and make them want to hear you.

- Create titles that produce the image of "sleeves rolled up and ready to go to work," not "cute," complicated, or hard to understand. Titles aimed at the business world in particular should be straightforward and indicate a high level of expertise.

- Use alliteration to make your title memorable. Titles such as "Secrets of Successful Speakers," "Marvelous Mentors," "Power of Positive Thinking," "Living Legends," "Invention Convention," and "Broadway Bound" stay in one's mind. Choose same-sounding letters and rhythms because people remember titles with alliteration. Dr. Robert Schuller is a master at this. One of his titles is: "Turn Scars into Stars." A very fine Los Angeles speaker, Rabbi Sol Rothstein, is the Chaplain of the LAPD. He uses a version of the Difficult People title: "How to Handle Hostile People."

- The human ear especially likes k and c sounds. Many products have been created specifically with these sounds: Kodak, all of the "crispy" products, Coca Cola, and many more. Words ending in o are also attractive to our ears. Jell-O, Dumbo, and jumbo are examples. We are not suggesting that you take someone else's title, just that you can learn a great deal by studying titles that are successful.

- Make use of rhyming words. Nursery rhymes have been used for centuries to teach children their ABC's and times tables. Notice the names of books and movies. See how many of them rhyme. A very successful book by Dr. Robert Schuller's is entitled, "Sift, Don't Drift; Lift, and Remember the Gift."

- Use contrasting ideas to make interesting titles. Titles such as "The Rise and Fall," "The Agony and the Ecstasy," or "Up the Down Staircase" make use of this concept. Remember, music and art are studies in contrast. Without contrast, music would be monotone and art would be a wall painted in a single color. Contrast makes life fascinating. Create titles with contrast, and you will catch the interest of the buyer.

- Every group is special. Its problems are unique. Each group wants to book an expert speaker who knows how to "fix" its particular problems. Put benefits and solutions into your title by adding the group's name to the benefit: "How Dentists Can . . ." etc.

- State the benefits to the buyer in the title. "Increasing Productivity," "Memory Made Simple," and "Conquering the Cold Call" are all examples of this concept.
- Make your title easily remembered and repeated. The titles that are repeated often, are repeated because they are so easy, they *can* be repeated!

Imagine you have a terrible headache. You walk into a drugstore, but cannot find a single remedy that says "Head" or "Hurt" on the bottle. What do you do? You leave to look for help elsewhere. If you create a title that talks about the problem your buyers need solutions to, and then deliver the best material to solve that problem, you will move steadily up the ladder of paid speaking success.

*F*rom Free to Shining Fee: Getting Bookings That Pay

A "booking" is a speaking engagement for which you receive compensation. Usually this compensation is a fee—money paid in exchange for the speaker's service. Speakers can also be paid in a variety of ways besides money: additional engagements, business leads for the speaker's profession or business, or payment in trade with the client's services or products.

This chapter shows you the steps you can follow to move forward, starting with no-fee presentations, eventually reaching high-fee speaking engagements.

Profiting from "No-Fee" Presentations

There is no reason to make a "free" presentation. There are many good reasons to present for "no fee." The majority of speeches in the world are done for no fee. Obviously, there are many benefits of speaking for no-fee, or so many people wouldn't be doing it! Many companies, hospitals, and legal firms train executives to do this kind of speaking. The payoffs are prestige, publicity, and fine public relations for the parent organization.

Here are more benefits of speaking for "no fee":

Correct Performance Problems

No one begins as a virtuoso in any field. We all need practice, and often the help of a great coach. Abraham Lincoln often used a story about a champion wood chopper who said, "If I had eight hours to chop down a tree, I'd spend six sharpening my ax."

The absolutely necessary way to sharpen your speaking skills and program content for the world of paid bookings is to practice your material before live audiences. Many successful professional speakers have prepared themselves for paid speaking by first presenting programs for no fee at service clubs. Even top comedians such as Robin Williams and Joan Rivers try out new material at comedy clubs to test audience reaction.

We suggest you often seek the counsel of a coach you trust. But, in addition, as the Roman orator Cicero tells us, "Nobody can give you wiser advice than yourself." Purchase a small tape recorder with a clip-on mike. Fasten the recorder to your belt, attach the mike to your lapel, and record every speech you give, so that you can listen carefully to the audience reaction to every story and each point. This is the key: how the audience reacts. Go off by yourself and honestly analyze the audience response to your material. If your audience did not laugh when you told a humorous story, perhaps a word was not understood. It may be that your pronunciation is not clear. Perhaps you did not build your story so that the audience could get the point. Maybe you did not visualize your story so that you could project it into the theater of the minds of your audience.

Exposure and Publicity

You can often use free (and paid) speeches for publicity. Send press releases out to the press that you are speaking to this prestigious group. (See more in Chapter 10: Becoming Famous: Promotion Strategies with Buyers, Bureaus and the Press.)

Educate the Public

Most large companies realize the tremendous marketing and goodwill benefits available to them by sending presenters into the public to teach them about their product and industry. There are thousands of "in-house noncommercial" speakers' bureaus that use presenters to spread the word of how their product or service can assist the community. Most noted for this are universities, government agencies, hospitals, and utilities.

Book Sales

As a no-fee speaker, you are often able to autograph and sell books after the talk. Many book stores and coffee-shop book stores bring in speakers for book-signing "parties."

Obtain Prospective Clients

Speaking for no fee is one of the best ways of obtaining prospective clients if you speak on a subject that will be valuable to their business or profession. You may begin your professional speaking career by speaking for no fee to promote your business or profession, as Dottie Walters did when she spoke to promote her tiny beginning advertising business. She built her advertising business using no-fee speeches as her method of promotion.

Many a business is sustained by this method. Attorneys speak to business audiences about "How to Avoid Probate" or "How to Keep Your Company Out of Court because of Wrongful Firing of Employees." A plastic surgeon, using "before and after" slides as illustrations, speaks to a sales organization about new surgical techniques to improve appearance.

These no-fee seminars and speeches, given as a means to attract new clients, do produce new business, and at the same time also obtain paid speech bookings.

Create Opportunities for Paid Bookings

You know you are good when someone in your no-fee audience comes up to you and asks you what your fee would be to speak for their event. Here are some ways to make this happen. We are not suggesting that you do all of these things at the same event to create opportunities for paid bookings. Try them out and see which you like best.

- In your written introduction, which you prepare and bring with you to be read by your introducer, close with: "*(your name)* has graciously agreed to stay after the program today to speak to those of you who are searching for a speaker for a future event. Now help me welcome *(your name)* from *(your hometown or company)*."

- Mention once or twice during your program, "My audience in New York last week loved this story . . ." or, "As I spoke in Tokyo last month. . . ." This puts the idea into the audiences' heads that you are a pro. (Naturally, you will use references that are accurate.)

- Use rating sheets. (See more on this later in this chapter.)

- Include something in your presentation that the audience would love to take home, e.g., recite a poem, or give ten rules of _____. Do not include this in your workbook. Ask the audience members if they would like a free copy. Instruct them to pull out their business cards and pass them to the people on the aisles, and your assistants will pick them up. Explain that you will mail a copy of the quote or poem to each person, as a gift. Then say, "Oh, while you have your card in your hand, if you are looking for a speaker for a future date, please just put a big S on your card."

- Have a small form made up and ready for this event, listing Who, What, Where, When, Why, and How. When someone asks you to speak for a group, smile and say, "Tell me about it." After you get all the rest of the information, ask this question: "What is your budget for this program?" Then be quiet. Let them tell you. What is happening is that you are being told what your talk is now worth. When this happens you are not a no-fee speaker any more. Get the contract out the same day.

How to Locate Service Clubs

Service clubs are always on the lookout for those wishing to speak. To locate them, contact your local library, Chamber of Commerce, and local newspaper. It varies from city to city, but these sources should be able to supply you with lists of the service clubs and their presidents. There are Rotary, Lions, Kiwanis, Jaycee, and many other service organizations in your area. These organizations hold weekly meetings at different times of the day. Some are breakfast clubs, some luncheon groups, while others always meet in the evening. There may be more than one chapter of the same service club, such as the Rotary, in the same city.

You may want to start with your personal friends who are members of various business service clubs. Ask your friend who is a member of Rotary to give you the name and phone number of the president of the club.

After you have spoken for a Rotary club, ask the president if you might have a list of all the local Rotary clubs' presidents. Say that you enjoyed presenting to this club so much, you would like to contact the other chapters. Ask for a letter of recommendation.

You must treat your no-fee presentations with the same professionalism with which you treat a paid speech. A meeting planner called us in a rage that her no-fee speaker had called three hours before the event and canceled. He had found out there would only be about 15 attendees, and he told her, "It is not worth my while, so I'm not coming." Bad call. This practical group was an association of meeting planners. This speaker's name will forever be "mud" in their (and our!) eyes. Even the most average of professional speakers will walk through snow storms to get to a presentation. If you decide not to show up for a presentation for any reason it will be viewed as a horrible breach of the most sacred pact a speaker makes—*to be there!*

How Speakers Set Fees

The question asked us most frequently by those beginning in the professional speaking business is "How and when do I set fees?" Novices ask this with fear and trepidation. "How can I be *worth* real money?" is their unstated question. We use this story in our seminars to help them begin to set fees.

Visualize a meeting of 300 well-dressed people. They have arrived at a glamorous hotel for a banquet. You are the featured speaker. Before the meal is served, the attendees gather in the cocktail lounge for the happy hour. What do you estimate they spend per person for drinks before the banquet?

Our seminar attendees typically give all sorts of answers, but the Hotel Association estimates it is an average of $10 per head, plus tips. Then we ask our speaker students to see a scale in their minds. On one side is the bar bill for this banquet. It is easily over $3,000. On the other side is the program presented by the speaker.

Now ask yourself: "Is one more important to the success of the banquet than the other?"

We know the answer to this, because we all have had the experience of attending a meeting at a beautiful site where we enjoyed the before-dinner cocktails and delicious food, then were bored by a terrible speaker. We have watched people walk out before the program was over, leaving the speaker to face empty seats. What will be remembered about such an evening?

If you are a good speaker with a message this group is vitally interested in, you are worth the price of the liquor.

You will implant your worth in your own mind if you post your fee schedule above your telephone where you can see it as you speak to clients.

You should start charging for your speeches when you have:

- . . . become an expert
- . . . developed a passion for your subject and your career of professional speaking, so that you never stop learning and improving every day
- . . . given at least 50 to 100 no-fee speeches
- . . . learned to be a good, reliable, exciting, informative, professional presenter who can handle any emergency
- . . . had members of your no-fee audience come up to talk to you after a speech and say, "What would you charge to speak at our meeting?"

Fee Schedules and Menu of Services

Fee schedules tell prospective buyers how much your services are going to cost them. A menu of services lists all the services you are able to offer the buyer. They are often combined onto one sheet which becomes an *a la carte* menu for your buyers that is most often referred to as a Fee Schedule.

If you have two or three varied topic areas, we suggest you have the same number of fee schedules. For instance, if you are an expert on dog training, but you also have a communication skills workshop, create two fee schedules. These topics are too diverse, and buyers will assume you are not an expert on either if you say you are an expert on both. You can always send both fee schedules to buyers who have an interest in both topics.

Some speakers have related topics, like Dianna Booher, who speaks on several dealing with "communication," including: "Communicate Care to Customers," "Communication from Boardroom to Bedroom," "The Gender Gap: Did You Hear What I Think I Said?," "40 Ways to Get the Paperwork Off Your Desk," and "Write This Way to Success - Business Writing." All of these are very appropriate to have on the same fee schedule. If she decided she also wanted to speak on voice production or drama techniques, these would be good add-ons to her menu. However, if she wanted to speak on "Prevention of Diseases in Children," she would need to create a second fee schedule for topics relating to this area of expertise.

What to Include in Your Fee Schedule/Menu

List all the things you might offer your buyers: consulting, panels, seminars, customizing, recording rights based on use of your recorded speeches, workshops, keynotes, media publicity days, your products, creating articles, special additional programs for groups at conventions, such as manager, presidents, children, spouses, etc. Think of all the services you could perform at a convention or retreat. If you do not list these things on your fee schedule, how will the client know that you offer them?

At our Walters International Speakers' Bureau we usually fax the speakers' fee schedule to the client before we negotiate the contract. The clients look at all the things the speaker offers, and we assist them in choosing the items that fit their needs. The contract is then written from their choices.

Factors Used to Set Fees

Speakers' fees may be set according to a variety of factors, including:

- the stature and expertise of the speaker (for example, a celebrity vs. an expert business speaker)
- the type of speaking session (for example, a main-room session, one or more breakout mini-seminar sessions)
- the amount of customization needed for the session
- the amount of time a speaker is asked to present
- the distance the speaker needs to travel to get to the event

Traditional Criteria vs. the New Way of Setting Fees

Traditionally, speakers would have a fee schedule that had many levels and variables, usually according to:

1. the travel distance from the speaker's home, and
2. the duration of the program. The length and type of presentation—for example, thirty minutes, two hours, two to four hours, four hours to full-day (usually 6 1/2 hours).

In the past, we suggested this sort of schedule ourselves. But over time and with the wisdom born of negotiating many bookings, we found flaws in using the criteria of travel and duration of program to set fees.

Travel distance   If you send a fee schedule like the one above that shows you have a lower fee for a local engagement, the client will want you to negotiate down to that fee ***no matter where the event is held.***

We now suggest you charge the same fee regardless of travel time (international travel is another issue, discussed later in this section). You don't need to offer a lower fee, the buyer is already receiving two discounts because they have no airfare or hotel room to pay for.

A fee schedule that offers lower local prices establishes the idea that the prices are not firm. Remember, if you insist on a lower local fee, not only do you take a cut, the speakers' bureaus take a cut too, because they earn a percentage of the contract.

Duration of the program   Offering several fees according to the length of the program can also be a challenge. If you say you will do 60 minutes for $5,000, but you want $6,000 for up to 3 hours, and the buyer only wants a 75-minute program, you find yourself haggling over that extra 15 minutes. How do you or the bureaus who represent you justify that extra $1,000 for 15 minutes? What golden gems will you be leaving out in the 60-minute program that are worth $1,000?

Now we suggest that speakers say their fee is "so much" for ***up to*** 4 hours, and another "so much" for ***up to*** 6 hours (a full day). If they want you for five minutes or four hours, the fee is then the same.

However you decide to charge your clients, it is imperative that you establish a fee schedule and stick to it. Meeting planners and bureau personnel know each other. People within the industry talk to each other. If you charge one client $500 and the next client $5,000 for the same program, the discrepancy will become known. The meeting planners and bureaus will not think simply that the client who booked you for $500 got a great deal. Instead, they will assume that you overcharged the one who had to pay more. They will always believe that the *lower* fee reflects what you are really worth.

Charging for Expenses

Before you skip this section as old news, we suggest you read it carefully. We anticipate a change about to occur in how speakers charge for expenses. First we will explain the accepted methods used now, then show you the way we see the industry moving.

Be very sure of your client's policy on travel. They are all different. But, no matter how it is done, it is the accepted practice for the buyer of a professional speaker to pay for travel expenses, hotel accommodations, airport to venue transportation, meals, and all other reasonable "out of pocket" expenses in addition to the speaking fee. This will be either included as a part of the fee you quote, or billed item by item after the event or lumped into a "travel fee."

If you plan to bill for expenses after the fact, be sure to include the phrase "plus expenses" on your fee schedule, your quotes to buyers, and your contracts. Whichever way you do it, do the same for all your clients! *Be consistent.* You should not charge one client first-class airfare and charge the next one nothing because you are using your frequent flyer miles.

Remember, the more restrictions you put in front of buyers and bureaus, the harder you make it for them to book you. We have speakers who want us to obtain all sorts of special privileges and concessions. If we have another speaker who is equally as good and who does not create problems over expenses, we will call that less-demanding speaker. Make it easy and simple for people to work with you—*and they will work with you.*

The Pitfalls of Prorating

It is most common for presenters to prorate expenses among all the clients within a trip or tour. Prorating expenses means dividing the travel costs proportionately among all the clients within the same trip. If you really want to know how to do this—step by painful step—E-mail us. We'll send you instructions. Prorating sounds simple, but the whole process causes a great deal of grief for buyers and speakers. For instance, if you are speaking for many clients on the same trip, you will need a series of one-way tickets. These are the most expensive type of ticket to buy. So, even though you prorate your expenses among several clients, it can easily cost buyers more than if they had purchased a round-trip ticket with no other clients to split the expense.

Tips for Handling Itemized Expenses

Should you decide to charge your clients by using the itemized billing method, make sure to follow these tips:

- Make sure the buyer knows well in advance what you will charge as fees and normal expenses.

- When unexpected expenses arise, discuss them with the buyer and speakers' bureau.

- Avoid surprises. Buyers generally do not mind paying expenses, but they do mind finding items listed that were never discussed or that fall outside normal expectations. Speakers' bureaus must be involved in disputes over expenses, because buyers hold bureaus responsible for the conduct of the speakers they recommend.

- Keep careful records of your expenses. Some will be deductible from your income taxes. Those that the buyer will pay should be carefully listed on an invoice.

Fees Inclusive of Travel and Travel Fees

As you can see from the preceding sections, travel expenses can be a terrible bother for buyers and speakers. This is why in the past two years we have noticed what we feel may be a trend. Several speakers are including total travel costs as either a set "travel fee," or as part of a flat bid inclusive of expenses. If they include a travel fee, for instance, their speaking fee may be $3,000, and their travel expenses fee $500 if they must get on a plane. This covers all air and car transportation, taxis, shuttles, car parking fees at the airport, and meals. It usually does not include the hotel room. The buyers put this on their own company credit card. The buyers can pay the speaker fully on the spot, so they can budget. There is less hassle and more benefit to the customer and the speaker.

This is certainly not practiced by the majority of speakers yet, but we think it is a growing trend. The Walters Speaker Services June/July 1996 survey of professional speakers showed 74 percent still send an itemized bill for expenses.

We asked 74 end buyers of professional speakers (other than sperkers' bureaus) the question: *Would you prefer that a speaker submit an itemized bill or just charge a flat fee inclusive of expenses?* Although most speakers prefer to send a bill after the event, the buyers want it the other way! Those buyers who included notes with their survey responses told us a flat fee inclusive of expenses would make their lives much easier.

In some cases setting your fee inclusive of the expenses offers a greater tax benefit. For instance, if you pay for meals yourself, you can often only deduct 50%. However, speakers must check with their own tax advisors.

Just be very clear (in writing) how all fees and expenses will be handled, and you will have no "ethics" issues on your hands. In all cases, ask the clients their preferences, and try to be accommodating.

When to Raise Fees

Name value, popularity of topic, professional delivery, and availability are the important factors that justify a fee increase. The famous law of supply and demand applies to fees. When your appointment book becomes filled to the point that you are uncomfortably busy, it is time to raise your fees. Raise your fees each six months to a year as your calendar dictates. Establish a date for the fee hike to go into effect, then put out a letter to all of your bureau's clients, announcing your new fee schedule. It is considerate to give six months' notice and to honor all past proposals at the old fee.

Another way to determine when to raise your fee is to check with fellow speakers, bureaus, and your potential buyers. Determine the fee range being charged for the same type of presentation and services you offer. Start a bit lower. Raise your fee as your abilities grow and your name becomes known.

Remember, household-name speakers receive from $10,000 to $120,000. These celebrities are used to draw the crowd of convention attendees or rally participants. Most noncelebrity business speakers who are experts present for $1,000 to $7,000.

Changes in fees can also be made to adjust for the difference between a standard presentation and one that you must customize. The increase should cover the extra research, study, consultation, field trips, and other work necessary to develop the customized material.

Nine Reasons to Consider a Lower Fee

You might be willing to accept a lower fee under the following value for value circumstances:

(1) Showcase opportunities to prospective buyers   If presenting the speech for this client has marketing opportunities for other speaking, consulting, or product sales. Audiences of speakers' bureau representatives, meeting planners, and association or corporate executives fall into this group.

(2) Barter part or all of your fee   If the client has a service or product that is of real value to you, barter part or all of your fee in exchange. Speakers have traded speeches and seminars for new automobiles, boats, fur coats, long-distance dialing credits, and many other valuable things! One speaker we know did a series of customer service programs for a chain of expensive toy stores. In addition to 75 percent of his regular fee, he accepted gift certificates at the stores. He told us he was all set for Christmas, birthdays, etc., for the next five years! In another case, a wine group paid part of the speaker's fees in beautiful gift packs, which the speaker used as gifts for his other clients. (Be sure to talk to a tax specialist about the appropriate way for you to report barter on your text forms for your own situation.)

(3) Exchange part of your fee for an ad   If the audience might prove a good market for your books, cassettes, products, and other services, exchange part of your fee for an ad in a national company or association magazine or event program brochure. These ads can bring you cash sales. An ad has a concrete value and a price which you can negotiate.

Note: Trades and barters should be taken at least in full dollar-to-dollar retail value of the item, or even more. The mark-up on items the client barters is often 75 percent over the wholesale cost. Exchange your normal "listed" full fee for double the value in retail list price of their items. Then both the client and the speaker receive a bargain.

(4) Sell a large number of products with the presentation If the buyer purchases a large number of your products as training materials or gifts for attendees, offer a volume discount. For example, if your regular one-hour fee is $3,000, the client needs 1,000 of your cassette albums on the subject to present to the attendees, and the albums retail for $89.95 each, you might offer them for 50 percent off retail with your full speaking fee. Or, discount your speaking fee to $2,000 and offer 30% off the retail album price. The client usually has a separate budget for educational materials. Although most speakers do not include these materials as part of their fee, Jeff Slutsky includes 100 hardback books as part of his "standard" fee. If the buyer flinches at Jeff's fee, he then has something to negotiate with by charging less, but not including the books.

(5) Sell a second presentation at the same event If you are skilled at several topics, do several at the same meeting. Visualize the twenty to thirty open slots the meeting planners must fill for a convention and offer to do one of your other topics at a lower fee at the same conference if they buy the first one at full price. They get the advantage of paying only one set of expenses (plane tickets and hotel rooms) and gain an additional program at a bargain price.

Sometimes, buyers are planning to book a speaker to create and tailor a second performance for the spouses, children, managers, presidents, etc., who attend the conference. Suggest they use you for this second program (if they offer it during the same day as your first program), and you will do it for no fee. They are able to combine the two budgets.

(6) Sell multiple dates in the same contract If the client needs several speakers during the year for different audiences or locations, offer to present a series of performances at a lesser fee. You might be told, "Cut your fee on this talk, and then we might use you in a series." In this case you reply, "This program will cost full price, but

I will be glad to add a clause stating: 'If a series contract is signed within one year of this date, $____ will be deducted from the series price.'" This is a business approach. Remember, this meeting planner may not be with the company or association next year. So get full price for this program and put the discount into the future contract.

Don't be afraid to ask for bottom-line promises. An alternative to the offer above is to write all of the dates of the series on the original contract, with a deposit due on all of them, including the first one. The balance on each contract date would be paid two weeks before each program day. Stay in touch and bill the client appropriately, with a copy of the contract sent each time, since bookkeepers also change employment.

While it may seem tempting to accept a "cut rate" on the date at hand in the hope of obtaining a future contract, it is not a good idea. This offer might be made only to reduce your fee, with no real intention of offering a future series. In addition, you might pass up other bookings because you are holding a series of dates. Without a contract, the clients could decide to cancel. If they are sincere in their promises, however, they will not hesitate to sign a firm contract for a series at the lower rate. If the dates are not set, just write into the contract, "four programs within _____ [their time frame]."

(7) Sell a set of articles   Offer to write a set of, perhaps, 12 monthly articles for your client's own publication. Discount your regular price for the articles because you offer a volume of 12 or 24 articles, but charge full price for the keynote presentation.

Example: Your generic articles on your subject might regularly sell for $300 each. For 12, you offer a quantity of $250 each. If the clients want them customized to their company or association, add the hours you spend in rewriting, at your regular consulting rate.

(8) Payment in full   You may want to offer a discount if the buyer is willing to pay you in full, including expenses, at the time the booking is made, instead of half with the contract and the balance two weeks before the date of the presentation.

(9) Vacations for the family   See if the buyer will pay for transportation, hotel, and meals for both you and your spouse that extend beyond the dates of the meeting, so that you can have a vacation.

Often, a large convention has complimentary rooms and discounts on airfares. This is a perk that costs them very little, but can mean a wonderful time together for you at a beautiful resort.

The Art of Contracting and Collecting

Speakers do not write contracts to protect them in court. We write them to help everyone remember what was agreed upon. We know, and the clients know, no one is going to go to court over a $5,000 fee. The buyer may contract for your services six months to two years ahead of the date. Working that far in advance makes it very easy to forget what everyone has agreed to, such as expenses for two in exchange for a lesser fee, ten extra banquet tickets for a family that lives in the area of the event, and so forth. Put these things in writing, and there will not be any hard feelings later. In case this meeting planner moves on and a new one steps in, everything you have agreed upon is spelled out. Having all the terms spelled out and signed off on by both sides will also serve to remind you, many months down the line, of your side of the bargain.

A few speakers use a formal, written letter to the client, with all the details of their agreement spelled out, instead of a contract. The client signs the letter and returns it to the speaker. A contract is better than a letter. Companies and associations are accustomed to working with contracts for hotel, catering, and all other services needed for a convention.

A nonrefundable deposit of 25 to 50 percent is standard to hold the date, with the balance payable on the date of the presentation. You take the date off the market with the receipt of the contract and deposit. You cannot sell that date to anyone else.

Some speakers insist on the final payment a week before the presentation date. Some buyers will only pay a month after the presentation. Again, make sure both of you understand what your expectations are.

Discounts offer a way to entice early payment. Somers White offers his clients a discount if the entire fee is paid in advance. Thus his speaking dates are paid for as much as two years ahead.

If you offer this option to your clients, you will have the advantage of having the money in your own bank account. However, the client may ask for an agreement that you will provide a back-up speaker on your same subject if you can't make the date. (You must make an arrangement with another speaker that you will stand in for each other.)

If an agent or bureau obtained the assignment for you, the negotiations, contract, and billing will be handled for you by the bureau.

Engagement Reminder

At Walters International Speakers' Bureau we send out two reminders, about two weeks before the event. One goes to the client and one to the buyer.

International Bookings

How to Obtain International Bookings

Unless you are an international celebrity, being booked into another country is always difficult. The company outside of your own country is thinking, "Why pay to bring someone from that far away when our own experts—people who know our needs and our culture—are right here?"

But, sometimes they do want an international person to provide an international perspective on the topic. That is what you can bring to the game.

The very best way to obtain bookings internationally is to ask for referrals from your national clients. Send a letter or call each of them and ask for the name of their counterpart in their international offices. If you do not have any clients yet within your own country *you are not ready to work internationally!*

Disadvantages of International Bookings

International bookings have several drawbacks:

- Clients are not used to paying the sort of fees U.S. speakers receive.
- In many countries the currency does not hold up to the U.S. dollar well.

- It takes you longer to prepare your program for an international audience, as you must do research on a culture with which you are not as familiar as your own.

- It takes a dreadfully long time to arrive at the foreign destination. For example, it can take over 30 hours to get a speaker from California to South Africa. You will find that you spend days just sitting in airports and flying.

- You need to add additional time onto the trip to adjust to jet lag. Some speakers can't function for a day or two.

We know of one speaker who was asked to do a public seminar in South America. The promoters left before the event was over, which the presenter thought odd. But not as odd as when he went to check out and 300 lunches and the meeting room rental were all on his credit card! The promoters' telephones had been disconnected and the hotel realized it was being "had." Since the event was billed as the "Mr. X Communication Skills Seminars," it seemed only fair to charge everything to Mr. X. This unfortunate speaker also did not have his airline tickets home. He was told by the local police to pay the hotel, or go to jail.

Here are a few tips that will make international bookings a bit less risky:

- When you can, schedule them in off times.

- Get a nonrefundable 50 percent deposit to hold the date and the balance ***before you get on the plane*** to leave your native country.

- Be sure you specify payment in funds of your own country, paid via wire to your bank account.

- ***Never pay for your own airline tickets*** with the client's assurance, "Oh, we'll pay you back later." Later often does not come.

- When you check into your hotel, make sure the group hiring you has given a credit card as the payment source. Do not give yours out, even for "incidentals" like room service and phone calls. Instead, put $100 *cash,* or your check, on deposit as a cushion.

- Check with your local embassy and travel agent for the appropriate passport and visa months before your trip.

Fees for International Bookings

So, how do you charge for overseas programs? Some household-name celebrities can charge by the day: from the day they leave home until they return. Unfortunately, the rest of us are stuck with a dilemma, to go or not. Although many speakers are paid their normal full fee and expenses, it is not the norm. Some speakers trade their work for airfare and hotel accommodations. At a large hotel chain, this can prove a great asset as you can use this credit anywhere around the world.

One speaker charges $5,000 U.S. for domestic bookings. In Australia, New Zealand, and parts of Asia he charges $5,000 in the currency of whatever country he is speaking in.

Do not do international bookings for the money. Go for the experience and the adventure. Take care that you are not lighter of purse when you return than when you left. Enjoy!

Who Buys Speakers?

When you approach a company with hopes of being booked for keynotes, seminars, and training, be sure to make your initial approach to the right person. Associations and corporations are the biggest buyers of noncelebrity speakers for their meetings, conferences, or entire conventions. Colleges are big buyers of celebrity speakers and entertainers, but they are also very interested in noncelebrity speakers for their non-credit classes.

Within an association the person who contacts you will most often be the Executive Director of the association, the Program Chairperson of this year's event, or a program committee member. Most often the decision as to whom they should hire is made by the entire committee.

Within a corporation, the final decision on whom to hire is less often done by committee, and more often done by a single person. This may be the vice president of something, the company's personnel manager, or the head of training and development. If you are contacted by a meeting manager or meeting planner, chances are someone higher up will make the final decision on whether or not to bring in an outside present. However, the meeting planner still has great power and should be treated with respect.

Where to Make Contact with Buyers

Your success as a professional speaker can depend, to a great degree, on your willingness to woo buyers. A rather important step in the process is, of course, finding them! Below we have listed several places to look for them.

- *In your audience:* One or more buyers will be watching and listening at your next speech. Ask for referrals to buyers on your rating sheets. This will be your number one source of new business.
- *At the library.* Ask the reference librarian to assist you. There are local, state, and national directories for virtually every kind of business and association. Write down the information you need. Or, better yet, copy the name and address of the company that publishes the directory, then write to them and order a copy for yourself.
- *Among friends and acquaintances of the person who is your current buyer.* Remember that referrals and word-of-mouth recommendations are the main avenues that buyers use to select speakers. Market yourself by asking for referrals from your buyer to other buyers.
- *Among groups related to your current buyers.* Build your connections laterally. For example, if you have begun with banking, approach buyers for banks in the same company first, then buyers at other banks. Work citywide, then statewide, then nationally.
- *Among businesses in related fields:* Keep stretching out laterally. After banks, to continue the example, the next step would be to try the buyers for financial planners, stockbrokers, and other groups or organizations in the financial world.
- *Right next to you:* Use the power of networking. You likely belong to associations, groups, or a church. Talk to the people you meet there and tell them what you do. They may open the

door to the best series of engagements you have ever had. Always carry your business cards with you and exchange yours with theirs.

- *The readers of publications for their own industries:* What does your current customer read? Find out and write articles for those publications! Buyers will soon call you.

- *In the news:* Study the news and advertisements as well. They are full of prospects. Watch for businesses, hospitals, or any other type of group offering seminars to their clients. Call and ask if they might like to use your subject for their next promotional event. By capitalizing on your observations, you will be able to find a sponsor for a seminar, do a joint venture in advertising, or find a client who needs a training session.

Showcases

There are many showcases offered to speakers which are sponsored by speakers' bureaus, speakers' associations, the National Association of Campus Activities (NACA), and others. The audiences at showcases are composed of meeting planners, such as Meeting Professionals International (MPI), the American Society of Association Executives (ASAE), or the International Group of Agencies and Bureaus (IGAB, founded by Dottie Walters), to name just a few.

A showcase allows buyers to audition several speakers in one session. The showcase program is like a Paris fashion show. Buyers come to look, listen, and *book.* When a speakers' bureau sponsors a showcase of speakers, all business is booked through the presenting bureau. At a bureau showcase, you will be expected to speak for no fee, and often help with the expenses of the showcase. You will usually also pay your own expenses for the opportunity.

Showcases are an excellent way to get started and are usually well worth the fee. Before you pick a showcase, however, ask the organization exactly which buyers will attend. That way you will know if the meeting planners coming to the showcase are interested in your type of topic. For example, if you are a sales speaker, you would be a perfect fit for the Sales and Marketing Executives group.

Much of the benefit of a showcase is in the catalog the sponsor creates and mails out. We have received calls from buyers several years after the event. At the time the buyers received the promotional piece, they just weren't ready to buy. When they were, they called.

How to Offer Your Programs in Less Time with More Value

It is not enough to just offer shorter sessions. You must find ways to deliver the information that will also change actions and attitudes.

- Consider offering your programs as "brown-bag lunches." Clients with billable hours like doctors, lawyers, architects, engineers, etc., want to feel they are not losing any productive time.
- Try a modularized training design that requires minimum time off the job or can be presented during off-peak work times with follow-up on the job programs offered in modules.
- Offer a program with back-up products and training materials that can be used on the job.
- Develop your program as on-the-job training or one-on-one coaching.

Making a Profit in Your Own Backyard

A wonderful marketing idea is to target your efforts to those groups coming to your hometown to hold meetings, conferences, and conventions. You are a good investment because they can save airfare and hotel bills if they use you. (We do not suggest that you offer a local "local-only fee." Other buyers see this lower fee and want you to give it to them, even though you need to travel! It just causes trouble.)

Take Advantage of Your Locale

In addition to attempting to sell our normal expertise locally, consider working up a second talk about your own area in which you cover local history, customs, shopping opportunities, and so forth. For example, one San Diego speaker wears a Mexican costume to present a second program on eating and cooking Mexican food. Conventions coming in from outside the San Diego area pay her for a regular business program, plus a second fee for a fun session about native cuisine.

Another San Diego speaker, whose regular business topic is negotiation, also offers a talk about what can be bought when shopping in Tijuana, the Mexican city across the border. Using props of beautiful Mexican leather, glass, and paper flowers, she teaches attendees how to negotiate for the best price.

Consider sending meeting planners who are coming into your area a small newsletter with news of your community and your topic. Offer to be of service and help in advance. Repeat the fact that by using you, they can save hotel bills and airfare.

Don't ignore the appeal of the foreign. Meeting planners sometimes think the speaker on the other side of the country is automatically better than the hometown one. On the other hand, those associations that are located somewhere else and come to your town for a meeting might think you are a much more interesting speaker than those they left back home. This is especially so if you can offer a "destination" program like the ones we have outlined.

Creating New Engagements from the Present One

Even after the event is booked, there may be ways of expanding the booking. For instance:

Do Multiple Tasks at the Same Event

When a meeting planner calls to book you for one session at a conference or convention, visualize that buyer working on a big chart with a least thirty speaker slots to fill. You should ask, "Is it possible that there are other slots still open? Perhaps I might be able to do two programs for you and save your association some dollars on airfare and hotel accommodations. If you could use me for both programs, I'll present the second one for half price. My only requirement is that you place me on the same day as my first program." This technique will help you cash in on the advantages of simultaneous bookings. Your $3,000 booking becomes $4,000, you increase the dollar value of your speaking day, and your meeting planner has another slot filled at a bargain price by a good speaker.

Book Multiple Dates at One Time

Also check to see if this same group is planning several events during the year. Suggest yourself for all of them. They have the benefit of a presenter who will be much better acquainted with their industry and their needs. You might suggest a lower fee if they book all at one time.

Cultivating Repeats, Spin-Offs, and Referrals

The best, most constant, and least expensive source of new bookings is your most recent audience. Since most people belong to several organizations and associations, they can and will provide many contacts, if you cultivate them. When you look out at your audience, picture each person as a door leading to future business. This business will come to you as repeats, spin-offs, and referrals.

Spin-off bookings are those that come from people who are in the audience the day you present, or from those who heard about you from someone in that audience who "referred" you to them. If you are very good, the same client who hired you for this current presentation may hire you for a "repeat." There is certainly a great deal of overlap in all three terms, "spin-off," "repeat," and "referral." Beware, all three of these are areas of potential great conflict with the bureaus and agents you work with. (See more on this in Chapter 11: The Advantages of Working with Speakers' Bureaus and Agents.)

When Dottie was building her advertising business using no-fee speeches as promotion, she had a clever system for creating her own spin-off business. She would pass around a small basket in which she had everyone place their business cards. Then she held a drawing. From the basket she would pull a winning card and give that person a gift. She took the business cards home, and used them to make her telephone sales calls for her advertising business on the following day.

There should always be some spin-off, referral, or repeat business from each presentation, whether no-fee or paid. Let's look more closely at all three.

Your #1 Source of Bookings: Referrals!

In August of 1996, Walters Speaker Services conducted a survey of those who book speakers and asked: "Of the speakers you have *actually hired* in the past three years, why did you decide to hire them?"

Figure 4:1. 1996 Walters Industry-Wide Survey, "Why Do You Hire?"

Their video tape	Their audio tape	Someone's recommendation	Other
15%	0%	55%	30%

As you can see, referrals are still speakers' #1 source of business. Find ways to encourage them.

To obtain more referrals

- *Give no-fee speeches to associations:* In our exclusive Walters Speaker Services 1996 Industry-Wide Survey of 1500 Professionals we found that speaking for no fee to associations was overwhelmingly cited as an excellent method of gaining referrals. These referrals led to multiple bookings in many cases. Jerry Fletcher, the Networking Ninja, told us, "I can trace multiple appearances and consulting contracts to a single referrer for whom I made an appearance at a neighborhood association breakfast that only 32 people attended."

- *Reward referrals:* Think about ways you can reward people who give you business. Joe Girard once was featured in the Business Book of World Records as the record holder for the most cars sold by one man. All he did, he said, was ask customers for referrals and reward those who gave them to him. In our bureau, we reward speakers who call in leads for bookings that they cannot fulfill. These may be jobs they are not qualified for or dates they cannot accept because they are already booked. We work on the booking lead, find the right speaker for the client, then share the commission with the speaker who gave us the lead. Everybody wins.

- *Ask for referrals after every speech:* After any speech, whether or not a fee was involved, send a thank-you note and ask again for referrals. When inquiry calls come in, always be sure to ask, "How did you learn about me/us?"

- *Always say thank you!* We send out a personal thank-you note to the referring person that very day.

Finding spin-offs in your audience　　There are several ways to dig for prospects in your audiences. Use one or all of these methods:

- *Paint your own professional image:* Otherwise the audience may assume that you have been asked to speak this one time "just for fun." Entertaining your audience is important, because what is learned with pleasure is remembered. But you also need to take positive action to be booked again. In the body of your program, plant the thought (discretely!) that you are a professional and would be a delightful and valuable speaker for other groups. Unless you do this, the idea that you could be booked for other appearances may never occur to the audience.

- *Include references in your introduction:* "[Your name] is available for other presentations. Your suggestions on the rating sheets identifying other groups who might be interested in this speaker are appreciated." Having the introducer read this announcement makes it seem "official."

- *Use references in your talk:* Talk about your other audiences, such as, "As I was on my way to speak in Chicago . . ." or "Great question. Just last week in Los Angeles I told an audience that. . . ." This plants the thought that you are a professional speaker who is in demand. "Nothing succeeds like success." So speak, think, and act the part of the successful speaker, and you will be one.

- *Always refer to yourself as a professional speaker:* Your business cards, letterhead, envelopes, and everything you print should feature your title as the "[your field] expert" and "professional speaker, trainer, and consultant."

Creating repeat business

- *First, last, and always, be so good that they can't wait to have you back again.*

- *Make it clear that there is more to be said on your topic:* Give as much information as you can, whether your program is a condensed version or the expanded one, in the time allotted to you. It never hurts to glance at your watch and say regretfully, "I wish we had more time to go further into this point, but we don't. However, I would love to come back and work with you again!" Remember, a professional speaker always finishes right on time and covers the topic he or she was brought in to discuss. Do **not** use this method if you are not really running out of time!

- *Let your audiences know that you have other topics:* They may not consider you for another presentation if they do not realize that you have more topics to offer. Try saying something like this: "Just last week that question came up in my seminar on _____. Here is an idea I gave them . . ."

- *Keep careful notes of each speech's content:* so that you can avoid repeating yourself in encore sessions. When you are booked again, your return speech must give as much new substance for the money as you gave the first time.

- *Show that you enjoyed being with them and can't wait to come back:* Have a good time with them, and for them. When you honestly enjoy them, they will honestly enjoy you and want you back.

- *Love your audience:* Let them know you care about them. Let it show in every gesture, every story, every inflection of your voice.

Lateral Marketing

Remember Benjamin Franklin's advice, "Go first to those you are sure will buy." Once you are successful, go to those whom you think might buy. Look at what business you are already getting, then look sideways, or laterally. That sales association you spoke for can supply you with a list of other chapters of the same association. The branch of the bank where you performed has a list of its branches and of financial associations they belong to. Then, ask for a letter of recommendation from the initial group. This letter will open the door to related groups. Call first, then send a letter of inquiry to the new group, mentioning the names of the key people in the first group, with copies of your letter of recommendation. The package of materials, literature, and letters of recommendation from your past buyers should show you as an expert on your topic for that industry.

These "lateral" referrals are an excellent method of increasing your bookings, because the new group will see you were well-liked as a speaker by others in their industry. Compile some of the best comments from the rating sheets and include these in the mailing. Follow up with another phone call to interested prospects. Remember, the odds are about one in twenty that you will be booked, so do not expect every call or letter to produce immediate results.

Market to Associated Industries

Next, approach clients whose interests are associated with those of the associations or businesses for which you have worked. For example, if your first successes were in banking, then try savings and loans, escrow companies, credit associations, real estate brokers, which might lead to building contractors and plumbers. Each group has similar and related problems and needs. You will be just as successful with them as you were with the first group. Each, in turn, will recommend you to others if you ask them to—and if you have done a great job.

Be sure to send a thank-you note to each person who helps you with lists or referrals.

How Rating Sheets Can Help You Get New Bookings

Rating sheets are a simple key to open doors and unlock business. It is possible to obtain several new engagements from the present one by using rating sheets.

Rating sheets are great tools for promoting your business, because they:

- gather feedback that will help you enhance future presentations and develop your material;
- automatically supply written testimonials to your effectiveness as a speaker;
- point out new markets to you with a direct referral from someone who has heard and liked you;
- give you direct booking leads; and
- put an order form right into the hands of the audience.

We have two ways of handling rating sheets: with or without an autograph table. If you do have an autograph table, you might print an order form on the back of the rating sheet, and the rating sheets may be deposited there with payments. You can modify this idea to fit your own situation.

How to Create a Useful Rating Sheet

In the past, many speakers have depended on numerical rating sheets that looked something like this:

On a scale of 1 to 10, with 10 being best, please rate my:

Appearance _____

Delivery Style _____

Material _____

Voice _____

Quality _____

Speakers, companies, and associations have all used this numerical rating sheet, but this system provides very little usable information for you as a speaker. When you study the results after your performance, you are left with nothing but numbers. A "10" rating depends too much on each listener's mood and personal belief system. Some people wouldn't give a "10" to the greatest treasure in their lives. Others give "10's" indiscriminately because they give *everybody* a ten.

Since we found the "numbers game" did not help us to improve, grow, find out what our audiences really wanted, or get more bookings, we redesigned the traditional numerical rating sheets and called it a feedback sheet. We developed a new idea based on what all speakers need and want from each audience: valuable information and additional bookings. Here are the types of feedback sheet questions we found are most helpful in attaining these goals:

- What basic message did you hear that you could use tomorrow? (Purpose)

- How will you use what you heard to increase your profits and/or productivity? (Practical application)

- Is there something else about my subject that you would like to know that I did not have time to touch on in this presentation? (New topics)

- Do you know of others (business, associations, etc.) that would benefit from the material presented today? Who are they? (Referrals)

- What is your opinion of my presentation? (Testimonials—make sure this is a permission check-off, so you can use their comments.)

Tips for getting your rating sheets returned　Here is a system that will ensure that your feedback sheets will be filled out and returned. You don't want to find them blank and left on the seats or the floor after the program.

- Put your feedback sheets on every seat before the program.

- Include instructions about filling out the feedback sheets as part of the printed introduction you have given your introducer. Explain in the intro that the feedback sheets will be picked up or else say where they are to be turned in. Always bring the one-page introduction typed, double-spaced, and ready. Rehearse with the introducer in advance and give the introducer a small gift.

- Reward the audience for filling out the feedback sheets. Hold a drawing with a prize. Have the announcer say, "There will be a drawing. One of the completed feedback sheets will be drawn for this special gift provided for the lucky winner by our speaker fifteen minutes after her presentation. She will be available at the autograph table." (The prize is your album or your book. This also gives the introducer the opportunity to hold up the prize, show it, and give a brief description, which will increase your back-of-the-room product sales.)

- The introducer explains there will be a pause at the end of your presentation, so that the audience will have time to fill out the feedback sheets. Then the introducer and assistants will pick up the sheets. Rehearse the introducer in a conclusion. (This will give you an opportunity to take your bows and still get to the autograph table in time.)

- If you have an autograph table, instruct and rehearse your assistants. Ask them to smile and say, "Thank you, we appreciate your helping us by filling out the feedback sheets."

Your introduction might look like this (keep it short):

> *Ms. _____ is speaking on _____. She is an expert on this because _____. We felt this topic would be good for you because _____.*

> *Ms. _____ is especially interested in ideas that will help her prepare information for her future audiences. After the presentation take a moment to fill out the feedback sheets that have been placed at your tables. If you know of someone else who could also benefit from our work, we would appreciate that information. There will be a drawing about fifteen minutes after her presentation. One of the completed feedback sheets will be drawn for this special gift provided for the lucky winner by our speaker. She will be available at the autograph table. She will wait until you are all done filling them out. Take all the time you need.*

For the conclusion:

> *Thank you, we appreciate your helping us by filling out the feedback sheets. Ms. _____ will be waiting for anyone who wants to ask questions at the autograph table.*

How to get even more mileage from your rating sheets

- After the break, pick up the feedback sheets in your hands, and stand in the traffic pattern by the coffee and refreshment area to read them. The late Anne Boe told us she did this after every talk. She said she never failed to have at least five members walk up to her, hand her their business cards, and say, "Please contact us. We want to book you."

- When the meeting is over, sit down with the meeting planner and review the feedback sheet results together. Especially, go over the things the audience wanted to know more about. Planners usually only hear from the two percent of the audience that is critical. If the results are 98 percent favorable, you may be re-booked on the spot. Positive, handwritten comments are very impressive.

- When you get back to your office, copy the feedback sheets and send a set to the meeting planner. The meeting planner will be sure that the appropriate boss or committee sees them. This is a good place to enclose a request for a letter of recommendation, and a proposal to speak on another topic.

- Follow up on the leads your audience provides on the feedback sheets. The odds are that one in five participants will give you specific booking leads. With good follow-up, one in five of those will actually book you. If there are 100 in the audience, 80 will fill out the sheets. Of those, 16 will give you multiple leads. This means you will gain about 32 referral leads for additional bookings. Thus, your feedback sheets may net you six additional paid engagements from the original program.

What to Do If You're Already Booked

If you receive a call for a date that is already booked, tell the client you are sorry, then add: "Let's nail down your program for next year, so that this will not happen again." If the client agrees, send the contract out at once with your usual deposit clause. You will find next year's calendar fills quickly if you use this method. Also, tell the client you will have your speakers' bureau find them a suitable speaker for this year. This will please your bureau and encourage them to remember you for other paid dates.

Sales Skills for Professional Speakers

We know very few *successful* speakers who are not also successful salespeople. Many *potential* speakers tell us, "Don't ask me to sell myself to get bookings." If you're not interested in "selling" yourself, then you are in the wrong industry. The most successful professional speakers work hard at marketing, publicity, negotiating contracts, and closing bookings, as well as at speaking.

Speak and Grow Rich is a book on marketing strategies for speakers. We cannot do the topic of sales skills justice here. There are many excellent books in every bookstore on the subject. But we do want to share a few sales strategies.

Don't Sell, Serve

If the word "sell" bothers you, consider these six pointers:

- The word "sell" comes from a Scandinavian root, "selzig," which means "serve."

- To serve, you must think in terms of your prospects' needs and wants.
- To learn what their needs and wants are, all you have to do is to ask them gentle questions.
- Use Dottie Walters' four magic sales words: "Tell me about it."
- Listen and take careful notes on what your prospects want.
- Give them what they ask for—joyfully, gladly. You must want them to have the very best.

The Humble Inquirer

Ask gentle questions. Bruce Barton, the great advertising genius, said, "Put on the role of the humble inquirer." Listen to the customer's voices, watch their faces, get into their minds. See what hurts and what pleases them. See their dreams. Your job is to help them get what they want.

Plant questions in their minds that will help them communicate and give you the tools you need to assist them. Unless important information is uncovered, they may not accept or even fully understand the benefits of your service.

Sample questions

- What does your group want to accomplish by bringing in this topic?
- Have you tried this topic with your group before?
- Why did they decide to use this topic this year?
- How will it be useful to your attendees?
- Are there other applications you could use this for?
- What can we do to make this concept work best for your group?
- What key results are you looking for?
- What do you want the return on your investment to be? (Lilly's personal favorite.)

Customize Your Proposal

Explore ways to adjust your proposal so that it fits the client's particular audience need. Be willing to change your material and terminology to suit the group you are addressing. Get the buyer to help you achieve the right focus. For example, dentists have "patients"; attorneys have "clients"; salespeople have "customers." Don't constantly refer to "salesmen" if a group also has saleswomen. Be aware of each group's problems and needs—and talk about them.

However, you should not fall into the trap of thinking you can simply change your material and pretend to be an expert on something you are not. Know when to say, "Let me have my bureau call you to find an expert in that field." Then add, "When you need my topic and area of expertise, I will be pleased to serve you." You will be remembered and respected by meeting planners.

Don't Give Up, Follow Up

You will not be able to turn every call you make into a booking. Only those inexperienced in sales expect to sell every "suspect," which is someone who might be interested in booking your presentation. Your job is to turn suspects into prospects, and then prospects into closed sales.

People in all fields do a lot of preliminary work before they win a job or a contract. Roger Dawson, a famous negotiation speaker, has his inside marketing person make fifty "cold" calls on brand new prospects every day. Of those fifty only five can say *Yes* to his four qualifying questions:

1. Do you hire speakers?
2. Are you interested in the topic of negotiating?
3. Is the fee within your budget?
4. Do you have a date set for your next meeting?

Only the five a day who respond *Yes* to those four questions get a press kit with demo video and audio tapes. Of those no more than one will result in a booking. Dawson does not do any further follow-up with those that do not meet the four qualifying questions.

So, for Roger's Dawson's office, final odds are fifty prospect phone calls to one booking. If you want to present three paid programs a week, you will need to call one hundred and fifty prospects a week.

This may not seem like a genius idea, but genius goes around disguised as intelligent persistence. Remember—Don't give up, follow up.

How to Handle "No"

Remember that a "no" now can turn into a "yes" later, particularly if you succeed in making a lasting impression. How you respond to rejections can have considerable bearing on your success. If you get angry or feel defeated, you may overlook opportunities to change a turndown into a booking or to sow some seeds for future appearances.

When a potential buyer tells you "no," you naturally feel dejected for a while. It can help to remember the words of Bill Marriott: "Failure? I never encountered it. All I ever met were temporary setbacks." Nevertheless, a "no" hurts. Take heart, there is a cure for rejection: positive action. An old football coaching slogan goes, "Show me a good loser, and I'll show you a steady loser." We suggest that you not be a good loser. Instead, be a great retriever of "lost" situations.

Here are some tips to get you over your hurt and into that frame of mind that creates stepping stones over the temporary setback of "no."

- Don't give up . . . follow-up!
- The buyer may have wanted you, but was vetoed by someone else in the company. Assume this is the case and stay on the buyer's side. A speaker we know sends a little gift to every buyer who rejects him. The card reads, "Hope you will keep me on your mind for next time." Buyers often move from one company or association to another during their careers. They will remember how helpful and charming you were and call you for another booking.
- If you are rejected this time, call the buyer and say you hope the meeting will be successful and that he or she will think of you for another occasion. Mention that if anything should happen to the speaker who was chosen, you would be delighted to stand by. Many a stand-in has had a start when the star "broke a leg."

- Call your contact when the meeting is over and ask how it went, or drop a card saying, "I hope all went well." Keep in touch. Make the buyer's success a concern of yours. Remember, people who hire speakers do so again and again.

- Ask the buyer who rejected you for a reference to a group he or she knows would be suitable for your material. Buyers know each other. Write thank-you notes for leads.

- Be like the friendly character in the poem by Robert Louis Stevenson, "Leary the Lamplighter." Leary went "posting up the street, lighting the oil street lamps each night." "You can always tell where Leary has been, by the warm light he leaves behind him," wrote Stevenson. The story, illustrating leaving the lights lighted in peoples' hearts was one of the favorites of Dr. Kenneth McFarland, the famous General Motors speaker. Leave the lights of caring on.

- Speak well of other speakers. Never criticize. Talk only about the future. This is the way to leave a warm light on and the door wide open.

- Stay visible.

- Stay friends.

- Try again.

Systems to Track Leads and Trigger Follow-Up Calls

One of the most important aspects of marketing is tracking *how* you are getting your leads, and *when* to follow up with them. In fact, if you don't develop a system for tracking, you will not be in business long. This will help you establish which of your advertising, direct mail, and publicity projects is the most effective and should be repeated. Also, your records will enable you to thank those who refer clients to you. Never fail to fill out your lead sheet for every incoming booking inquiry. Use it for calls from bureaus, clients you solicit yourself, and those who call you direct.

It is imperative that you track incoming inquiries not only for your own benefit, but also to maximize the use of multiple nonexclusive bureaus that obtain bookings for you. If the caller heard you at a program, ask which program. Check your records. How was that program booked? If it was booked for you by a bureau, get all the information first, then call the lead to your bureau. The bureau will appreciate your honesty about the client and will work for you enthusiastically on many new bookings. If the lead came from a fellow speaker or business client, send out a thank-you letter the same day.

Tracking Leads without a Computer

We hate to even suggest you *can* track clients without a computer. However, computers are expensive, we know. So, although they and a good software program supply the best systems for tracking data, to get beginners started as professional speakers we do have a few other suggestions. But, please, *make that laptop with a modem your first investment.*

Until you have your computer, make up some kind of form to keep by your phone to remind you to ask all callers how they heard about you and to record their answers. For example, you can use 8 1/2 × 11 file folders that are filed alphabetically according to the buyers' company names. Also, you can use a small file box to create a tickler file. Each client or potential client should have a matching 3 × 5 card with the date listed when you need to call that client again, and the cards should be filed by date. A tickler file created in this manner is easily portable, ready for follow-up in your office, or to be taken with you so you can make phone calls on the road.

In your office, as each date in your tickler file comes up, you can pull all the client records you need to take action on.

Before our speakers' bureau became computerized, we used the new client inquiry form shown in Figure 4:26 to help us keep track of essential information.

Create forms to suit your own business.

Tracking Leads with a Computer

Now that we are computerized here, what we see on our screen is basically the same "sheet" we used to work with. We type the information right in while the client is talking to us. We do not need to write it once and type it later. They talk, we type. Often, while the buyer is discussing needs, Lilly is able to fax them a list of suggested speakers while they are still on the phone.

Figure 4:2. Manual New Client Inquiry Form

New Client Inquiry   Today's date _____

Lead origin/referred by   _____

Contact _____   Company name _____

Care of _____   Address _____

City _____ , State _____ .   Zip _____

Home phone (_____)_____ Work phone (_____)_____

Best time of day to reach you? _____

Assignment information:

Date _____ Time of talk _____ Hours to speak _____

Location of event?   _____

Objectives?   _____

_____

Theme of meeting?   _____

Type of company _____

in audience _____ Age range _____ Ratio of male/fem _____

Business responsibilities of audience members

_____

From which part of the world?   _____

Budget for presenters? _____

Budget for educational materials? _____

Budget for registration gifts? _____

Speakers used before?   _____

Decision making process?   _____

What other service might we help them with? _____

Sample Computer Worksheet

Many computer screens are smaller than the average piece of paper, so a bit of condensing is often needed. For instance, in our form Lilly uses "com" to mean "company," and the full word, "com-

Figure 4:3. Sample Computer Worksheet

Master Planner Worksheet

Nme _____ ____ Com _____

c/o or Title _____ Address _____

City _____ State____ Zip____ Cnty _____

fax _____ Phone _____

email ____

Cd. ____ Originated _____

Dates _____ Loc _____

Theme _____ Airport_____ Time_____

Event _____

Objectives _____

Company _____

Types
Audience _____

Speakers Used Before _____ Didn't Want _____

Dec. Maker _____ Call Back _____ Report____

Priority ____ Old Con _____

Alternate Contact _____

pany," to mean company type. That may be difficult for you to remember, but in your own database you are able to make up your own fields and the titles for those fields. They'll be very easy for you to remember if you create them yourself.

Have your database of clients constantly open on your computer screen. When someone calls in you hit a quick "find" and, *wham,* all of their information is in front of you. If they are new, you just hit "new" and type as they talk. You will be amazed that all callers slow down when they hear you typing in the background. As a society we have been trained to talk to typists!

Are You Available?

Speakers sell dates. The speaking dates on your office calendar are your inventory, your stock in trade, as are your products. You must have a quick, efficient method to track dates, times, and locations of your speaking engagements, meeting with potential clients, and other important matters. The following tips can help you develop better scheduling habits and a highly efficient scheduling system:

- The information must be easily accessible from your computer, in a program whose files can be opened and the data available to you in less than ten seconds.

- If you use a computer to keep track of your dates, make sure the software you use is quick and accessible for all of your team's computers.

- One person or calendar must be the master that is checked before a date can be confirmed for you. If you are on the road and book dates, someone back home might double-book you.

- Use a three-or-more-year calendar. Successful speakers often are booked a year or more in advance with inquiries several years out. Even as a beginning professional speaker, you must be able to track your future whereabouts for several months ahead of time.

- If you don't use a computer system, try a wall calendar that hangs on the wall directly in front of the phone, next to your menu of topics, your fee schedule, a mirror, and your goals.

- If you work with a manual calendar, use self-adhesive tags or markers of different colors to indicate pending dates, definite contracted dates, and personal days such as dental appointments or special family events. Buy plastic markers or tags that are easy to write on and to change.

- Keep a United States map and a world map with time zones close to your phone, along with a book that lists zip codes and telephone area codes. Speaking can be an international business. Lilly has a map of the U.S. with zip codes and time zones on the wall next to her desk, in addition to an electronic touch-sensitive clock with a map of the world that tells her the time anywhere on earth with the touch of a finger.

- You should not book a date until you check carefully that you can meet the travel-scheduling challenges.

Meeting Travel-Scheduling Challenges

When a client or speakers' bureau calls to inquire about your availability, don't just look at the blank spot on the calendar and say
"Yes, it's clear." Always consider the travel time from one speech to
another.

- Look at the dates on either side of the proposed event. Note
  your location the day before, and the travel time from venue to
  venue, to be sure you have time to move from one day's
  engagement to the next, allowing for canceled flights and
  delays.

- Figure the estimated travel time involved so that you will arrive
  in a refreshed and alert manner. Allow for late plane arrivals, to
  be sure you will have time to get some rest. It is always best to
  arrive the night before an event.

- **Never** accept a date if there is only one flight available to get
  to the engagement! If that flight is canceled, you let down a
  great many people. Not to mention the liability problems
  involved in who will then pay for all the travel expenses now
  incurred for a speech you can't make. Ask them to schedule
  you later in their program, or on another day. If they can't, just
  say no; you will make a much better impression declining this
  date.

- When booking flights, never take the **last** possible plane that
  will get you to the speech on time. If that flight is canceled, you
  have no other options left to get you there. Speakers are paid
  not just for the time they are present on the platform, but for
  taking the personal responsibility to be at the presentation site
  refreshed and on time. For example, we booked Lilly to speak
  in Louisville, Kentucky, for a full-day presentation, starting at
  8 a.m. Lilly insists on being in the room 90 minutes before the
  event starts (she wants the planners to find her in the room
  when they arrive). This meant she needed to arrive the night
  before. From our local airport there were two flights, one that
  left at 7 a.m., and got her there at 3 p.m., or one that left at
  noon and got her there at 10 p.m. Yes, the later flight would
  have been more convenient, but if anything happened en

route, there would have been no way she could have made the date. You are being paid to *be there.*

- Consider the time of year the meeting is being held. Are there likely to be any weather problems? What are the alternate means of transportation in case of a blizzard or storm?

- Check the "real time" it takes to arrive at the venue in question. On a map of the United States, for example, Wyoming looks close to Denver. Denver is easy to get to from most other major cities. Therefore, you may figure that you should be able to make a Wyoming date on time with no problem. But this may not be so. Check with your travel agent. How many local flights actually go to that area of Wyoming from Denver? How far is the venue from the airport? One hour or six hours? What is the ground transportation situation? Until you know the answers to these questions, you cannot confirm your availability for a booking.

- Go over travel arrangements with the meeting planner. For example, your client may plan to send a limousine or small plane to transport you to an isolated resort. They get very unhappy if they pay for a limo driver and you go and rent a car (and expect them to pay for it!). Find out exactly how you are to get to the program and how long the trip will take. Check to be sure the transportation they want you to take runs when they want you take to take it. Often, event coordinators forget that you are arriving very late and the shuttle they want you to take will not be operating.

- Carry with you the clothes and materials you must have to give the speech. As "Cowboy" Bob Walters says, "There are only two kinds of luggage: carry-on and lost." Find bags that you can carry on comfortably. Keep a set of the smallest size necessities (toothpaste, brush, etc.) packed and ready to go, and pare these necessities down to a minimum. Also pack a small travel steam iron. The hotel's dry cleaning facilities may be closed when you arrive. You can usually ask the hotel staff to supply an ironing board in your hotel room.

- If you must ship your materials ahead, have an alternate plan for when they are lost (which they often will be). Using Second

Day Air, for arrival two days before you get to the venue, is the best way to insure it actually will be there when you are. Call the day before and confirm your materials' arrival with the bell captain at the hotel or conference center to which they were sent.

Become the Expert and Leading Authority

Once you have found a suitable topic to market, search diligently for a new approach to its presentation. Be unique.

You may know a great deal about your subject when you begin, but you will undoubtedly find there is much more information to learn. When Rodin created the statue of *The Thinker* he left the top of the head unfinished because he wanted to symbolize the thought that mankind is never finished, always creating more, understanding more, growing more.

Bringing attendees together in a meeting is expensive. Time itself becomes more precious as so much information pours into the business world. To be successful as a speaker, the information you present must be not only well delivered, but challenging and unique. This comes from your diligence to become *the leading expert*.

Speakers Are Booked Because They Are Experts

The 30,000 professional speakers listed by our bureau are categorized by topic, fee, markets, and speaker's home location, so our first question to a new caller is, "What is your topic?" We wince when the answer is "Oh, you just name it. I can speak on anything!" We heave a weary sigh, knowing that this is another would-be presenter who is an expert on nothing. The caller is immediately classified in our minds forever as "a jack of all trades . . . a master at none."

Speakers are booked because they are experts: experts at humor, motivation, or with information and insights in a specific area of knowledge. Today expertise is much more easily accessible by the average person than it was even five years ago. On-line systems, phone hookups, and videoconferences open a floodgate of information to anyone. Therefore, to be competitive with the average ten-year-old it becomes ever more important for you to be on top of the information pertinent to your field of expertise.

In the 1930s, the highest-paid speaker of his day was Will Rogers. He presented himself to his audiences as a simple cowboy who had a wry, homespun wit, and some canny remarks about politicians. He gave the impression he could barely read, which made his famous line "I only know what I read in the papers" a great laugh-getter as he delivered his political commentaries. What the public didn't generally know was that he regularly read ***every*** major news publication in the U.S.—***daily***! To be a success as a political humorist, he worked hard at becoming one of the leading political events experts in this country. His humor was built on public amazement that a rope-twirling "bumpkin" had such insight.

Study Enhances Your Uniqueness in the Marketplace

Diligent observation and deliberation over relevant information in your chosen field also makes you more marketable because you will automatically become unique. As you study and re-study your topic, you will gain a perspective on the material that is uniquely your own.

Through your passion for your topic, you will find your own views and opinions taking form. As Goethe said, "All the knowledge I possess everyone else can acquire, but my heart is all my own." This personal emotion and passion will lead you to your own special slant. It will send you beyond what has been said and thought by others up to this point. Then the magic begins. You become like Captain Kirk on the bridge of the Starship Enterprise—boldly going where others have not dared to go before.

Where Paid Experts Find Knowledge

Study all the material available on your subject in your field and related fields. By this we mean: If your topic is sales, also look into communication, personal relationships, listening skills, body language, and various kinds of sales, such as in-person, via phone, via direct mail, etc.

Be so very familiar with your subject that no one can stump you with a question. There is nothing more embarrassing than losing the confidence of an audience because you do not have the background to speak on your subject.

There are many ways to find the knowledge you need to be "the leading expert." Here are a few of the obvious—and not so obvious:

Academic Courses

It is very difficult for most professional speakers to attend classes. However, most colleges have now jumped on the "distance learning" bandwagon (see Chapter 8: Virtual Seminars: Correspondence School to Net Classrooms).

Having a degree is not essential to being a highly paid professional speaker. Having the knowledge that goes with deligent study is! Look for classes that are flexible enough for you to do your studying on the road.

Local and County Libraries

What sadly neglected places are our public libraries! The wisdom of the greatest minds of the ages is waiting there to assist you in giving the best informed talk ever given. But so many do not consult these experts for their advice. What did Einstein say about innovation? Caesar about leadership? General Patton about strategy? What are Mother Teresa's thoughts on compassion? All these great minds are at the library waiting in a wonderful quiet setting, wanting to tell you what they know. Libraries have books, magazines, newsletters, audio tapes, and videos, and on-line services ready for you.

Jill, the reference librarian in our Glendora Public Library, has been a fantastic asset (as has the entire staff there) to us in our professional pursuits. Often while working on a book, Lilly will fax a difficult question to the library. Usually within just a few hours, Jill calls back with the answer to the sticky research question. If Jill does not know the answer, the library submits the question to the huge research system of which they are a part. Libraries are often ready, willing, and able to order what you are looking for from another library.

We highly suggest your local library staff. They are a *valuable* resource. And don't forget to send them cookies or a gift occasionally to show your appreciation.

New and Used Bookstores

Let us give you a quick billion-dollar business success tip: *actually read the books and use the principles.* Dr. Edson Bueno is the founder and president of the fastest-growing company in South America, the Amil Grupo (they gross over a billion dollars a year in medical insurance, hospitals, and restaurants!). He considers himself not just the Chairman of the Board(s), but the Chief Trainer. He reads business books constantly. He devoured Tom Peters' *In Search of Excellence*. When he got the chance to hear Tom do a full-day seminar, he was almost disappointed! He told us, "The material was the same as Tom covers in his book! Why bother going to see him in person?" Now, Dr. Bueno was amazed that no one else at Tom's seminar that day seemed to notice it was the same material, even though they all claimed to have read the book. You see, unlike 95 percent of all readers of business books who only read the first chapter, Dr. Bueno actually *reads* business books.

As you honestly read business books, consider yesterday's best sellers. Out-of-print books can offer all kinds of insights that will seem like new ideas to your audiences. Joke and quote books, collections of anecdotes, and biographies are great to search for in used-book stores. Collect quotations and proverbs.

Quotations and Proverbs

Books of quotations and proverbs will be a wonderful help when you prepare special material for your clients. The easiest ones to use are those in which the quotes are listed by subject, not by author. We use several but particularly like the *Rubicon Dictionary of Positive, Motivational, Life-Affirming and Inspirational Quotations* by James Cook (Rubicon Press).

We find quote books a tremendous source of inspiration when writing a presentation. For instance, you know how you want to customize your material to this particular audience. Let's say the subject is "determination." You look that up in your quote books. There you see what many, many great minds through the ages have thought about "determination." We find the ideas begin to flow when we use quote books.

There are also several great quotation software programs you can purchase for your computer. These are a blessing to anyone creating a speech, writing articles, or authoring books.

Your Own Reference Materials and Software

In addition to gathering materials on your specific topic, you must have immediate and easy access to reference materials. For many years, our office boasted three sets of encyclopedias, at least ten dictionaries, and well over one thousand books of all sorts.

Today they often gather dust while we just point and click on our faithful computers.

Using an electronic reference source is so simple, fast, and far-reaching, it seems almost silly to think of actually standing up and walking across the room to grab an encyclopedia and physically search through it. We also have several CD-ROMs with massive amounts of material.

We have not taken our old friends—our dictionary or encyclopedia sets—off the shelves. Frankly, they have more information in them than the CD-ROMs do. But just one set of these encyclopedias cost well over $1,000 only a few years ago. Our little CDs cost about $50, they take up the same space as a sheet of letterhead, and take much less time to use. The world of reference is changing.

Associations

Most of the real learning you will need about your topic will come from people in your industry, working on the same sorts of problems that you face. Attend their meetings. Meet people. Make contacts. Talk, discuss, get involved. Take careful note of which speakers and subjects are most often booked and which are the most successful.

You need to join two sorts of associations. One is to enhance your knowledge in your chosen topic area and niche market. The second is to enhance your education in the craft of professional speaking. In the industry-wide survey Walters Speaker Services conducted in 1996, professional speakers voted the National Speakers Association, Toastmasters International, and the American Society of Training and Development as the best associations for learning how to better your speaking skills.

Magazines and Newsletters

Subscribe to all the magazines and newsletters that apply to your topic area. Being able to access the actual data from magazines and newsletters through a computer search is a more usable way for you to quote it in your materials (see later in this section). These publications sell their mailing list to others in related fields. So subscribing will put you on other desirable mailing lists. Soon you will get announcements about new products and seminars offered in your subject area. This will enable you to keep your fingers on the pulse of your industry.

In addition to subscribing to publications to advance your knowledge in your topic, subscribe to those that give you inspiration and ideas for the craft of speaking and marketing ideas as a speaker. For free information on the Walters' *Sharing Ideas Magazine* for speakers call (626) 335-8069.

Seminars and Lectures

Continue going to seminars and lectures regularly to hear what other speakers have to say.

Beware! If you feel, "I am so much better than these people! I don't need to listen to them!" you are in a real danger area. Find ways to force yourself to keep growing and looking for the interesting tidbits in what others are doing. If nothing less, learn from them things not to do yourself!

If you use or adapt other speakers' material, give them credit.

Research on the Information Superhighway

Professional speakers need on-line access to vast knowledge bases. The information available is mind-boggling! Telling you about all the whats and hows of the information superhighway is a bit like trying to tell you all the whats and hows of all the information you will find in the public library. The Internet is so varied, constantly changing, and vast as to seem infinite. You could compare the Internet to a huge, electronic, international library of knowledge with electronic search engines that point you to the appropriate areas.

The information superhighway is not actually here yet. Vice President Gore coined the reference some 17 years ago and everyone ran with it. But it is frankly still under construction. What we do have is the Internet, which could certainly be considered the "foundation" for this highway. The dream of the superhighway is a mega-super-library with every book, magazine, and newsletter ever written right at your fingertips, searchable electronically with a flick of your finger—and for free! You can get into a great deal of information via the Internet, some for free, some for a price.

On the Net you will find everything from NASA images to where your FedEx package is at the moment, Letterman jokes, today's news, and message areas for groups of people who like to discuss almost any topic you can think of. It is amazing to see all the people and businesses creating a presence on the Internet: small companies, multinational corporations, elementary schools, senior citizens, governments, rock bands, political parties, and Walters International Speakers' Services! (Come and visit us; our website address is http://www.walters-intl.com.)

Using five things—a computer, telecommunications software, a modem, a phone line, and an Internet Service Provider—speakers are now able to find out *something* about just about *anything* from *anywhere* that has a phone line.

The Internet satisfies a professional speaker's need for information at odd hours in that it never closes. A physical library has hours of operation. Best of all, once you find the text you need, you can copy and paste the information directly into your documents (always crediting the source from which you found it).

Once you have access to the Internet, it usually means that you also have access to a number of basic services: electronic mail, interactive conferences, information resources, network news, and the ability to transfer files.

Basic Terms

Here is a quick overview of the terms you need to know to navigate this superhighway.

Network: Two or more computers hooked together so they can share information.

The Internet: The catch-all word used to describe the massive, worldwide network of computers. The word "Internet" literally means "network of networks." The Internet is actually made up of thousands of smaller regional networks scattered throughout the world.

E-mail: This is the most widely used on-line option. It allows you to send private messages to anyone else who has an E-mail address.

Bulletin board: An area on a network where public information is posted and read. This is a computerized community bulletin board.

On-Line Services: Interactive providers of information and services. CompuServe® and America Online® are two of the biggest.

World Wide Web: The Web is a site on the Internet; they do not technically mean the same thing. However, most people don't know the difference and use the terms "Web," "Net" and "information superhighway" interchangeably.

Web Reference Areas

It can take a bit longer to "surf" the Net in a quest for information on specific businesses than to use a commercial on-line database product (see the following section). Much of the free data provided on the Web is sponsored by the companies themselves, so you might find more about a company at its home page than you would find on a commercial subscription service, unless you're visiting a company-sponsored forum. You can find great in-depth sources of basic, up-to-date data about a company's products, services, and support resources. Of course the amount and quality of information varies greatly from company to company, depending on how well they design and maintain their websites. Because they are sponsored by the companies, you will not be likely to get the negatives about your prospective clients or their competitors from websites. Think of these websites as in-depth advertisements.

There are vast treasure troves of facts and figures available free from national and state government sources as well as from universities. Use your Internet provider's search engine and look for an area you plan to travel to as you speak around the world. Many cities have websites telling about themselves. Before you speak there you would do well to study some of the history and customs, and events being held there during your stay.

If you are making a speech let's say, to Hewlett-Packard, you might go to their website (www.hp.com). There you would find press releases, product descriptions, reseller lists, and technical support services—all up-to-date information, which Hewlett-Packard wants you to know about. Now you will be able to relate your presentation and information to what HP is currently doing.

It is estimated that by the end of 1997 there will be at least 2000 newspapers on-line; many will have searchable databases for you to find articles; some will charge a fee and some will not. They sponsor their areas by selling space to their advertisers.

Should You Get On-Line?

While on safari in Africa at the Umhlametsi Game Reserve, Lilly went into the food hut where the one phone for the entire reserve was kept. She plugged her Macintosh Powerbook® into that phone line and called the local number for CompuServe® there in South Africa. Within three minutes she completed several tasks:

- Received E-mail from her office in Los Angeles,
- Sent E-mail messages back to them,
- Did research for the book she was working on by looking up an entry in the electronic version of an encyclopedia kept there on-line, and
- Left a message in the Trainer's Forum about a question she had on a new training program.

This tool is just *new,* not impossible; it is not even difficult. Remember when the microwave seemed confusing?

To begin your quest as a twenty first-century expert, you must buy a computer and get on-line. We suggest to everyone just entering this new technoworld that you purchase the most user-friendly computer you can find. Then subscribe to the most user-friendly on-line service. Get started. Figure out how to turn your computer on and off, how to get E-mail, how to send information to your clients, etc. Once you grasp these basic things, you can move on to the other services with a broader range of information, more targeted to your needs, like on-line subscription-based database services.

On-Line, Subscription-Based Database Services

An on-line service is a company you reach through a phone line by using your computer. Like going to different types of restaurants, you are going to get a different menu of services depending on where you go. Each company serves it up in different ways, quantities, qualities, and costs. They don't all serve the same thing and many overlap in the types of information you find when you get there. But this sort of information is just what you need to keep current on your expertise.

Data is only as good as the "search" engine you must use to locate it. The most valuable aspect of any on-line subscription-based database service is how "searchable" it is. As a rule, we have found that the more proprietary the information and the faster and easier it is to obtain, the more it costs. A fairly modest search can rack up some sizable bills on a premier research service. With serious business intelligence, you get what you pay for. If you're looking for vital statistics on companies, a wide range of information on why and when a company has hit the news, and you want it fast, you will do better with the databases supplied as part of a professional commercial subscription-based on-line service than you will on free areas of the Net or the free areas in your consumer on-line service.

There are basically two types of subscription-based on-line services: consumer services, and business/professional on-line commercial database products.

Consumer On-Line Services

We suggest that you start with a consumer on-line service, like America OnLine® or CompuServe®. Once you get familiar with it, get an Internet account also. We subscribe to both and have an Internet account.

Although not specifically for business use, there is a great deal of business information available on the consumer services. The electronic versions of Hoover's Handbooks of company profiles are getting tens of thousands of visits per day by users of America Online®, CompuServe® and other on-line services. The Hoover's profiles typically include an overview of the business, company history, names, ages, and salaries of top management, and financial information. Hoover's on-line information is updated monthly. The reports are well-written, complete, and include lists of competitors, a particularly useful feature for speakers who want to prepare a presentation and use information on how their host's competitors are shaping up. This information is also available through the business/professional on-line commercial database products discussed below, but it is much cheaper through the consumer services. Consumer on-line services offer E-mail, travel news, encyclopedias, dictionaries, and much more.

Currently these consumer services run about $19.95 a month for unlimited access. In some cases, the special premium research services have additional charges (more later in this chapter).

Business/Professional On-Line Commercial Database Products

Business/professional on-line services are commercial database products. They are more expensive, faster, and have a much broader range of information. They search literally thousands of databases in *one* search. The best ones highlight the word(s) you used in your search criteria and fast forward you right to the spot in the articles. Lexis-Nexis, Dialog, DataTimes, or Dow Jones are some of those that provide searchable full-text versions of newspapers, magazines, wire services, and more. Their premium pricing shows that these are intended for the business user. When you are customizing your programs, writing articles for your clients or the media, or preparing marketing strategies for product sales, these tools are invaluable.

In the past few years on-line information providers have become easily accessible. We use several and now can't imagine life as a professional speaker without them! The one that is best for you simply depends on what you need. If your topic is "finance," you need the ones that have the best up-to-date information on finance.

If your topic is related to "hobbies," you need the ones with the best information on that, etc.

Telling you which information provider to subscribe to is rather like telling you which car to buy. Whether you need a mini-bus, sports car, truck, or RV depends on your individual needs.

Research Using On-Line Newsgroups and Forums

Newsgroups and Forums are an excellent source of information and networking for speakers. They allow you to take part in communities of people interested in particular topics. They offer the unique opportunity to participate in discussions on a wide range of subjects.

You are able to post questions. Then a "thread" develops as people give their input to that question. These threads are smaller conversations within the larger topic of the newsgroups or forums. For example, a group about pets may contain threads about dogs, cats, iguanas, or other animals.

When you get to an area you think you are interested in, look for FAQ (Frequently Asked Questions) documents. These documents are very valuable to point you in the right direction. They also generally discuss etiquette for participative areas.

On-Line Forums

Forums are on-line discussion groups. They're the electronic equivalent of the office watercooler. A speaker can use them for PR or for research. People gather in on-line forums in areas of like interests. These areas are as varied and vast as anything your imagination can conceive. All the major on-line services have forums, although the service you use may refer to them as clubs, bulletin boards, roundtables, or special interest groups (SIGs).

Go to the search engine for your on-line service or on the Internet and search using "Forum" for lists of what is available. Look for groups that discuss your topic area. It is a great way to network and learn.

Newsgroups

Usenet Newsgroups (also referred to as Usenet, newsgroups, or just News) connect millions of people around the world. These newsgroups are distributed through the Internet—you'll find over

20,000 topics (and millions of people!) in these globe-spanning discussions.

You can access newsgroups from your on-line service or directly from the Internet. Go to the search engine for your on-line service, or on the Internet, and search using "newsgroup" for lists of what is available.

Tips to Enhance Your Image as an Expert

Whenever your name appears, make sure you also list your topics. It helps to create recognition of you as an expert. Here are areas where you should do this:

- When you sign your letters,
- On your business cards,
- On your letterhead, and
- As part of your "signature" on your E-mail.

Have an E-mail address and a website address on all your correspondence. We highly recommend that you list your mailing address, fax, and phone number and your personal and company names on your E-mail. We often get requests to mail information by E-mail, but find none of this information listed.

Marketing Tools for the Speaking Trade 6

The expectations of life depend upon diligence; the mechanic
that would perfect his work must first sharpen his tools.

—Confucius

To gain prestige and publicity, and to market your topics to those
who pay for speeches and seminars, you must have the right tools
of the professional speaker's trade. To this end you will hear many
in the speaking industry tell you that **you must have a superb
video and an expensive brochure to get started.** Wrong! It's a
myth! You do not need, and in fact we strongly suggest you do not
create, a video nor an expensive brochure in your first year!

You will create these expensive tools when you are ready to
compete for paid speaking engagements in the $2,000 per talk and
above mark, *after* your career is beginning to bring you some decent
and *consistent* bookings (at least 50 dates per year in the $2,000 cat-
egory). To arrive at that point you must develop **all** of the nine skills
we discussed in Chapter 1 and become . . .

- . . . a passionate expert on a topic
- . . . compassionate toward the audience
- . . . a target-specific marketer

- . . . able to customize the topic to a particular audience within their market (for free)
- . . . a creator of marketing tools
- . . . a salesperson
- . . . a serviceperson
- . . . a businessperson
- . . . a great speaker

Invest your efforts in obtaining referrals by developing all the skills we mention above. Get the right topic, the right market, the right business and speaking skills. Without these all of your promotional materials are a waste.

We have never met a speaker who didn't hate their first two or three or even ten efforts at creating marketing materials, often throwing out thousands of dollars in wasted brochures and videos. We could weep over the many speakers who attempt to *enter* this industry and make expensive video demo tapes and brochures to start themselves off. No one in any profession is at their best in their first few years. You will find yourself making drastic changes in content, styles, culture, and even in the markets you will target during those first hundred speeches. While you are discovering who you and your markets are, you must create smart, rather than expensive, marketing tools.

These tools must be flexible and expendable as you outgrow them. This chapter is about the first tools you should use and ones the highly paid professionals use.

You may not need all of the tools we will discuss in this chapter, but all are valuable and worth considering for the many stages of your speaking career. Without *proper* marketing tools, you and your speakers' bureaus are like carpenters trying to erect a building without power tools or blueprints.

Design Materials That Market You

Designing materials that will sell you comes easily if you have done your homework as to what *your* market is asking for. Before you begin, think of all the materials you hope to create and design them to match each other in style, content, and color.

In this section we will discuss the items that must be on your materials, and how to choose designs and colors that will help sell you. Keep in mind that some modifications will be needed depending on the media by which you are sending the material: mail, fax, or E-mail.

Essential Ingredients for All Your Marketing Materials

Inexperienced speakers sometimes send us introductory materials that are covered with sea gulls or beautiful designs—unrelated to their topic. They print their materials in expensive full color. Their front page copy reads only, "professional speaker." This is somewhat like a restaurant menu with one word printed on it—Food. This is rather a *given*. We need details!

As you look at your proposed design for a promotional item, ask yourself these questions. Does it **show**—not merely tell—the prospect that:

- the audience likes you?
- you are an expert on the topic the buyer wants?
- you speak well?
- your topic solves a problem?

By the way, the worst way to show a prospective client that audiences like you, is for you to tell them: "Audiences think Mr. Speaker is wonderful!" Being "wonderful" does not create interest, because everyone in this business is *expected* to be a "wonderful speaker." We see numerous variations of the "I'm wonderful" theme. Sometimes the adjective claims the speaker is "unique" or "charismatic" but the point is the same. The buyers are not nearly as interested in your opinion of yourself as they are in those four items above.

Keep it simple and to the point. Use this rule for all the marketing materials you create. The front page of your presentation folder, demo tape cover, business cards, and stationery must include:

- Your benefit-laden topic; big
- Your name; small

- A line or two of your key qualifications on this particular subject;
- How the buyer can find you. (Actually this does not need to go on the front, but it must be on at least every other page: your address or the speakers' bureau that recommended you or one or the other.)
- Your picture (for all non-E-mail and most faxable materials).

Design your materials with the thought that the buyer may never look inside! Right on the cover you must have the words or pictures that will show prospective buyers that you have the answers to their needs. We lose interest fast when we must go digging through the materials and still have difficulty finding what the heck the speakers are offering to the audience, besides the fact that they "speak."

Beginners often mistakenly list the benefits of their program on the last page, hidden inside the folder. Highly paid speakers place the benefit full title in the largest size type on the top of the outside front cover of their presentation folders and demo tapes.

Your presentation kit is your silent salesperson. Be sure your design and colors transmit the idea, "Let's book this one! Here is what we need!"

What to Include in Contact Information

If you are not sending material out for a speakers' bureau, you *must* include contact information so the prospect can find you! For those items bureaus will use, you will need to have them printed without your contact information, instead center stickers with the bureau's name and phone on everthing.

Business cards are much too easily separated from your other materials. Include your contact information on every sheet of every item you produce, including your workbooks and giveaways. Always include your:

- Name
- Phone number
- Fax number

- E-mail address
- Your website address, if you have one.

Send one set showing how you book yourself. One set ready for the bureau to use.

Note that we do not say your address must be included on your own packs, although of course they are on many professional speakers' packages. Consider that speakers are not in the "walk-up" business. Rarely will a buyer come to your office. So why bother listing your address? Why encourage them to write to you, when you *want* them to call?

A separate dedicated fax number and E-mail address on a speaker's contact information are immediate clues that the speaker is a pro, and a real businessperson. Without these we ask ourselves, "How would we contact this speaker if we have a booking on this subject?" So, not only for the convenience of the bureaus and buyers, but to create the image of a savvy speaker, include these, or the bureau data.

Creating Faxable Materials

You will lose many beautiful options in design if you make an item faxable. But in today's world you have little choice. Many people will ask for your materials now, which means they must be faxed. So why not design them so they will look good when they arrive at their destination?

To make your materials faxable:

- Keep them on as few pages as possible. This saves you money in phone bills and the receiver in paper costs.
- Do not use large areas of black; these take a long time to fax.
- Remember that all colors will come through on the other end as black. Look carefully at your materials. That lovely light blue background or colored paper may make your whole fax look like a big black blob. Print everything on white paper with black or a dark ink.
- Use black and white photos with a light background if your skin tone is dark, and a dark background if you are fair.
- Reproduce your photos in "lower resolution" (fewer dots per inch). This looks grainy for normal uses, but nice on a fax.

- Have an artist do a line drawing of you, and use this instead of a photo.

- Set your fax machine to send "half-tones" or "gray scale" (depending on your fax machine's criteria). This makes a huge difference in how the sheet appears as it is received.

- As you create new materials, fax them to yourself to make sure they look nice on the other end.

Creating E-mailable Materials

There are many ways to send a full brochure to someone with graphics, color, and photos via E-mail. We do it all the time in creating our magazine, *Sharing Ideas for Professional Speakers.* However, the average user, especially those that buy speakers, are not likely to have the equipment, not to mention the savvy or the software, to open a document that is sent as an attachment to E-mail. In order for the receiver to read an attached file, they *usually* must have the same software in which you created it, or software with the appropriate filters. If you did anything fancy to your document that used graphics, chances are very low that the average receiver is going to see your marketing piece the way you created it.

Today (the technology is advancing quickly!) it is most effective and usable by the receiver, if you just send your marketing items as actual text within the E-mail, not as an attached document. You lose all color and all font options, but at least they can read it. If you have never seen an E-mail, think in terms of what you used to see when you only had a typewriter to work on, could not use **bold,** and had only one font and one size type.

If you have someone else create your marketing items for you, make sure they give you a copy of each item on a disk, in a format from which you can pull the text off as "text only." Keep these on your computer. These will be your E-mail marketing materials.

Customize Those Packages!

With today's easy-to-use technology, customizing the copy on most of your materials to read, "Customer Service for Tellers in Hectic Traffic Areas," from simply "Front Line Customer Service," is just too easy to be ignored. Besides, it can make all the difference in the world to a buyer choosing one speaker over another. Think of ways you could customize your topic for the inquiring client and add those thoughts into your outline.

Speakers often send our bureau a presentation folder on one subject with a note saying, "This subject is not what your client wants, but send it anyway." We can't think of a better way to lose a client than to do this! Customize the presentation kit to meet the objectives this specific buyer wants. Use your computer.

Designs and Colors That Sell!

We caution you to remember to use color on your materials (except the faxable versions.)

We receive many speakers' presentation kits that are completely blank on the front cover. Visualize a board room table with all the speakers' materials in color with benefit-filled titles and pictures, and yours completely blank. What product or book have you purchased that was packaged with . . . nothing?

Or, what if your presentation folder only shows your picture and name ten times? Bureaus and buyers react to this kind of material with the frustrating thought, "Yes, but what the heck is her topic?!"

Remember, they will not open up your folder unless the front of it has a mind-catching title in large letters, your picture, your name (much smaller and at the bottom), and a qualifying line explaining why you should be heard on this topic.

Matching Colors and Themes Look Elegant

Choose a color scheme and design theme for your business materials, then stick to it in everything you print so that your content one-sheets, demo tapes, business cards, envelopes, stationery, and related materials will all match. This is the easiest way to look elegant.

Somber materials in shades of gray and black are uninviting and not likely to draw many bookings. Warm-spectrum colors ask for action. Cool and dark colors put your buyer to sleep. If you use a dark color, be sure to put your topic title in a bright warm-spectrum color against it—red or gold against black, for example.

Dotties' Grocery Store Presentation Kit Design Method

Take a walk through your neighborhood supermarket. Look only at the colors and designs. Let your eyes roam. When you see packages that attract your eye, buy them. Study those packages. Especially note the titles, benefits listed, type styles, and the attractive pictures of what is inside on the front.

These packages are designed and tested by marketing experts, at great expense, to catch the eye of the buyer. (They caught your eye, didn't they?) Note the colors. Acquire inspiration and knowledge by studying successful marketing packages closely.

Project the Image of Excellence

As you become more professional and your fees increase, the image your promotional materials project must take on a higher quality and more expensive image as well. You and your materials must "look the part of excellence." Like the clothes you wear on the platform, your presentation kit must express you. A little foil on the front will look elegant and gain attention. Foil comes in many shades, and can make your lettering come to life. For example, speaker Maxine McIntyre has beautiful, coppery-red hair. Her presentation kit and demo tapes feature foil in the same shade. The impact of her color picture and the foil title is stunning!

Always keep in mind that it is not possible for you, or your bureaus, to obtain bookings with high fees, such as $5,000 or $10,000, for a one-hour program if your presentation kit projects your image as a $500 beginning speaker. Like a beautiful business suit and a great haircut, your promotional materials make a first and lasting impression.

Of course, excellent promotional materials can never take the place of top talent and superb presentation content. But the materials can have a powerful impact on your career. They are an important and essential part of your professional image.

What Goes in Great Promotional Packages

Usually, the entire presentation kit is contained in a presentation folder, or sometimes a plastic container, filled with many marketing tools. These important packages are called by many names.

Buyers call them the "speakers' package(s)." If you call them that around your office, it might be confusing, as it would not be descriptive enough. We used to call them "press kits," but since they are most often not going to the press, this seemed rather silly to us. Now within our office we call them presentation kits or promotional packages. This kit must *sell* you when you are not there to do it yourself.

How to Use Your Presentation Kit

The presentation kit is used in two ways:

- First, the presentation kit is sent to prospective clients who want to consider you. It is often used at a board meeting where the clients are considering several speakers. The purpose of the kit is to show them who you are and what subjects you cover in your presentation. In this instance, the presentation kit is an invaluable asset in helping you find and close bookings.
- Second, presentation kits are sent to media personnel to interest them in considering you for publicity interviews on TV and radio, or for magazine and newspaper interviews and articles.

You fill the kit individually for each prospect. Be sure that you send only the most appropriate materials.

Never ask a prospective buyer or speakers' bureau to send back your kit if you are not booked. We recall a speaker who hounded our bureau for the return of an audio demo tape, wholesale value about $1.00. The bureau does not want to hound the client, nor should you. Moreover, when your presentation kit is in their files, it is an instant reminder of your ability and may bring you a booking for this program or future ones.

What Goes in Your Presentation Kit

In this section, we will go over each of the many items that speakers *might* include in their packages. Here is what we feel are the *minimum requirements:*

- The presentation folder.
- A content one-sheet flyer *on the topic the buyer has asked for.*
- A letter on your attractive letterhead, and business card (if this is not a bureau lead).
- A video and/or audio demo tape of your live presentation, *on the subject requested!* Color cover—spine, back and labels.
- Your complete fee schedule, which is a menu of the services you offer.

Once you begin to be successful in the market, you will be able to customize the materials in your kit to be a closer fit with your customers' needs. You will also begin to include other items in the package. It is a *very good idea to include:*

- Lists of clients for whom you have spoken or copies of letters of recommendation, or a sheet of testimonials with 2- to 3-sentence comments, giving the names of the buyers and their companies.
- Mail-back card addressed to you, (only when you book yourself—not when you send your kit to a bureau.)
- Biography information (often referred to as a "bio").
- Black-and-white glossy photo of you, taken both posed and while you are in action before an audience.
- A copy of your contract (not needed when you send presentation kits to the media or to speakers' bureaus).
- Reprints of articles you have written *on this topic.* (white out dates)
- Reprints of articles *about you* and your work, written by others. (white out dates)
- Product(s) you have developed: your book(s), or book cover(s), or copies of your newsletter if you have articles on a subject the buyer is looking for.

Note that we did not mention brochures. Presentation folders have replaced them. If brochures are used at all they tend to be simple 4- to 8-page affairs. Think faxable.

Letterhead, Business Cards, and Postcards

How many times have we been approached by speakers who say to us, "Please book me!" When we ask for them to send materials, they don't have the most basic of marketing tools: letterhead and business cards! The immediate impression is that this speaker hasn't a clue as to how this business works.

Business Cards

In any field, a business card is required. A special one is necessary in the world of professional speaking. The card features your picture, your main area of expertise, and of course all the information on how to locate you.

Business cards can be the usual rectangle, or they can be created in the form of a rol-o-dex card with your topic on the tab. There are many people who do not have a computer database of suppliers, and still use card files. Dottie especially likes the rol-o-dex kind, "So handy to slip right into your holder on your desk." All are filed by subject topic.

Postcards

Postcards can be a super marketing tool. Carry your customized postcards around with you. You will be able to fill that time on airplanes by jotting thank-you notes and quick inquiries to your buyers, bureaus, and those who have assisted you in your programs. Put your picture and your name on the same side as the message. Use a pen in a complementary color ink. Keep a small notebook with you to jot down names and addresses of people you want to thank, such as your introducer, buyer, the company secretary, others on the panel, and so forth.

We all get a great deal of mail, and often we breeze through much of it. But what do we read every word of? Handwritten postcards! In this computer age, a handwritten note is one of the only items that is rarely tossed out.

Letterhead

Cover Letters to Potential Buyers. Your letterhead is a sheet of writing paper with a heading that includes your name and address at the bottom and your services as a speaker. If you plan to have two sets of materials, one to fax and one to mail, then consider including full-color picture photos of you on your letterhead. Create your letterhead to match your business cards and presentation folder. In addition to your cover letter, many of your promotional items—fee schedules, one-sheets and endorsements—can be reproduced on your letterhead for a professional look which matches.

Your cover letter, printed on your letterhead, should be in the first place the prospective client's eye will fall. Do not use watermarked or rag content paper. These things will look dirty when you use your stationery for faxing.

Less is better for content in your cover letters. Let the buyer know:

- What event you are sending these materials in regard to,
- What is included in the information package,
- A quick synopsis of what you understand their needs to be and how you can fill those needs, and
- When you (or your bureau) will be calling.

Content One-Sheets

After the cover letter, the most important item you will need for the first several years of your speaking career is a content one-sheet. Create an attractive content one-sheet for each topic for which you want to obtain bookings. It should be just what it says—one sheet, one-sided.

One-sheets tell the customer:

- What you are selling
- Topic title big across top
- Points you will cover in this program (short outline or bullet points)
- Who this topic is most appropriate for
- A few endorsements
- A short bio stating why you are the leading expert on this subject

- What you look like (your photograph or a drawing of you—face picture towards copy, not out.)

The first thing at the top of your content one-sheet should be a **very small** line that says what you are selling: Seminars? Books? Dog grooming? Then, print your topic very bold and large. Often—*way too often*—we receive one-sheets that say in huge, bold letters that take up a quarter of the page: PROFESSIONAL SPEAKER! No, no, no! Clients are buying expertise on a topic. That is what needs to be prominent.

Your one-sheet should also include a short outline that shows the points you cover in this presentation. Head this part up with something that says openly, or at least implies: "Your Audience Will Learn . . ."

The person making the decision to buy wants someone who will specialize in their particular type of audience. Somewhere on the page, either in the title or as a line of its own, you must say or imply clearly "who should attend this program," managers, salespeople, front-line personnel? Salespeople need a different approach than do front-line people. If you say your program is "appropriate for all," *all* will think you don't know what you are talking about.

Even though you include a full sheet of endorsements and testimonials (see later in this chapter for details), including one or two endorsements right on your one-sheet is an excellent way to show you are liked by buyers on this particular subject.

A very **short** biography under your photo allows buyers to see the best of your background without searching through all your materials. And remember, one-sheets must be faxable (especially those photos!).

There are several ways to put all the material together on your one-sheet. Just remember that what you want to jump off the page is the benefit-laden topic. You might try something like the one-sheet.

Presentation Folders

Top presentation folders are often printed in full color and sometimes have foil accents or elaborate die-cuts. These high-quality types of presentation kits are both beautiful and expensive.

The most popular presentation folder is printed on good quality glossy cardstock with pockets on the inside bottom. All of your marketing materials are then placed inside this folder. Without the inside pocket, your items fall out on the floor. It is also a good idea to have a tab along the long side, which extends to display your name and topic title when the package is placed in a file cabinet.

Please do **not** go out in your first few years and spend a fortune on a customized presentation folder! Great materials will not get you bookings if you are still working on finding a market and developing your topics and skills. Your presentation folder can become obsolete overnight, so create one that is flexible, can be changed easily, and won't hurt as badly as you watch the trash man haul off a hundred copies.

Instead of having a printer create a customized folder, go to a high-end stationery and office supply store or catalog company. These companies have many styles of ready-made deluxe presentation folders. Use these to create your own customized folders in small quantities.

There are several ways you can customize them.

- Print a customized label from your own laser printer on label stock that has no perforations. In other words, 8 1/2 × 11 or smaller sheets of paper that are one giant, adhesive-backed label. Print your presentation folder cover on this and trim away the excess. This allows the color of the folder to show around the margins of the sticky paper. Using your own laser printer and computer allows you to experiment with creative ideas and designs on a budget, often in full color. If your laser does not print in color, go to a high-end copy store. They will rent you the use of their computers and color printers, or they will do it for you.

- You can also easily customize your folders by using a metallic gold or silver and printing your topic.

- Glue the cover from your book, tape, or other product to the front of the folder.

- Use a combination of all of the above!

Answers About Top Competitive Video and Audio Brochures

Video and audio demonstration (demo) tapes are actually brochures in another media. When you wish to rise above the $2,000 per talk mark, a good-quality demo tape is a *must* to compete for higher-paid speaking engagements. But until you are making $2,000 a talk, you will do better to work on referrals, and keep creating an even better talk.

Unless you are a celebrity, bureaus and agents will not want to book you without a video demo, because their buyers insist on them for each topic. Highly successful speakers get about 40 percent of their bookings from bureaus and agents. Most bureaus will not be interested in booking you anyway until you are well on your way to being a highly successful speaker (See Chapter 11, The Advantages of Working with Speakers' Bureaus and Agents). In that interim time, ***please*** don't put your money into producing a "bells and whistles" video demo before you are earning at least $3,000 per program. This is a complete waste of money—*a great deal of money!* Wait until *after* your career is beginning to bring you some decent and *consistent* bookings. Wait until you have completed at least 100 paid engagements, and your calendar is too full of low-fee dates, before you worry about creating a video. Use audio demos first, then create a video demo *as a means of raising your fee,* not as a means of starting out.

Other advantages to audio are that you can easily and quickly have one for each separate subject, which clients like. Buyers tell us they like audio demos, since they can listen to them in their cars, as they exercise, etc.

If you make fifty audio demo tapes you will spend from $100 to $500 for production and duplicating costs for a high quality audio. If you must bring in a professional recording company yourself, production costs on fifty video demos are about $1,000 to $3,000 for the very *lowest* quality, and duplication costs are about $4 to $15 per tape after that. Many speakers report that a good quality video cost them over $10,000 to produce.

CD Demos

As we write this a few speakers have begun to use CDs as demo tapes. The trouble with CDs is they are still very expensive to produce in small quantities. But they will no doubt be the trend in another few years. As for today, ***all*** of your buyers will have audio tape players, ***most*** will have video players, but how many will have a CD player? Many people still don't, especially at work.

Many of the emerging forms of electronic marketing tools are interactive, searchable, and portable. Buyers can do things with these new tools that they simply could not do with the paper versions. They can copy the information or graphics you send them directly into reports for others on the selection committee. Once they book you, they can copy your data right into the event promotional materials with incredible ease.

Demo Tapes on the Web?

Another trend in demos is audio and video clips that are downloadable from the Internet. These are not easily usable yet, but within a few years we feel most buyers will review speakers this way. Today, a 60-second video clip might take as much as 20 to 30 minutes to download with a 14.4kbps modem. Tomorrow, it will be faster.

How Long Should Your Demo Tape Be?

Another enduring myth in the speaking industry is that demo tapes must never be more than ten minutes long. This is because buyers are very busy people.

How long does it take you to decide you don't like a song you are listening to on the radio? Thirty seconds? You have about the same amount of time to prove to the buyer or bureau that you are:

- Liked by the audience
- An expert
- A good speaker

If you make a good impression, they will want to hear more. They will often sit through an hour to listen *to someone they like and are seriously considering.*

How Many Different Demos Should You Prepare?

We suggest you prepare a separate tape for each of your topics. If you have four very different topics, you *must* have four separate demo tapes (another good reason to use audio). It does not work to tell a buyer or potential client, "I really speak on leadership, but this tape on time management will give you a sample of my style!" They will assume that you are really a time management person who is experimenting with leadership as a new topic, and they will reject you. People who buy presenters are looking to buy *experts.* It is all right to mention on a tape that you also have programs on _____ and _____ at the end of the tape. You might suggest that you could be of service by presenting more than one topic at the same event. But don't try to demo them all on one tape.

What Is the Best Format for a Demo Tape?

Never send a prospective buyer an unsatisfactory or unflattering tape. You will never get a chance to change that first impression.

In the first 60 seconds the buyer should hear or see (in order of importance) that:

- The audience obviously liked you, as indicated by their wonderful response.

- You are an expert on the topic the buyer wants and have great, unique information to impart.

- You speak well, and have original material.

These points should not be made by an announcer in those first sixty seconds, but through your live examples in front of a real audience.

Arrange a demo tape that begins with your best segment, clearly showing your knowledge of the topic with lots of audience reaction. A rousing audience reaction, with you at your very best, is one of the most effective sales tools you can use. At the point when the applause fades out, edit in a segment of you speaking to the buyer, with a very brief sentence or two on who you are and what the audience will learn from this topic. Fade back into a live presentation, making sure there is audience background noise or a short music segue so the listener will understand you have changed segments. This should be you making a brilliant point in a presentation. When the applause fades out again, come back in with you (you in a recording studio) speaking to the buyer, explaining more about the topic and the services you provide, and how these will help a group. Now fade back into another portion from a live presentation. Repeat this process for anywhere from five to ten minutes, cutting in and out of other items that are effective to include in demo tapes.

Other Effective Items for Your Demo Tape

- *Testimonials:* A brief vocal testimonial by a prestigious person is great. Be sure the person is a buyer of speakers or a well-known person in your field, not another speaker. A speaker we know recently sent out video demos to speakers' bureaus that featured seven of his speaker pals endorsing him at the beginning of the tape. At a meeting we attended, we heard several bureau owners laughing about such endorsements. When you use an endorser, identify the person by name and company.

- *Products:* Using videos is a great way to show a display of your products. These help to establish you as an expert.

- *Full presentations:* Some speakers have a full presentation at the end of their tape: "Now, listen to a full one-hour speech as performed for the _____ Association."

- *Biographical credits:* Give your own credits and biographical information at the very end. Be brief about credits. Do not have a long intro by someone else. Buyers want to hear *you*.

Tips and Tricks for Creating Good Demos

- Your video demo must show you presenting in several different settings. This creates the image of someone who is used at many meetings and is in demand.

- Buyers want your audio or video demo to be live, recorded in front of a real audience, as you perform your speech on the topic they have asked for. Buyers do not like to listen to television and radio interviews, to see or hear marching bands or fancy swirls and designs.

- The listener must see and hear the audiences! What they want from you is an audience learning and having a good time. Show this to them on the tape! Always make sure there are two mikes, with a double feed, one on you, one on the audience. That way the audiences' reactions will be recorded on the tape.

- While giving a speech, always repeat questions from the audience, otherwise they will not be heard on the tape.

- Never use canned laughter! Never, never, never!

- Remember to say at the end, "Please call the phone number on the front of this tape. I look forward to working with you to help you achieve your goals for your meeting." Do *not* print or record your phone number or address on the tape. If you do, bureaus cannot use it. If a bureau has asked you send out this tape, do not put your label on the front, put theirs.

- Select unique material for your demo. Never use a story that is well known, or is not original. Bureau owners and buyers of speakers have heard *all* the old stories. Edit a section of one of your speeches where you give new material on your subject and your audience is at its highest point.

- If you have a good audio segment, but not video, consider having the audio play while stills of you are flashed on the screen with the logos of the companies you have spoken for. Flashing just the letterheads of these big companies across the screen while a good audio is playing is also effective.

- Some speakers who use audio demos have the recording studio leave 30 seconds or so blank at the beginning of their audio demo tape. They slip the demo into their own cassette machine before they send it out and record a brief, customized message to the buyer they have just spoken to on the phone. Use the buyer's name and the suggesting bureau. Mention the things you discussed over the telephone. Customizing the tape takes just a minute, costs nothing extra, and can be a very powerful closing tool.

How Do You Get Your Presentation Taped?

Since your demo must be selections from several presentations, try to have every presentation you give video or audio taped with professional equipment. If you obtain just a few minutes of usable material from each you are doing well.

Many beginning speakers hear everyone tell them, "You must have a video demo!" so they go grab a canned audience and try to create one. The results are almost always embarrassing.

Many meetings already have equipment at the event to tape other sessions. If you are trying to develop a good demo, make it a standard part of your contract to suggest that you will allow them to video your presentation, and use the tape for training purposes later, for fee. Always specify that you are to receive a master of your program the day of the presentation.

Before you accept no-fee jobs, ask if they have taping equipment with a double feed. Offer to trade your program as a fund-raiser in exchange for their doing a professional job of recording your presentation and furnishing you with 200 demo tape and 100 audio tapes ready for sale.

Most colleges have wonderful taping equipment, and some have television production courses in which the students are looking for experiences, like taping your programs! Contact one of the business class teachers, and see if they would like a 30-minute presentation.

How to Package Demo Tapes

Be sure your demo tapes are attractively packaged with your picture, using appealing type, and in colors that match your presentation kit. Consider using the same material reduced in size. The same three things that go on the front of your presentation folder go on your demo tape:

- Topic title in large type in a bright color at the top.
- Great color picture of you.
- Under your picture, run your name and one line that explains why you are the expert on this topic.

Be sure the spine repeats the topic title in large type, bright color, and with your name following it in small type. Both audio and video tapes are stored flat, so a good spine title makes it easy to find the demo when it is urgently needed.

At Walters International Speakers' Bureau we often receive audio or video demos in commercial boxes with nothing but the name of the tape manufacturer on the front. Sometimes the title of the program or the speaker's name is scribbled on it in pencil. It is not possible to send this kind of material to our clients. We only deal with professional speakers. Everything has to look right and be right.

Prepare your demos, as you do all of your materials, in two ways:

1. When you book yourself, with your address, phone, fax, E-mail number, etc., on the outside of the tape box, and inside on the label, ready for them to use for their clients.
2. To send to speakers' bureaus with the individual bureau's name, phone, fax, etc., on it, and on all of the rest of your materials, ready for them to use for their clients.

Sending Out Materials for Bureaus   Often a bureau will ask you to send materials directly to their clients. Be sure your address, phone, fax, E-mail, etc., do not appear on any of these materials. This includes the backs of your photos, letters from clients, etc.

A speaker who sent his materials to our bureau recently had his contact information all over the demos, the presentation folder, in fact on every single page. He called to ask if we received it. (He had not called us prior to sending it.) We explained that no bureau could use what he had sent because his contact information was everywhere. He got very angry and said, "Oh, just stick your dumb label over the top." End of story, end of speaker.

What a crummy look one label pasted over another gives! First, it won't fit. Second, it looks cheap. Third, a speaker who says this to a bureau is saying he has no respect for the bureau. This is not a good way to get the bureau enthusiastic about working with you.

Our reaction to this man was that if he would treat a bureau owner in this rude and inconsiderate manner, we could expect the same poor treatment for our clients.

An easy way to accomplish customizing demo tapes for each bureau you work with is to print labels up with just your name and topic. Purchase fancy labels that will run through your laser printer, perhaps in gold. Have them ready in your computer with your name, topic, and title. Before you print them, add in the bureau's contact information. When the bureau sees that you have prepared your materials so beautifully just for their use, you will have begun a long and lucrative relationship. So simple. So inexpensive. So powerful.

Testimonials and Letters of Recommendation

Testimonials and letters of recommendation are very valuable to your career. Some will come to you unsolicited, but most require time, effort, and planning on your part. They are well worth it. Testimonials can be used in many ways:

- included live on demo tapes,
- scattered throughout your materials as quotes,
- reproductions of the full actual letterhead,

- bits and pieces of reproductions from the letterhead pasted together in an artist collage.

How to Get Letters of Recommendation

There are several ways to obtain written recommendations. Like all good things, they seldom happen by themselves.

A speaker once called us to complain that he was having trouble obtaining letters of recommendation from clients who had booked him. When we asked what method he was using, he explained that he had prepared six-page sets of extensive questions with rating totals at the bottom of each page.

It's no wonder no one mailed them back. He was asking his clients to spend too much time. Make it easy for people to give you testimonials.

Here are some tips to help you.

- Make it a habit to discuss a letter of recommendation with the buyer before each program. Explain that the letter is very important to your career and that you will especially appreciate the effort and thoughtfulness of the planner in giving it to you.

- Help your buyers write the letter of recommendation. When you have finished a program, and someone important in the group gives you a sincere compliment, say, "I am so honored by our comments. Would it be acceptable if I quoted you in my materials?"

    When they say yes, make it easy for them. "Super. Let me drop you a note with that phrasing as you just said it." (Some speakers use recorders for this, asking first if they may record their comments). Follow up, and always send a note of thanks.

- Use audience rating sheets each time you speak. (See the section on "How Rating Sheets Can Help You Get New Bookings," in Chapter 4: From Free to Shining Fee.)

Which Recommendations and Testimonials to Use

If this potential client is likely to be interested in your program on leadership, add to your presentation kit some copies of your most impressive, complimentary letters from other groups who have heard you speak on leadership. Highlight the word "leadership" in the letters of recommendation. This backs you up as an expert on the topic.

Next, choose letters from the prospective buyers' own industry. Make it easy for them to see that you are experienced in their industry.

Also, highlight the portions of the letters where your clients mention other benefits the prospective buyers have told you they want. For the buyer looking for plenty of humor, highlight sentences such as, "Kept us all laughing."

Another idea, used by several prominent speakers, is to pull out the most important line from a letter and print it across the top of the page in large type, underlined in red. For example: "You've done it again. Even better than the last three times you spoke to our group!" (signed) Mary Smith, CEO of XYZ Corp.

Send only testimonials from paid speaking engagements. If all of your endorsements are from service clubs, the buyers' and speakers' bureaus will raise their eyebrows and think, "This speaker has never been paid to speak. She's not a professional."

Letters from celebrities or leaders in the industry you speak for should go into every presentation kit. Be careful not to include material from controversial people. Your circle of friends might think this person is wonderful, but the CEO of a large company can take one look at such material and reject your program, out of fear that you will not talk about the desired subject, but will get off on a controversial subject instead.

Use Current Letters

Do not use letters that are more than two years old. If you get a particularly good letter, perhaps from a famous or high-ranking person or prestigious company, white out the date before you reprint the letter for use in your presentation kits.

Calendars

Many speakers mail us their updated calendars monthly. This serves several purposes:

- keeps your name in front of speakers' bureaus;
- shows that you are busy and therefore must be a good speaker;

- the bureau may see you are scheduled to be in a specific location and can make a match for a client there

When you mail your calendar, keep it simple! A bureau will spend about five seconds looking at it. As with all other marketing materials, your name, your topic, and your photo should be where they can be easily seen.

"Bio" Sheets

Your speaker's biography should also be included in every presentation kit. Speakers often send our bureau a curriculum vitae (see the glossary at the end of book) thinking it will suffice as a bio. The two are quite different. A CV lists the educational, professional history, and job qualifications of the speaker and may be several pages long. A speaker's bio is one sheet or less. It lists the reasons *this* speaker is an expert on *this* subject.

We once had a speaker send us a bio that began with her birth weight. Your bio is not your life history. The buyer just wants facts about your *qualifications to speak on your topic*. If you have owned a business in your field, worked with many companies in your area, written articles or books on your subject, and spoken for major companies or been presented with honors, these are the things you should list in your bio. Keep is as short and simple as possible. Put speaking credits first, then other publicity, such as media appearances. Your picture and topic title should go at the top of the page.

The Importance of High-Quality Publicity Photographs

Presentation kits don't always contain a separate photo. But you will need hundreds of copies of black-and-white and color glossy publicity photos. You'll use photos on book jackets, album and tape covers, brochures, business cards, letterhead, magazine articles, and websites.

What Sort of Pictures Should You Take?

Your publicity photographs must help convey the image of a competent, polished speaker and expert. Therefore, the quality of your publicity photographs must be top-notch.

Hire a photographer who has a studio or a complete set of portable lights and is familiar with the process of shooting good business photos. Do not choose an "artsy," soft-focus, or outdoor-shot specialist. Women especially get trapped into taking glamorous shots rather than photos that give the impression of someone you would trust to balance your checkbook.

Gentlemen and ladies, go to someone who has a makeup artist. Studio lights always do odd things to your skin. You need makeup to look normal and healthy. There are currently small inexpensive photo shops in most malls that offer "glamour" pictures. They do your makeup and supply some costumes. But they also do good business shots of you in your own clothes.

Lighting is the key to good photography. Be sure the background is light if your skin tone is dark, and that the background is dark if you are fair. A brunette against a dark background gives the effect of a face peeking out of a black bag. Contrast makes an interesting picture. Tell the photographer you want pictures with sharp contrast for media reproduction.

Your eyes should be lit so that your expression snaps out of the picture. A good photographer will "capture your spirit." Take along to the photographer's studio the props you use on stage—such as a telephone, a sign, or a microphone. Your apparel for the session should include a sports outfit, formal attire, and several business costumes. The photographer may take as many as 100 shots of you with the different costumes and drops showing you in a variety of business poses and action shots. Suggest that color pictures be shot at the same time as the black and white ones. Be prepared to pay extra for this service, but remember that it does save you the time of a separate shooting session.

Beware of having your photograph printed on your materials in pastels or bright colors. Colored ink on a photograph looks ghastly. Use either black on white, very dark brown or full color for photos.

How Do You Get Action Shots?

Quality action photos of you speaking are wonderful for your promotional materials. However, they are difficult to obtain. You need shots that capture you speaking and the crowd responding. This works very well if you work with a hands-free or long-cord microphone and are able to go down into the audience.

Here are several ideas to help you obtain action shots:

- Hire a professional photographer to cover your speeches.

- If you cannot afford to hire a professional photographer to cover your speeches, ask the buyer if anyone in the group is an amateur photographer and would be willing to take pictures of you. Give this person a gift, perhaps one of your books, to thank him or her.

- Often, the group you will be addressing already has hired a photographer for the event. Ask the photographer if he or she can take some shots of you while you work. Offer to pay for the pictures.

- Carry a 35mm camera with you to your speaking engagements, loaded with black-and-white film. Keep it at the ready and ask someone from your audience to take live shots.

- Call a camera shop or college with a photography class that is near the venue you will be speaking at. Ask for a recommendation of a student or amateur photographer to come and shoot two 36-exposure rolls of black-and-white film while you are presenting. Then have the film developed yourself at a quality developer. Most corner "quick and fast" photo shops are not going to give you the quality you want for your promotional photos. Do some checking in your area to find out where the professional photographers go to get their film developed.

Try for "Name-Dropping" Photos

Many savvy speakers always carry a loaded camera with them. If there is a celebrity or well-known speaker on the program with you, ask for a shot of them shaking your hand or looking at your book. These pictures are great for publicity. Another good photo is of you with the buyer or president of the group that booked you. Send a copy of this picture with the articles you write for them in the future, or use the photo to help illustrate their testimonial letter or letter of recommendation.

Articles by You and About You

Our 1996 survey found the number one choice for best passive marketing is *exposure through the press and writing articles*.

When you send presentation kits to prospective clients, enclose copies of the articles you have written, or those that were written about you, that are on the topic the buyer is interested in. Highlight those sections in the articles where you discuss the issues and problems in which your buyer expressed an interest.

When you have an article published, ask for or buy copies of the publication. Some magazines (such as *Sharing Ideas*) offer reprints of just the page you are featured in backed up with the front cover. These single sheets make super additions to your presentation kit.

Twenty First-Century Electronic Desktop Marketing Tools

To market themselves for the past 100 years, speakers have been using: brochures, newsletters, catalogs on paper, phonograph records, then audio tapes, and now video tapes. Although the information is very similar to what speakers have used for years to obtain bookings, we are seeing new marketing tools emerge as speakers become "cyberpreneurs" and use electronic desktop marketing. The ability to connect to a million or more people on a commercial information service makes the modem an extremely effective marketing tool when combined with such features as the Web, Fax on Demand, E-mail newsletters, and on-line forums.

Electronic desktop marketing, when used wisely, is a proven and profitable method with a global market and it requires a much smaller investment than conventional marketing.

This section will give you ideas on how to use twenty first-century marketing tools and help your materials stand out among the piles of materials that buyers receive constantly.

Marketing with Wide-Area Hypermedia! (Web Pages)

The Web has changed the way people view and create information and marketing tools. The speakers who are currently doing a huge number of bookings from the Internet are those with high-tech topics. For instance, Peter de Jager of Canada tells us he does a great many bookings at excellent fees with his topics: "Managing the Impact of Technological Change" and "The Year 2000 Computer Crisis." People who buy these are also on the Net, so they look for expertise there first. If your topic has any connection to programming, computers, business futurists, technology, software, etc., then you *must* have a Web presence.

Check Out Your Market Before You Get on the Web

If you decide to create your own Web page, see how others in your own industry are benefiting. A good way is to use one of the many search engines and check out the newsgroups, mailing lists, and special interest groups related to your product or market. Subscribe to a few and follow the threads. Ask others what their Internet experiences have been and what has benefited them the most.

Web Malls and Directories

Some on-line directory services are like the yellow pages of a phone book. If you just have a sample listing, then there is no fee. If you want an "ad," it costs. If the directory service specializes in an industry, then there is almost always a charge to be involved.

Some companies set up a "mall" and sell you space. This is something like a directory, but on a grander scale. They create a spot for you, and advertise it on the Web. When someone is looking for "speakers," then their site, and others like it, appear with the results from the search engines. The buyer clicks on that name, and the link jumps them right to the directory. Then there are search engines within the site to help the buyer find a speaker. It was simple and easy for us to be involved with these directory services. We just mailed them a simple package of information. They took what we gave them and made it look terrific. We did not have to know how to use E-mail or a computer in order to use this sort of advertising. We could simply use the Web page like a telephone directory ad that said, "Call us here!" Using this sort of service was a great way to get started on the Web.

Creating Your Own Website

You have several options on how to set up access to your own website. You can host the site on your own computer or put it on a "server's" computer. Either way you need Internet access, which a service provider will supply for you.

If you do it yourself, you will need to leave your computer on at all times so the line stays open. If you have your server host the site for you, you will need to have a way to go into it and "fix" and update the information. Servers are very eager to do this for you, for a fee of course. But you can learn how to do it yourself.

We decided we could not in good conscience tell you the benefits of using a service to create your site, if we had not tried to create one on our own. But even with the "easy" Mac programs (we used Adobe's SiteMill®), creating our site meant Lilly spent an entire weekend poring over the program and manual, learning how to use it correctly, then about 30 hours in creating a 30-page site (http://www.walters-intl.com). Not horribly difficult, but after that weekend she was grateful to hand the project over to the experts at our internet provider, Mike Frick of Speakers Platform.

E-mail on Demand

If you cannot afford your own website, there are several companies that will have your article available via E-mail on demand. You just list the "address" in your materials, and they post the articles, press releases, outlines, or any sort of documents you wish to have available to the public. There is a small fee for this.

Forums and Newsgroups as Marketing Tools

Forums are a good way to "network" with others in your related field, not just other professional speakers, but those in your targeted industries and areas of expertise. As you haunt these various message areas you will become involved in conversations. But make sure to have something to say rather than "Hire me!" Otherwise, it is just like walking up to people having a conversation at a party and butting in with some odd, unrelated remark.

Less is more when it comes to buyers. You can't come on strong, especially in this new on-line world. Buyers who are put off will just back off as they throw flames at you. He spent his time on-line creating *relationships* with these potential buyers. He was soon being booked and referred by members of the forum worldwide! When a speaker does a good job for a forum member, they post it for everyone else to see. In this case 2000 members—many of them potential buyers—saw the rave reviews about Tom. This can be more effective marketing strategy, and certainly more cost effective, than a standard letter of recommendation.

You can also create your own newsgroups or forums as a service to your customers. Go to your on-line service, or the search engine on your Internet server and do a search using, "create newsgroups." You will find many articles that explain how it is done within your own computer and Internet set-up.

Tip: Sign your E-mail! Every day we get E-mail in which the sender forgets to add a signature at the end. E-mail automatically tells the receiver the E-mail address of the sender, but does not tell the receiver who you are. All we see is your E-mail address. Something like "CyberCutie@aol.com," is not very informative in a business communication!

Fax Mailing Campaigns

We do a great deal of fax campaigning and find it very beneficial. *Note:* Some businesses get very annoyed if you send them faxes. The federal government has passed laws prohibiting *advertising* by fax. Make sure those you "campaign" to are those that have *asked* to be on your faxing list! Or, make sure that you have an 800 number listed where they can call and request that they be deleted from your list. It is always a good idea to check with a fax company in your area, or an attorney, for updates on this issue before you do a fax broadcast. You can quickly clean your fax list so that only those who want to be on your list receive your faxes.

Fax campaigns can be done in three ways:

Using Your Fax Machine

Most fax machines are programmable to develop a phone book of your clients. You just need to program them to send, say, your newsletter, to everyone within the group you have selected. (Many copy machines now have this same option.) You just put the newsletter into the fax, and say (more or less), "Send this to group XYZ." Then the fax machine just keeps dialing the phone until it reaches everyone on your list.

Using Your Computer's Fax/Modem

Faxing people from your computer is the faster way to send a fax. We generate almost no paper documents anymore. We create everything within our computer, and fax it to our clients or speakers from our computer's fax/modem. When a buyer calls in, we input the information about the meeting into our computer as they are talking. (A good headset is needed if you plan to type and talk.) Often, while they are still talking, we are able to fax the buyer a list of speakers that fit the needs of the event being planned.

When we want to do a fax marketing campaign, for instance a speaker going to a certain city, we create the message, grab the clients' names in the same geographic area, and schedule a time for the computer to send it off. Then the computer and the fax/modem send the faxes, one at a time, usually all through the night.

Fax Broadcasting Services

Fax broadcasting is a fast and efficient means of distributing document information to a large number of recipients all at the same time. Using a broadcast service is an inexpensive delivery alternative to direct mail.

To use a fax broadcasting service, E-mail or mail them the database with fax list of, for example, 5000 people. Then you fax them the item you want faxed. ZOOM! All 5000 are sent at the same time! Amazing. Having your own computer dial 5000 phone calls one at a time is time consuming, even if you have it done after hours while you are out doing something else.

You can send all kinds of document types via a fax broadcast. Usually a good service can send near-laser-quality output on standard fax machines. Once they are done, they send you comprehensive transmission reports for each broadcast. They can also delay the broadcast to off-peak hours, which allows you to save money on jobs.

Fax-on-Demand

Fax-on-demand is a convenient central repository of document information that is accessible from a telephone and deliverable to any standard fax machine anywhere in the world. Speakers are able to give their buyers the fax number. Then, when the buyers need introductions, bios, outlines of presentations, articles on specific topics, etc., they are able to call the fax numbers and a voice prompts them through document selection.

Fax-on-demand is accessible from any touch-tone phone and does not require calling from a fax machine. Selected documents can be directed to any fax number. You can buy your own fax on demand machine for your office, or use a fax on demand service.

It's an efficient and easy-to-use 24-hour fax information service for your clients.

1-800-Fax-Response

If you sell a great deal of products, you might also consider a fax service that can centrally collect unlimited data—surveys, inquiries, orders, membership updates, as well as other information—and speedily forward it to you. These services have the ability to handle large quantities of incoming fax responses. Some have an 800 number assigned for your buyer's use, 24-hour availability, rapid delivery of received fax responses, and are "never busy" to your clients.

To *Speak and Grow Rich* you must have the tools of the trade. In addition to your skills as a speaker, you will constantly develop these marketing tools. We have tried to give you an overview of the many tools available to you. No one uses all of them, but you will need some. Start with your one-sheets, then expand to all the wonderful ideas that will occur to you as you progress. Remember, your materials are often compared by the buyers with materials from many other speakers. Do everything in your power to make your materials eye-catching and impressive so that the speakers' bureau representative or buyer will reach for yours first.

*H*igh-Profit Public Seminars

Public Seminars have the highest profit—and the highest risk—of any enterprise in the speaking industry.

Public seminars are sold to the public (individuals) rather than to corporations or associations. Often corporations look for public seminars to send their people to when they have a need for training, because either they can't release large numbers of people at one time or they only need a few of their people trained in the specific topic area.

Many speakers produce their own seminars and market them to all sorts of specialized public audiences. The possibilities of those who might attend a public seminar are endless: investors in real estate or precious metals, people who want to start their own businesses, and thousands of other business and personal interest groups.

Seminars are held all over the world. Anthony Robbins offers seminars at his own private hotel in Fiji, as well as at other exotic locations. Several companies provide "adventure seminars" that take place during mountain climbing trips or on sailing ships.

Many specialty technical seminars, such as those for consultants, doctors, dentists, and other professionals, charge attendees $1,500 or more per person. Those who register are willing to pay these fees because a good seminar can help enhance their careers by increasing their knowledge and income-earning potential.

Twenty-five participants at $1,500 each translates into a gross of $37,500 just for registrations. Additional income is gained from back-of-the-room (BOR) product sales. A real estate seminar leader reports typically that his seminar BOR product sales usually equals the amount his seminar grosses from registration fees. Therefore, he brings in about $75,000 for each seminar that registers twenty-five attendees.

Weekend personal growth seminars often are marketed at $1,500 per attendee per day. Multiply that figure by 200 participants and you get a gross income of $300,000 for a two-day weekend retreat. As a rule, the attendees also pay for their own transportation, hotel rooms, and meals. It is easy to see why speakers add special public seminars to their speaking-fee repertoire.

Many famous speakers and business leaders began their companies with seminars in their homes. Barbara de Angelis, author of *Are You the One for Me*, and Jean Nidich, creator of the Weight Watchers company, started out this way.

Anthony Robbins started very small, but today he presents live public seminars all over the world. Sometimes he presents the program live through the network of United Artists Theaters. The theater seats contain keyboards so that attendees can ask questions of Mr. Robbins. His presentation is broadcast to theaters across the country. In each location his products are offered for sale at the back of the room.

Producing and Marketing Your Own Public Seminar

To offer a seminar to the public, you must make all of the arrangements yourself. This includes locating lists of good prospects, writing advertising copy, printing flyers and posters, sending out direct mail pieces, faxing and E-mailing announcements, telemarketing, reserving a seminar site, and taking care of refreshments, meals, and lodging. In short, you must act as your own sales agent, publicist, buyer, site arranger, promoter, playwright, finance manager, and then star in the show. You wear all of these hats, and more, when you create your own seminar.

If you decide to create and market your own seminar to the public, the following ingredients are essential for success:

- Your seminar must appeal to a specialized market. In other words, it must have a niche, such as meeting the information needs of state income tax preparers, dog lovers, women going through divorce, those who wish to expand their profit in the world of paid speaking, etc.! You might consider a high-priced seminar for a small market, or a lower-priced one for a large, competitive market.

- You must be recognized as an authority in the seminar's subject matter before you take the program to the marketplace. People want to learn from successful experts, not unknown orators.

- You must develop good marketing skills and make astute use of direct mail, advertising, and promotion.

Seminar Marketing Tips

The secret to profitable public seminars is good marketing. You can pull in responses and registrations by using direct mail to specific markets, newspaper advertising, publicity stories, and specialized magazine advertising in trade publications aimed at a particular market. We explore these, and much more, in greater depth in Chapter 10: Becoming Famous: Promotion Strategies with Buyers, Bureaus, and the Press. But we'll give you a few tips here with specifics as they apply to public seminars.

Create the Right Image in Your Marketing

We recently received a call for advice from a man who had lost more than $5,000 promoting a seminar. His advertising had brought in only two registrations. His topic was "Making Money Fast." The registration fee was just $25. What happened? He had bought expensive ads on the financial pages of his local daily newspaper. He had guaranteed a large attendance and paid a high price for a seminar room in a very expensive hotel.

We believe he went wrong in his focus. First, his program and price did not appeal to the financial page readers, who probably thought both the title and fee were a con. If the fee had been $500, if his name had been known in financial circles, and if his title had been "Careful Investment Strategies," he might have obtained ten attendees and a profit. His title and price, however, were aimed at people with lower incomes, most of whom were not readers of the financial pages. Notices posted in laundromats might have pulled attendees at this price range.

Second, he could have reached the right audience if he had used the local radio talk shows for publicity interviews, advertised in the shoppers' column, and held the meeting at a lower-priced location. If he had raised his seminar fee from $25 to at least $100, his title might have worked, and given him a profit instead of a dead loss.

Start a Newsletter

Consider starting a newsletter aimed at your market. Mail or fax it it to your prospective attendees at least twice a year, or quarterly. This keeps them thinking of you as an expert, and gives you a place to announce seminar dates. Note that if your newsletter is not filled with must-know information they will simply trash it. If the information has enough value, you can charge for it.

Publish a Yearly Updated Seminar Calendar

We publish an updated calendar of our upcoming seminars in the United States and internationally. We include the location and contact phone numbers of all of our public seminar sponsors and partners. This list goes out with everything!

- We publish it in *Sharing Ideas.*
- We mail it with every sample copy of *Sharing Ideas.*
- We include it with every product order we ship.
- We list it on our website.
- We fax it with our other letters and information.

We find that listing the whole year's seminar dates is very beneficial. If you only advertise one date at a time, many people will not be able to attend. We have been surprised that people from one state often register for our seminars at other locations. When we presented our *Speak and Grow Rich* seminar in Dallas, one attendee flew in from Brazil. We asked him why he chose Dallas. He explained that his daughter lived there, so not only would he obtain the knowledge he wanted, but he would be able to visit with her at the same time.

Giving prospects a choice of places and dates increases the chance that they will register for your seminar. Listing a series of dates also lets prospects know you are successful at what you offer.

Try Postcards

Our experience with direct mail shows that what works best is a series of three large postcards mailed to potential attendees in the geographical area where our seminar will be held. We give new information and an update on each card. We mail these three weeks apart to our entire mailing list in each area.

List Your Seminar with Seminar Companies

Two companies who will list your public seminar topic and dates on a nationwide computer network are the Seminar Information Service, 17752 Skypark Circle, Suite 210, Irvine, CA 92714, and Skiebo, 44 Forster Ave., Mount Vernon, NY 10552. Many daily newspapers have a seminar section where you can advertise the seminars you sell to the public.

Search the Internet for sites that will list your seminar.

Develop Your Own Mailing Lists

Develop a mailing list, Fax number list, and E-mail list of your own from every attendee and inquiry. We find that 75 percent of our seminar attendees come through recommendations from past attendees. We use our rating sheets at our public seminars to ask current attendees for names of others who might benefit from this program. At least 50 percent of our attendees give them to us right there. We mention the referring person's name on our first mailing to the referral.

Trade Mailing Lists

Consider trading mailing lists with others who offer seminars on topics related to yours. People are creatures of habit. If they will attend one paid seminar, they may be very interested in another on a similar subject.

Try the Two Step!

The Dale Carnegie organization and many, many others have found a "two-step" to be effective in increasing attendance. They offer a no- or low-fee seminar. At this seminar they give such great value, and create such excitement, that attendees want to sign up for their complete, more expensive course.

Other Income Opportunities with Public Seminars

Taking Advantage of a Three-Way Profit Possibility

You may be able to sell tickets to a cruise or rooms at a resort to your attendees and make a markup on those, at the same time that you sell registrations to your seminar. Sometimes these venues will help you with beautiful advertising materials to send to your prospects, and some will even assist you with mailings. You also can sell your products during the program, giving you a three-way profit possibility.

Selling Products at Seminars

We have an entire chapter on creating and selling products (Chapter 9: Speaker Products: Triple Your Income) but it is so important to your income for seminars, we want to reinforce it here with some specific ideas for public seminars.

If your seminar has the right ingredients and back-of-room (BOR) products to sell, it can be a great revenue producer when you present your own programs. Seminars charge from $39, on the low end, to $5,000 a weekend on the high end. A good seminar at $39 should easily attract 100 attendees if marked properly, and bring in $3,900 in registrations. However, you will easily bring in another $3,900 from the same group if you develop valuable products: a continuing newsletter, books, tapes, and often a hot line or consultation service via phone after the event. At these less expensive seminars the products are offered at the back of the room as "bundles" or "systems."

Many seminar leaders think of their BOR table as a miniature information store that stocks the best of materials available on their topic. Starting the "store" and keeping it stocked does require an investment. But most publishers are glad to offer you their materials at from 40% to 50% off retail. The back-of-room display saves the attendees time, since they do not have to search through stores and catalogs to find the products they have been inspired to explore by the presenter.

At more expensive seminars the product is often, but not always, included as part of the registration fee. These packages are aimed at a particular audience, such as salespeople or managers.

Barney Zick, who is well known and successful in real estate, developed a major mailing list of people interested in investing in income property. Now he markets his seminar to his mailing list. Zick charges an average fee for the seminar, then offers his special materials on income property as back-of-room products. He reports that his average product sales alone are $20,000 per performance.

Working with Others to Produce Public Seminars

If you work with someone else who will produce your seminar, your profit will be much less, but so will your risk. All you do is show up, speak, and sell products. You are either paid a flat fee (smaller than you will receive for corporate or association work) with a cut of product sales, or you arrange to "share-the-gate."

The types of companies that host public seminars are well-nigh endless! Look at any business or association that might want to increase their visibility, or make use of a facility that is not full seven days a week:

- Colleges
- Churches
- Public city buildings and town halls
- Urban Independent Seminar Companies
- PTAs
- School Booster Clubs who want to raise money for athletic or musical equipment, trips, or uniforms
- Hospitals
- Chambers of Commerce
- Service Clubs (Rotary, Kiwanis, Lions, etc.)
- On-line seminar classes
- Associations or groups that wish to offer their members seminars, and are glad to book them on a share-the-gate basis
- Local television stations, newspapers, and radio shows

As we go over a few of these in more detail, open your mind and see what other ideas come to you of businesses that might want to do public seminars!

Public Seminar Companies

Some of the more famous public seminar companies are CareerTrack, Fred Pryor, National Seminars, and Dun & Bradstreet, but there are many others, all with various ways of doing business.

A number of seminar-producing companies contract with speakers to deliver a given topic several times a week on a specified circuit. One circuit might be the Far West, while another would cover the Northwest and Alaska, and yet another covers the Southwestern United States, etc.

Speakers are contracted to present a seminar that is owned by the seminar company. The seminar's subject may or may not be one that you already know. The main requirement is that you are an experienced speaker and seminar leader. You learn the seminar and deliver it, adding your own stories and personality. Attendees at this type of seminar range from 25 to 300.

Speakers for this sort of seminar company may be paid in a share-the-gate arrangement (see more on this later in this section), but most often they are paid a flat fee of from $200 to $2,000 a day, with the average being about $400, plus travel expenses. Most presenters for these public seminar companies double that, or more, with their cut of the product sales made that day. Although these fees seem low, a series of programs and payment are assured. For example, a contract might be signed for 15 seminars in a four-week period, at $400 per day plus all expenses and a cut of product sales. The presenter is fairly well assured of bringing home $9,000 for that month. Many of these presenters end up doing a total of 70 to 100 paid dates a year for these companies, netting from $40,000 to $100,000 a year.

If the seminar company buys a seminar you have personally created, they usually pay you a fee or a royalty when other speakers present it for their company, as did CareerTrack when they used Tom Peters' "In Search of Excellence" program and Wes Roberts' "Leadership Secrets of Attila the Hun."

At a public seminar company, the subject matter is the star, not the speaker. These companies often have a number of speakers on the road at one time, each giving the same seminar and using the workbooks provided by the company. Each circuit is set up so that the speaker can complete one program, get on a plane or bus or rent a car, and go on to the next program for the following day. A typical schedule is two one-day seminars, a day off, then two more seminars.

Several of these companies create products such as audio or video recordings of the speakers' work, and offer them to the public through their catalogs. Royalties for these products also can be very lucrative.

New Wave Seminar Companies

As an emerging industry they call themselves by several names, including Urban Independent Adult Education and most recently New Wave seminar companies. One of the most famous of this type is The Learning Annex, but there are now similar companies in almost every major city in the U.S. with a population of two million or more. They offer noncredit adult courses. Each of these seminar companies publishes large catalogs several times a year that offer seminars on popular topics.

These classes are usually presented in a two- to four-hour format. Presenters are more often than not paid on a share-the-gate basis from which they pay their own expenses. Fees generally run from $39 to $99 per attendee. The average class pulls in about 40 attendees, while the more popular classes may pull in up to 150 attendees. Although the fees are normally split with the seminar company, product sales are normally all kept by the speaker. This is where the real money is made.

These companies feature famous speakers, and those with topics which are interesting to the public. Deepak Chopra, Brian Tracy, and Dottie Walters are featured regularly across the country by these seminar companies. Their catalogs are mailed or distributed in stands on street corners and in markets. In addition to the more traditional topics like business skills, self-esteem, or how to start a business, these companies look for many more subjects.

Colleges and Universities

Numerous public and private colleges offer noncredit classes. They produce catalogs of these programs which usually are mailed to every resident within their district. Most are offered on a "share-the-gate" basis. These classes are arranged on a per-head, per-session, or per-day basis. Call and discuss the possibilities, requirements, and financial arrangements with nearby colleges. Ask for the person who is in charge of the programs. When you are successful at one college, expand to the county, state, national, and international counterparts. Some speakers work in this field exclusively.

The college seminar market can be very lucrative and an excellent way to begin right in your local area, to promote yourself and your topic at no expense to you. These seminars also lead people who are interested in your topic and your other services to you.

Share-the-Gate and Fund-Raising Seminars

A variety of organizations sponsor seminars as fund-raisers for their treasuries. They work with speakers and seminar leaders on a "share-the-gate" basis. This title comes from an old circus term, which means that the performer receives part of the fees paid by the attendees. This kind of seminar is often done with sponsors such as hospitals, churches, colleges, universities, "New Wave" seminar companies (see previous section), Chambers of Commerce, school booster groups, and other organizations that need to raise funds, or that offer these seminars as their regular business.

Any group interested in increasing revenue will likely listen to your proposition for a seminar project, especially if your topic is closely suited to their members. For example, a woman speaker who presents "Parenting" programs works with the booster groups at schools. Instead of selling chocolate bars to raise money for the children's uniforms or other gear, parents enthusiastically sell tickets to the seminar. The trick is to find groups that will tie in best with your subject.

How to "Share" in a Share-the-Gate

In a share-the-gate, the speaker supplies the presentation and often pays his or her own travel expenses. The sponsors provide attendees, the hall, refreshment breaks, advertising, their list of prospects, postage, printing, the labor to send the flyers out, and, occasionally, travel expenses for the speaker.

The usual arrangement is a fifty-fifty split of the gate for ticket sales although different organizations work at various percentage levels. For instance, one speaker we know does a great deal of work for a South African seminar promoter. They pay him 15 percent of the gross ticket sales, but they also pay for his travel between the U.S. and Africa, and two days of hotel and meals for each one day of seminar.

Some seminar companies want to split the "profit." We strongly suggest you do not make this arrangement with any promoters. *We have* **never** *seen this work to the presenter's advantage.* There just does not seem to be a profit left at the end of the day.

How to Start with Share-the-Gate

Contact groups within 100 miles of your home that might want to "share the gate." Let's say you get 20 groups interested. Suggest that you offer at least two programs a year for them, perhaps a first program for beginners, and a follow-up, advanced program. This means you have 40 dates booked a year. Non-name speakers in smaller facilities can make from to $50 to about $2,000 per date on this sort of booking if they **don't** sell products. If you create products and sell them at the back of the room, you will do even better. But let's be cautious and say that to start you make an average of $200 per date for these "share-the-gate" seminars. That's an extra $8,000 a year, a nice start to your speaking career. Once you develop products— manuals, workbooks, books, tapes, any items attendees will need to accomplish the subject you are teaching—you can double and triple that amount. (See Chapter 9: Speaker Products: Triple Your Income.) Often the attendees will want to consult with you on an hourly basis for more individual help, which increases your total income per event even more.

These sort of "share-the-gate" programs are an excellent way to develop your talent and gain the experience you need. The more experience you have, the more marketable and valuable you are to bureaus and other buyers. In addition, you will begin to get spin-off business. People in your audience will begin to say, "That was terrific. How much would you charge to come to our company and present the same program?"

Adapting Your Seminar for Cruises and Resorts

Cruise ships, exotic spa resorts, and other facilities dedicated to comfort and pleasure are an increasingly important marketplace for professional seminars and speakers, not to mention a whole lot of fun! Seminars of all types can be held at these exotic settings. Also, you can create an exotic adventure seminar in *any* location.

Cruise ships usually pay a fee only to the evening entertainers, such as magicians, singers, and dancers. Professional speakers will not be paid a fee by a cruise ship line unless they are celebrities (and often not even then). Of course, the association corporation that books your program might use a ship as the venue. Many new cruise ships with meeting facilities have been launched, the ship becomes the venue for the meeting instead of a hotel on dry land. The group who books you will often pay your regular fees, plus you are treated to a vacation at the same time.

There are two other ways you can be booked on cruise ships:

- Exchange your programs for a working vacation at sea.
- Hire the venue and sell tickets as a public seminar at sea.

Exchange Your Program for a Working Vacation at Sea

Cruise ships also feature four to five "enhancement" speakers per trip for regular vacationers. Numerous speakers present their programs while sailing in the South Seas, traveling up the Amazon, or even stern-wheeling it up the Mississippi River.

Many seminar subjects are offered to passengers: gourmet cooking, self-improvement, how to invest, fitness in the fast lane, astrology, history, and hundreds of other topics. There seems to be no limit to the subjects that cruise ship travelers enjoy in a seminar or speech.

One type of speaker who is popular aboard cruise ships is the "destination" presenter. This speaker's program topic ties in with the history of the destination or with the flavor of the cruise. To catch a cruise company's attention, tailor your area of expertise to the needs and interests of a cruise ship audience. For example, Eskimo culture is explored and explained during Alaskan voyages, while Britain's

Crown Jewels are a popular subject on the cross-Atlantic run to Southampton on the QE2, and someone who tells the stories and lessons of Marco Polo would be a great match for travelers on China cruises. A speaker performed as "Mark Twain" during some of the Halley's Comet cruises to the South Pacific. The real Mark Twain, it was pointed out, had been born on one swing of the comet and died on its return.

Finding that special niche can make all the difference. Believe it or not, a speaker who presents a three-dimensional show on the sinking of the Titanic has appeared many times on cruise ships.

Speakers and seminar leaders typically work for cruise lines on a trade basis. They are given passage for themselves and sometimes a guest in exchange for presenting one or several sessions during the cruise.

Hire the Venue and Sell Tickets as a Public Seminar

To put on your own seminar at a resort site, or on a cruise ship, you proceed just as you would in arranging your own seminar anywhere else. The resort or ship lends itself very well to a high-priced executive or family retreat program. We have found they do not work as well for the normal business program that an attendee must receive permission to attend. Often the seminars are sold most successfully to entrepreneurs, couples, or families. When selling them to corporations, the business applications and benefits must be very clearly stated, along with the reason that the learning will better be accomplished at a resort or fun venue over a traditional venue.

Famous seminar leaders, such as Ed Foreman, offer seminars for executives in this manner. Often 50 to 100 attendees come to spend the weekend, be inspired, learn stress-reducing and other health skills, and come away refreshed and motivated. Fees per attendee can be from $2,000 on up for this type of weekend seminar.

Tax Tips for Seminars Held Aboard Ship or at Resorts

You may offer executive retreat seminars that can qualify as a double win: knowledge plus tax deductions. However, the rules can get trickier when cruise ships or resorts outside of the United States are involved. Before planning to sell such a seminar, you should check with the Internal Revenue Service or your tax attorney and find out exactly what you must do so that your seminar registrants can qualify for a full or partial income tax deduction. Tax rules change each year, so be sure to update your material frequently.

Virtual Seminars: Correspondence School to Net Classrooms

The "virtual seminar" is the next wave in speaking industry trends. The Internet, satellites, and computers are changing what a "meeting room" looks like. The meeting rooms of the future actually could be your attendees' living rooms. With telecommunications and computer technology, a new "anytime-anywhere" world of information has become available to everyone through long-distance learning.

Virtual classrooms are already being widely used in business and academia. The benefit of having the attendees simply log on their computers at a specific time for a teleconference of some type will make 16-hour business flights even less attractive than they are now. In addition, pay-per-view seminars will soon be available via cable on home television sets.

Distance Learning

Distance learning simply means teaching attendees and students who are not in the same room with you.

The idea of classes given through the mail via correspondence school is well established. It became official with the educational system in the United States in 1926 when the National Home Study Council was formed. There is still a bit of skepticism in academia toward "correspondence school," but call it "distance learning" and

141

it immediately becomes chic and acceptable in both the academic and the business world, probably because now the magic of "technology" is involved. For years, colleges have offered distance learning by way of lectures on your home television.

In addition to businesses, we find reference after reference about the many schools and universities using virtual classrooms. Most modern distance learning uses telephone lines. Telephone companies give grants and training to teachers to encourage them to use distance learning.

Technology today has brought distance learning right to the brink of drastic change. The medical industry was the first to adopt new distance learning the way we envision all business eventually will use it. Doctors are extremely busy, and don't want the additional downtime of travel.

Benefits of Distance Learning

Professional speakers might well use some of the many types of distance learning available today as ongoing training opportunities. There are many benefits to both the attendee and the presenter.

- Homework can be sent back and forth via mail, fax, or E-mail.
- There is a higher ratio of students to teachers than can be maintained in ordinary schools. This extends the presenters' productivity.
- Much less space is required to hold the class.
- Little or no travel costs are involved.
- Attendees don't have to commute or relocate.
- The presenters' geographic reach is extended.
- Distance learning is boundary-less as it levels the playing field and provides opportunities regardless of location. Information at the same level of sophistication and training can be offered to urban and rural locations.
- Updating electronic books and workbooks in the virtual seminar is simple and the production costs are a fraction of the cost of normal paper materials.

- Distance learning provides up-to-date information. The presenter is easily able to use only the most current information and does not need to worry about actual heavy costs of workbooks and materials.

- Participation and attentiveness are improved, particularly with interactive video, which provides a stimulating teaching environment.

- By its very nature, distance learning lends itself to just-in-time training. The attendees log on when they are ready to learn the appropriate "lesson" and download the information. If needed, they chat with the instructor via phone or E-mail.

Distance learning has been of great importance to speakers' income. Advances in technology will make it even more so as distance learning begins to use the newer tools of teleconferencing, business television and videoconferencing, desktop videoconferencing, and classes on the Internet.

Teleconferencing

Teleconferencing is a conference held among people in different locations by means of telecommunications equipment, such as closed-circuit television or phone lines. This could be a conference call or business television or videoconferencing.

Several speakers add value to their services by offering a miniseminar via a conference phone call either before or after the live talk. Some do this before a real-time, in-person presentation, to help establish the exact needs of the clients. Some sell this as an additional service after the talk—perhaps just for the managers, depending on the size of the group.

Business Television and Videoconferencing

Videoconferencing offers two-way video and two-way audio. The presentation is delivered to the audience's eyes and ears, as an interactive, electronic forum, using television and or telephone. Participants can watch and listen to experts in their field, ask questions, and share views from the comfort of an on-site meeting room.

For example: At Philips' fourth annual "Customer Day," they wanted to create an event focused on improving customer satisfaction. A Business Television network was created that transmitted the program via satellite to more than 300 sites in 55 countries over 3 continents. Philips' president, Mr. Jan Timmer, was able to broadcast his keynote speech to all the employees and customers at the same time! Different speakers were set up to speak at the same "meeting," actually delivering their presentations from different countries around the world. From their own offices, factories, hotels, and theaters they watch on normal or wide-screen televisions, cinema screens, videowalls or superprojectors 17 different languages saving millions for large international companies by bringing training to the employee." This sort of medium is excellent for training as well.

Desktop Conferencing (Text and Audio Only)

In addition to traditional videoconferencing, professional speakers are now able to offer programs that train people who sit at their own computers at their own workstations (or anywhere they have a laptop): desktop conferencing, and desktop videoconferencing. In a "live cyber-lecture" the speaker sits in front of his or her computer and "speaks" to hundreds of people who sit watching their screens at their offices, or at home.

Desktop conferencing is communicated via written words typed live to the students' screens. Desktop videoconferencing uses live video and audio projection of the speaker, and written words or graphics as the presenter chooses.

Currently there are millions who are able to use the written word technology through on-line services like AOL, CompuServe, and Internet servers, all of which provide ways to "chat" in this manner. Indeed, most of what you hear about people "talking" to each other on the Internet is done through typed messages, not with live video and audio. However, video and audio are being added to this medium in many businesses daily. It will not be too far in the future before the norm will be for every personal computer to come with a video camera and modem as part of the standard equipment.

Desktop Videoconferencing

More and more vendors are making all kinds of videoconferencing systems and centers available: AT&T, Kinkos, and many, many others. A little camera is fitted to the top of everyone's computer. A live picture of everyone at the "meeting" is then sent to all their screens. Normally this is done for small groups of 4-10. They see each other and the multimedia on their screens, all controlled by the seminar leader.

The best programs for trainers and speakers to use include interactive tools such as videoconferencing, hand-raising, annotation and electronic whiteboard with multimedia authoring.

Some of these new desktop video applications allow attendees to share their digital work by creating a small video picture window on the computer screen. Some products also let multiple users view applications running on each desktop. Thus a spreadsheet, for example, can be simultaneously seen and adjusted by several people. (See the Glossary for more explanation of these terms). In other software products, the student is able to ask a question by just clicking on the "hand" icon. The seminar leader sees a hand go up on his or her own computer. The instructor decides if and when to give the "floor" to the attendee, allowing everything the student draws or types on the screen to be visible to the others.

Today teleconferencing or videoconferencing companies rent "Public rooms" for these videoconferences. You can rent a room for your meeting in many of your local Kinko copy centers, local hotels, and schools.

Virtual Seminars on the Superhighway

These virtual on-line seminar classes are taught combining the traditional correspondence school format, E-mail, and live on-line chat. Some seminars also require that the students use off-line resources like books, audios, and videos.

On-line chat is a bit deceptive. It implies communication that is as fast as talking. Since you are keyboarding which is much slower than talking, it requires that the presenters be innovative to keep the pace moving. Speakers must reduce their best thoughts into "sound bytes," or type bytes as the case may be.

On-line classes are held through the Internet at websites or through on-line services. An on-line service creates a virtual campus. As in a real campus, you are restricted to the buildings they have constructed. The college wants you to follow their rules and procedures. You are limited to the results of their marketing brilliance—or lack thereof!

You could equate presenting a seminar from your own Internet website with offering a seminar at a site you went out and rented or bought yourself, your own personal seminar center. You make all the rules, pay all the expenses, reap all the profit, and cover all the losses.

Earning Income Teaching Desktop Classes

Presenters teaching through their own websites—especially those teaching computer-related classes—seem to make a greater income than those teaching through on-line services.

We found the highest income for presenters through on-line services to be about $30,000 per year. On the other hand, the presenter who was earning this amount was doing the seminars in addition to his full-time teaching job. He has no materials costs, as everything is sent via E-mail (therefore no postage costs either), and no travel—he never leaves home to teach these classes. Nor does he need to worry about packaging and having snappy clothes.

Presenters who teach from their own websites and also sell products, especially high-technology computer-related products, earn a great deal more. According to our research, these presenters can earn over $80,000 per year.

Classes Through On-Line Services

As we write this, AOL seems to be the most active of the on-line services in offering seminars. They offer classes from "Resume Writing," to "Basic Japanese." Fees are from $25 to $50 for a 4 to 8 week course. Some presenters charge separately for materials, and some include them in the seminar fee.

We anticipate that classes at Internet sites will grow faster and offer more to attendees than those offered through on-line services, as they are not limited by on-line service procedures. On the other hand, if the on-line services begin to truly market the classes they offer, they could be a much better venue.

Classes Through Internet Sites

As in all other aspects of speaking, you must market your program to make it successful. On the Internet this means:

- Listing your programs in all the available search engines.
- Developing an E-mailing list of potential attendees.
- Writing articles for magazines that potential users of the Internet and your product are most likely to read.
- Linking your site to other sites on the Web that are complimentary to yours.
- Asking your current clients and potential clients for referrals.

Broadcasting Back to the Home

There is a great deal of talk in the speaking industry about pay-per-view business public seminars. Companies like CareerTrack, one of the largest public seminar companies, are seriously considering offering their seminars to viewers in their own homes. While this is not being done yet, we predict it coming in the future for all professional speakers.

Speaker Products: Triple Your Income

Speakers are actually in the *information* business. As you develop your subject, study it, write articles about it, and come to new conclusions, your body of knowledge becomes more valuable and salable in many other formats. You can create videos, audio albums, workbooks, consulting sessions, CD ROMs, training materials, reports, calendars, posters, magazine articles, screen savers, software programs, T-shirts, hats and even toys based on your expertise. These products are the valuable offshoots of the body of knowledge in your speeches. They not only add significantly to your speaker's income, but are also reminders that leave a trail that prospects follow back to you.

Sales of speaker products can do more than boost your level of income. Creating excellent products also adds credibility and prestige to your position as an expert. You're much easier to publicize when you are the author of professional products.

Product is cited over and over by every successful speaker we know as one of the best marketing tools and sources of income for your speaking career.

Studies show that people only absorb and remember ten percent of most presentations. We learn best through repetition. Products provide that repetition and help attendees retain the knowledge you give them. They can continue learning from and enjoy your expertise—at work, at home, while driving in their cars, as they jog, etc.

Self-Publishing vs. Traditional Publishers

As you create your products, you will need to decide if you wish to publish them yourself, submit them to a traditional publisher, or both! Most people don't realize just what makes creating product the most lucrative part of a speaker's income, whether you self-publish or go with a major publisher. The big secret is that products must be "pushed" by the authors in the many ways we suggest in this chapter. It is nice to imagine someone will publish your product, invest thousands of dollars in promoting it, and then sell 10 million copies. That happens with about 30 books a year: over 147,000 are published annually!

We create our products both ways. We find we often make the same amount of end profit, whether we self-publish or use a major publisher. We may sell more with a major publisher, but our net is so much higher on our own products that we tend to make about the same. Let's explore both avenues.

Traditional Publishers

Traditional publishers have two categories: "big house" and "small house." As you can guess, a big house is a major publisher, a small house a smaller business. A large publisher is harder to get into, but has more resources. A small house has fewer resources, but has a greater focus on pushing your product—you are a bigger fish in a smaller pond.

If you sell your products to publishers, they will edit them, design the cover, market them in bookstores, and often sell them to book clubs. You receive an advance deposit against royalties. You normally pay for your own writing expenses—travel, research, and time.

Royalties are usually 10 to 15 percent of the retail list price. To sell these books yourself, you purchase them from your publisher at wholesale and you sell them at the retail price, earning the difference in addition to your royalties. Usually you will be able to buy the product from a publisher at anywhere from 35 to 50 percent off the retail list price, depending on the publisher and the quantity of your purchase.

Advantages:

- These publishers reach a worldwide market that normally you would not have contacted or known about. You will make contacts, sales, and speech bookings you would otherwise never have made.
- A major publisher has everything in place so that your book could sell into the millions.
- You do not need to worry about production issues and costs: typesetting, editing, printing problems, ISBN, bar coding, cover design, etc.

Disadvantages:

- Finding a publisher can be difficult.
- You have no control over production issues: typesetting, editing, how many copies will be printed, cover layout and design. You may end up with a product produced that is simply awful from your perspective.

Getting Your Product Published by Major Publishers

Like speaking, the business of writing and selling products to publishers is competitive. The odds against your product being published by a major publisher are high, especially on first product. Do not be hurt by rejection letters. If getting published was easy, everyone would do it.

Dan Poynter, who offers seminars on self-publishing, says: "Each large publisher receives 15,000 to 20,000 unsolicited manuscripts per year." It is estimated that 350,000 books are actually written annually, but not submitted to publishers. Only 32,000 books actually go into print each year in the United States.

The average nonfiction book has a run of only 5000 copies before it goes out of print. But you as the speaker on the subject of the book can personally sell this amount in a very short time because you have a continuous, built-in steady market for your product among the members of your audiences. Many "authors-only" do not have this advantage. Publishers like the advantage of working with "speaker-authors."

Steps to Help You Get Started on a Product Proposal for a Major Publisher

- If you have created a workbook for your seminars and speeches, you already have a viable product in the embryo stage. If not, tape your full-day program, and have it transcribed onto a computer disk.

- From this disk create at least three of the chapters in product form. Then, create a table of contents and a chapter-by-chapter outline of the rest of your proposed product.

- In your proposal tell the publisher why people will buy your product and why it is unique.

- Mention that you are a speaker and will sell the books as part of your programs. This is a big plus in the eyes of the publisher.

- Be sure to approach only those publishers that publish the kind of materials you present. Some publishers look for recreational books on humor, science fiction, travel, or cooking, while others concentrate on business.

- If you don't know which publishers handle your type of product, go into a bookstore and examine a number of books on your topic, as well as related subjects. Note the length of the chapters, the number of pages in the books. Get a feel for a commercial product. Buy the best examples of books on subjects similar to yours. Study the books you have purchased. Then think of a new angle or "slant" for your material and send a query letter to suitable publishers.

Self-Publishing

We have met many beginning speakers who scoff at the idea of self-publishing. "No successful author was ever self-published!" they presume. Not true: Mark Twain, Zane Grey, Carl Sandburg, Edgar Rice Burroughs, Edgar Allen Poe, George Bernard Shaw, Elizabeth Barrett Browning, T.S. Elliot, Ernest Hemingway, and Walt Whitman are only a few self-published authors.

"Oh sure," they say, "what about author-*speakers?* Real *professional* speakers!" Okay, how about Dr. Ken Blanchard, Joel Barker, Mark Victor Hansen, and Jack Canfield (the last two now famous for their mega-best-seller series, *Chicken Soup for the Soul*? John Gray's (of *Men Are from Mars, Women Are from Venus* fame) first book, *What You Feel You Can Heal,* was a tremendous success and was eventually picked up by Harper. Zig Ziglar sold thousands of copies of his famous book, *See You at the Top,* before interesting a big publisher. He also created and sold thousands of copies of his audio albums before Nightingale Conant decided to publish and market them.

In fact, self-publishing is the rule, rather than the exception for most in the speaking industry.

Advantages of Self-Publishing

- *You* won't turn *your* proposal down!
- No one knows your market like you. You are in the best position to develop a marketing plan and a vision and to implement them.
- You already are committed to its success.
- Your product is published much more quickly.
- You have complete control. The cover, the text and the copy all look the way you want them to look. There is no reason a self-published product cannot be of a higher quality than the average quality that is produced by a major publisher.
- Producing a product yourself is relatively inexpensive. Audio tapes can be produced for 75¢ up to $3 each; books for $2 to $4 each (for runs over 5,000 you can bring print costs down lower).
- You receive all the income from sales because you personally did all the work a major publisher usually does.
- If your self-published product sells well, you will have proven that there is a market. Successful self-publishing can set you up as a good prospect for a book contract from a major publisher.

Disadvantages of Self-Publishing

- You must take all of the risks and do all of the work, or alternately, job it out. The process requires an investment of money.
- You will need to hire the services of editors and designers to ensure that you create a quality product. Often self-publishing has been given a bad name because the author does not take

the time, nor hire the talent, that is needed to produce a quality product.

- You must take on the task of distribution. This means you must have the facility and labor to wrap, address, and ship products in a timely manner.

- You will need to store the products in an easily accessible location. The first run should be at least 3,000 to 5,000. This is about one bedroom full of books stacked fairly tightly.

- Recordkeeping is of prime importance when you self-publish!

Publishing on Demand

New print-on-demand technology (from companies like Xerox and Kodak) allows print shops using high-quality photocopiers to actually "remember" your complete print job on disk and recall it for future reprints. The marriage of these two developments has created an innovative approach called "publishing on demand." Imagine that customers of your product can locate your materials over the Internet and order your materials, paying via credit card or other means. The product—the books/manuals/documents—is then manufactured *afterward* to fill each individual order.

Publishing on demand involves no major up-front printing costs for the self-publishing author, no warehousing of preprinted books; it's efficient, the contents are always up-to-date, and there's no waste.

One option to speakers to take advantage of with this on-demand publishing concept is to do it yourself: Most of us have laser printers that will print at 600 dpi, which is what most print-on-demand machines use. Promote yourself on the Internet, solicit orders, then print out a copy as each payment is received.

For those of you not ready to approach the technology needed for this sort of project, there is at least one company that will do it for you—a new Canadian group, Trafford Publishing (www.trafford.com). You still need to create your product, but they have a "virtual warehouse" of authors' products and an Internet Web bookstore. You set the retail price for your products: Trafford sees that you get 85 percent of the markup over wholesale price as your "royalty."

We see this as an approaching wave in the publishing world.

How to Create Products

Creating product can be wonderfully simple, and terribly complicated! It depends on how you do it. Books are the most difficult, time consuming, and *important* to your speaking career.

The trick is to know when to create your products and how to gather the material. Then devote the time and effort to create products you are proud of.

When to Create Products

If your audience is asking you for more material, you know you have a market for your product. If they are not, go back over this book. Something is wrong with the topic you have selected or the market you have chosen to market it to.

Constantly gather new material and update the material you already have on your topic. Soon, you will have enough for some type of product.

Performance Support and Expertise on Demand

As you ponder what products you wish to create to supplement and advance your speaking career, think in terms of "performance support" and "expertise on demand." Many companies are reluctant to let people off work to attend a seminar. Training materials that continue the educational process while the employee is on the job are the easiest of all products to sell.

Today our world moves at the click of a remote control device. Businesses are willing to invest in products that help them improve productivity and efficiency, and to access expertise with the click of a button. People learn 80 to 90 percent of their job skills *on the job*. As presenters, we will do well to find ways to meet this need.

Develop products that can go to the job site and teach while the attendees are on the job. Make a list of what products would be beneficial in assisting businesses and individuals to get the job done more efficiently. If such products already exist, consider acting as a distributor for those products and selling them yourself. If you can think of a way to do these things even better, or in a newer way, than existing products, then create a version yourself! This is the way all products are created and marketed.

Gathering and Protecting the Material

Before you create a product you must begin to gather information. In Chapter 5: Become the Expert and Leading Authority, we told you in great detail where to find that information. But you must know how to gather and store the material.

The best system for storing the material you gather is to scan it right away into files on your hard drive. Lilly has created her own database using FileMakerPro® by Claris. She tracks the topic and the text, and for each item she creates a follow-up date. This way she stays on track and on time with products we are working on.

If you are still in the process of setting up your computer system, a simple way to begin creating products is to obtain a large legal-size accordion file, which can be purchased at any stationery supply store. On the outside list your subject/chapter titles. Then on each division, attach a card that lists the title and the items you wish to cover in that chapter.

When an idea occurs to you, write it on a pad or in your database and slip the note into the proper section. This often happens as you speak to someone on the phone or are doing something else. Get into the habit of capturing your ideas instantly. Dottie likes to write herself a note as to how she thinks the idea can be used on the same piece of paper.

When you see articles, hear someone speak, watch the news, or read a quotation, ideas will come to mind that tie into your material. Write them down or tear the articles out and place them into the proper section division.

The Line between Research and Robbery

It is very easy to do so much research, and to use a bit of information so often, that you feel it is yours. As you gather material for your products, please cite where and when you found it. Keeping careful records, and citing your sources gives you credibility.

Adapt it, don't adopt it! There can be a fine line between research and robbery of other people's material.

Public Domain and Copyrighted Material

Material in the public domain is available for you to use as you see fit. If the material has a copyright, you will need to gain permission to use it.

Deciding whether or not the copyright has expired and the material is currently in the public domain can be difficult. Some material that's well over a century old still remains under copyright if the publisher who purchased it reprinted it on a steady, continuing basis ever since its conception. The copyright on other material may have run out years ago, even though the publication is fairly recent.

The records of the Copyright Office are open for inspection and searching by the public. Moreover, on request, the Copyright Office will search its records at the statutory rate of $20 for each hour or fraction of an hour. For information on searching office records concerning the copyright status or ownership of a work, request Circulars 22 and 23. Records from 1978 on may be searched via the Internet.

When Do You Need to Ask Permission?

If you are using someone else's ideas to make money, they are going to want a piece of the pie. The old rule of thumb, that you needed official permission to use a quote if it was twenty-five words of text or up to five lines of poetry, no longer holds at all. However, recent changes in federal law have tightened that up. You must now be very careful if you quote song lyrics, lines of poetry, even pet phrases coined by comedians, sportscasters or other media personalities and celebrities.

The trouble is, there is so much confusion in copyright law, no one seems to know what is really allowed anymore. To be safe, we try to get permission from everyone.

As a tip, getting permission to quote something from a major publisher is like pulling teeth with no pain killer. There is no standardized policy from publisher to publisher, nor consensus on how much they might charge for the use of copyrighted material. Many, not all to be sure, take months to get you a response, if they respond at all. You will often find it easier to simply call the author of the work directly and ask for a five-minute interview, which most are very willing to grant. Now you have original material which you *can* quote!

Many of us who are trying to gain permissions are forced to just rework information and create our own from it. When you reword it in your own thoughts, and you don't need to gain permission, it's called research.

Granting Permissions—Say Yes!

We would much rather grant anyone permission to use our work and credit us than to see it "reworked" under someone else's name! Many beginners in the industry guard their material and only allow others to quote a sentence or two. This is a mistake. The harsh reality is that people are going to use "adaptations" of the things you have said and written—*whether they ask your permission or not.* They only need to change the way it is worded and it is no longer "yours." If you are lucky enough to have people *ask* if they can quote you, for heaven's sake, say yes!

Being quoted by others gives you greater prestige, credibility, and exposure. So just say, "Yes! Thank you! I'd love you to quote me. By the way, how were you planning on crediting me? Can we just double check that you have the correct references?"

Copyright Your Material

In general, copyright registration is a legal formality intended to make public record of the basic facts of a particular copyright. Even though registration is not generally a requirement for protection, the copyright law provides several inducements or advantages to encourage copyright owners to make registration. Among these advantages are the following (from the Library of Congress's documents on Copyright):

- Registration establishes a public record of the copyright claim.
- Before an infringement suit may be filed in court, registration is necessary for works of the U.S. origin and for foreign works not originating in a Berne Union country. (For more information on when a work is of U.S. origin, request Circular 93.)
- If made before or within five years of publication, registration will establish prima facie evidence in court of the validity of the copyright and of the facts stated in the certificate; and
- If registration is made within three months after publication of the work or prior to an infringement of the work, statutory damages and attorney's fees will be available to the copyright owner in court actions. Otherwise, only an award of actual damages and profits is available to the copyright owner.

- Copyright registration allows the owner of the copyright to record the registration with the U.S. Customs Service for protection against the importation of infringing copies.

For additional information, request Publication No. 563 from: Commissioner of Customs, ATTN: IPR Branch, Room 2104, U.S. Customs Service, 1301 Constitution Avenue, N.W. Washington, D.C. 20229.

International Copyright

You have heard the war stories about products—books, software, audio albums—that are reproduced outside of your own country without your permission or recompense. We got the following from the Library of Congress public documents on International copyright:

> There is no such thing as an "international copyright" that will automatically protect an author's writings throughout the entire world. Protection against unauthorized use in a particular country depends, basically, on the national laws of that country. However, most countries do offer protection to foreign works under certain conditions, and these conditions have been greatly simplified by international copyright treaties and conventions. For a list of countries which maintain copyright relations with the United States, request Circular 38a.
>
> An author who wishes protection for his or her work in a particular country should first find out the extent of protection of foreign works in that country. If possible, this should be done before the work is published anywhere, since protection may often depend on the facts existing at the time of first publication.

Tape Your Programs: An Instant Product

Many a wonderful product is created by simply turning on a high-quality tape recorder during your presentation. Lilly's first audio training album, "Persuasive Platform Presentations" (Royal Publishing, 1989) is a 4 1/2-hour radio program with a 70-page workbook. She had a two-day session recorded live at a program she gave in Africa. When you have your program taped for use as a product, be aware you must have it transcribed onto paper so you can tell the producers where to edit it. Lilly later used the transcripts of this album to create her best-selling book, *Secrets of Successful Speakers: How You Can Motivate, Captivate and Persuade* (McGraw-Hill, 1993). Make sure when you tape a live program you have a microphone on the audience as well as on yourself!

Rules for Taping: Sales and Royalty Rights

When your clients want to tape your session and sell audio or video tapes to attendees at a convention for a lower price than your materials, you have a dilemma. Associations often sell such tapes for $5 or $10. Of course, it is not the same highly edited material you sell as product, but it will certainly kill the sales of your higher-priced BOR package, or in advance educational packages to your client. If you plan to depend on tape sales for a part of your income, bear this in mind when you negotiate fees.

Recently a speaker opened his mail to find a catalog listing an audio album he himself had not created. He called the catalog company and was told the audio album had been created by an independent recording company who recorded many conventions. The speaker had signed a "release of all rights contract" with the client who hired him. Do not do this. Negotiate your own recording rights and licensing contract in advance. Go over the recording use and the recording rights contract as you negotiate your fees.

In another situation a speakers' bureau arranged for the speakers' program to be rewritten, customized, and updated two years after the original program. Then the speaker was paid $10 per employee of the company, for all the worldwide employees who they estimated would be trained with the tape for a two-year period. Including the keynote fee, speaker products the client purchased in advance for all their worldwide employees, the customization fees, and the recording rights, the total contract was over $100,000. Each of the items the client ordered were listed on the fee schedule, and negotiated in advance.

How to Charge   If a client wants to record your presentation and offer it for sale, ask for an additional fee for these ancillary rights. One way is to charge an additional 50 percent of your normal speaking fee. For example, if you charge $1,000 as your initial base fee, you would instead charge $1,500 if tapes of your presentation are sold. If you agree to such an arrangement, be sure you do not sell your own reproduction rights when you sell the rights that allow the client to sell your tapes at an event. Specify in your contract that the client's tapes will be "for resale only at the _____ Convention, etc., and not to be sold in any other way, or at any other time." (This is called "First Rights Only.")

An alternative to the above plan is to charge the client a set royalty fee of, let's say, $1 per attendee at the convention. Note that this is not $1 each from those who buy the tape, it is $1 for each registered convention attendee. This amount is added to your contract in advance in the space you have provided. The same rule applies to the sale of video reproduction rights. (See our sample recording rights contract below.)

Get a Copy of the Master   If you are going to allow clients to tape your performance, always specify in the contract that you are to receive the master and several copies of the tape. Often, you can use these professionally-produced materials by editing them for use as demo tapes, albums, and other products. They can be very valuable to you.

List Recording Rights on Your Contracts and Fee Schedules   Your speaking contract and fee schedule must stipulate that there will be no recording of your material by the clients unless your separate recording rights contract is signed before the date of the program.

We have a clause in every contract that leaves our speakers' bureau: NO RECORDING OF ANY TYPE, AUDIO OR VIDEO, WILL BE ALLOWED DURING THIS PROGRAM WITHOUT PRIOR RECORDING AND LICENSING CONTRACT.

Often when the client sees this, they call and say, "but, but. . . ." Then we can open up the negotiations.

Welcome a client's desire to discuss the uses of your taped talk. Sometimes, the client will want to used the video to train field office people. Negotiate a deal for the additional use of your material. Discussion of this opportunity can lead to selling books, workbooks, audio albums, video albums, articles, and other materials—all to be used in the client's training program. You have the opportunity to negotiate a very large contract.

Recording Contracts   A recording contract will let everyone know the exact use of the recorded material allowable and states the recording rights amount you are to receive for this use. Bring a couple of copies of your recording rights contract with you to the event in case you need them. Hand one to the recording people as you arrive.

What Can You Sell for Profitable Products and Materials?

In order to keep your product sales as a major part of your income, try to create at least one new product a year and revise and reissue old ones to fit changing times and new technology. Remember, every prior satisfied buyer of your products becomes an annual prospect for continued purchases.

The very best products for you to sell are the ones that are so obvious, you are most likely to overlook them! Do you talk on time management? Do you tell audiences they must have a special kind of calendar? What kind? For heaven's sake, call the company that manufactures them and set up a distributorship!

Do you talk on leadership? Do you love to quote "The Art of War?" Then offer it for sale in your programs! It will be an easy sell.

Doug Malouf, one of the most successful speakers in Australia, creates new products each year. He raises his speaking fee rates as each product is announced. Still wondering what to sell? Consider one of the following:

- Books
- Workbooks
- Single audio tapes
- Audio albums that contain your speeches or related subjects
- Video tapes
- Materials on computer disks and CDs
- Articles
- Special reports
- Task checklist pads
- Desktop reference guides: a job aid for details that participants aren't going to memorize anyway
- One speaker offers decks of playing cards imprinted with his body language material.

- Screensavers. A company now offers the creation of computer screensavers that contain quotes or valuable information. They package them with the speaker's picture on the front and on each screensaver inside.

- Speakers on time management often create special calendars and appointment books or charts.

- Inspirational plaques and posters (often sold to clients in quantity orders for their many offices)

- Sets of special quotes on cards

- Personality analysis tests that enable attendees to figure out what makes employees or customers tick

- Join with other speakers in your field to produce anthologies and team products.

- Create generic and custom training materials for specific clients, for high consulting fees and continuing product income.

Do not offer to furnish products as part of your speaker's fee, unless you have already added the cost of designing and manufacturing these items to your fee. All extra materials you provide should be sold to the client for an additional fee. Some speakers sell rights to the client to reproduce and use their materials. Others supply the required quantity of the finished product, on a per-item per-attendee basis, offering the client quantity discounts. Do not offer to furnish free handout sheets. Instead offer generic or customized workbooks.

Sell Someone Else's Products

In addition to your own products, you can sell products someone else has created on your subject. For example, attorney Linda Bulmash speaks in her programs of the wonderful book by Viktor Frankl, *Man's Search for Meaning*. In a consultation with Linda, we suggested she call the publisher of the book and arrange to become a dealer. This means Linda could buy books by the case at wholesale, then offer them BOR to her audiences at retail. Linda now offers the books singly and in a package of six, so that her buyers can use the books as gifts.

Create Kits

Look at what you tell your attendees they must do, or read, or learn or have. Do you tell them they must read a certain book? Use a special type of organizer? Both? More? Well, put all of the items you feel they should have into a "kit." You can save your audience members a great deal of time and effort, and make an excellent profit, if you make them available yourself!

Create an Anthology

Speaker anthologies are a sophisticated method of combining self-publishing and regular publishing. A number of speaker/authors are gathered together in one book. The anthology should have a unified subject such as humor, communication, stress, sales, etc. Each author writes one chapter on the topic he or she is an expert in.

For some anthologies, a group speakers get together and self-publish a book or audio album. With others, anthology companies do all of the work for the speakers. They find the other speaker/authors, handle all of the publication details, then sell each author the books or albums at wholesale so that they can make a large profit when they sell them to their audiences. Some publishers offer individual dust jackets for each author, feathering the author's name and picture on the front and back.

In any kind of cooperative book, video or audio album, each participant agrees to purchase a minimum number of products. The larger the purchase, the lower the wholesale price per item, and the higher the profits at retail will be.

Video Tapes and Audio Albums

Companies that publish speakers' video tapes and audio albums also look for quality materials that fit their markets, just as book publishers do. Your topic and their marketing and distribution capabilities are the keys to success. You can approach these publishers in the same manner that you approach book publishers, but you should send them complete programs rather than snippets and outlines. This approach works very well for audio albums as well as books.

Another way to profit is to offer long-term training materials for clients. For example, you could produce a series of 12 different training sessions on audio or video cassettes, customized for a client's sales management team. on a different topic for each month of the year. The client is then able to host a motivational sales meeting, with your video and materials, instead of you in person.

Electronic Products

Electronic products are the wave we are all either riding or trying to catch. Floppy disks, CDs, software, motivational screen savers, and palm-top time management and calendar tools are all here already and valued by your audiences.

Electronic products make "expertise on demand" an easy reality. Your audience can quickly access your ideas and concepts in a "virtual trainer" as they sit at their desks at work. This decreases the need to pull everyone off their jobs for an in-person presentation.

Although electronic products are not going to replace presenters totally, they are making up an increasingly larger percentage of product sales. Look at what you are currently teaching. Could it be done better with a "tool"? Are you in a position to design this tool? Are there already some in the marketplace? then add them to your menu of products.

Databases

As you develop information and contacts, consider ways to turn them into products. For instance, early in our own marketing efforts, we started gathering information on speakers' bureaus. Today we have the most complete list of bureaus available anywhere. We sell this as a directory. There are over 500 bureaus in the eighteen countries. For information call (626) 335-8069.

Products on the Web

The World Wide Web is likely to be the site of the next wave of speakers' products. It is reported that the electronic market is growing over 100 percent a year, whereas the bookstore market is growing at just 4 percent annually. The future of publishing maybe in on-line publishing, which is cheaper than books because there are no paper or printing costs.

Articles for Profit

Not only will magazines pay for articles, but you should also consider writing a series of educational articles for your client's in-house magazine. We work with several speakers who sell a series of twelve generic articles on their topics, one a month at $300 per article, a total of $3,600. That can be a super add-on to your speaking contract with a client. If the client would like the articles customized, many speakers charge an $500 or more per article.

Your articles can also be sold directly from your web site. Prospective buyers long-on, and preview a "brief," then make a purchase which can be automatically E-mailed to them upon verification of their credit card. (To see the Walters website: Walters-intl.com)

Special Reports

Try gathering copies of articles you have had published on specific topics within your area. These can be offered at an excellent fee via B.O.R. sales by mail order or E-mail. Ten dollars for a package of five pages of crucial information is not an uncommon price. Special reports can be profitable by themselves, but they also can lead to other profit centers and products. For several years, we kept copies of tips Dottie's used in her talks on small business, "101 Ways to Promote Yourself and Your Business." We sold these in our catalogs and at our seminars. A national radio show saw one, which prompted them to have Dottie do a series of "motivational business minutes." This later was expanded into our book, *101 Simple Things to Grow Your Business and Yourself: Easy Ideas for Improving Sales, Productivity and Service!* (Crisp Publishers, 1995), a paperback book filled with quick ideas, lighthearted cartoons, and wit.

Newletters as Products

One of the best ways to become known quickly and to promote your speaking topics is to publish your own newsletter. We talk about newsletters in Chapter 6: Marketing Tools for the Speaking Trade, because they are also excellent promotional tools even if you simply give them away to your customers and prospects. On the other hand, many speakers earn a considerable part of their income by selling their own newsletters and magazines.

Consider starting a newsletter aimed at your market. Twenty years ago we started a little newsletter *Sharing Ideas for Professional Speakers*. Today it is the largest newsmagazine in the world for professional speakers with all the issues, tips, news, and trends of the speaking world. You can mail, fax, or E-mail your newsletter. Our E-mail is Dottie@SPEAKANDGROWRICH.COM.

Electronic Newsletters

Electronic newsletters, done via fax or E-mail, are wonderfully inexpensive: no paper, no postage. They also arrive immediately instead of a few days after they are mailed.

An electronic newsletter gives the client a feeling of receiving fresh information. When you pick up a reference book, you wonder, "How old is this?" When it's on-line, there's a sense that this is fresh, the latest. That's something people don't mind paying for.

How to Profit from Customizing Products

Many clients are quite pleased when you agree to customize your materials for them, such as books, workbooks, training manuals, and audio or video tapes. Many successful speakers establish a standard price for products sold as they come off the shelf, then set up higher fees based on the amount of customization.

Although you can and should consider customizing all your products if it will help your clients better achieve their goals, we will focus on customization of workbooks and manuals as being the most common. Please apply the ideas you will gain in this section to customization of all products.

Technically, a workbook is something the attendee writes in as you present. It is more or less an outline of your presentation, in which you have copies of statistics, charts, clip art and photographs, and quotes, items you don't want them to bother writing down. The workbooks help them visualize the information you are trying to impart.

You might also create a booklet or handout for them to take home filled with information, which they would not necessarily be expected to write in and follow along with.

How to Charge for Customization

When you work out how much to charge your customers for your customized products you must ask yourself these questions:

- Will the product be "personalized" or "customized?"
- Will the cost be added into the package price? Or will you itemize the bill: speech, workbooks, etc?

Personalizing vs. Customizing

There is a huge difference between personalizing a workbook and customizing your products:

- *Personalized* (custom cover with the name of the client): Your current materials are simply rearranged and tailored with the appropriate pieces the clients will need for this presentation. Personalization can be done easily by:
  - ✓ adding a note or message by the client in the front;
  - ✓ placing the client's logo on the front cover;
  - ✓ scanning the client's logo onto your computer and adding a small version of it into the head or footer of every page;
  - ✓ putting the date and time of the meeting on the cover or title page;
  - ✓ creating the cover page in the client's corporate colors.
- *Customized* (designed and written exclusively for the client): A highly customized workbook might have the client's own logo and buzzwords used. It is geared specifically for a single client, and would not be usable elsewhere. Products of this type command the highest prices, including consultation and writing fees.

If you are booking more than 70 dates a year, you will be hard-pressed to actually customize your products.

Itemized Fee or a Package Fee?

An itemized fee structure might look like this:

Figure 9:1. Itemized Fee Structure

Items	Investment
One-Day Seminar	$5,000
Workbook Design	$1,000
Workbooks @ $35, for 100 attendees	$3,500
Total Due	$9,500

Figure 9:2. A Package Fee Sample

Our program for you will include:

> One-Day Seminar
> Workbook Design
> Workbooks for 100 attendees

All included for $9,500.00 (plus travel and other expenses)

There are two schools of thought on whether you should charge a package fee or charge for the products separately.

1. An itemized bill spells out the high value of each item the customer will receive. If you do not place a value on these products, neither will your customer.
2. Customers prefer a simple, package fee that will include the R&D costs of the workbook, the speaker's fee, and all other expenses.

You will need to experiment within your own unique environment to see which works best for you.

Value Your R&D Time

It is vital to remember to place a value on the time it takes to create handouts, workbooks and manuals when you quote your fees.

Even personalizing an existing workbook for your customer takes at least three hours and sometimes up to two days. Highly customized materials can take weeks or even months to develop.

If clients ask you to develop a totally new workbook, they will be expecting to pay a higher overall fee or a fee for R&D. There are many methods of charging for these custom materials.

Methods of Charging for Customization

There are four main methods speakers use for normal customization and highly customized materials.

- *Flat Research and Development Fee:* A flat R&D fee would be charged in addition to the speaker's fee to present, or quoted as part of the total package
- *Per Attendee:* Per-attendee fees may be thought of as a licensing fee, or as a per-item cost, depending on how you have approached the client.
- *Per Hour:* A per-hour fee is best used when clients are unsure of what they need you to do. Per-hour fees are often in connection with other fees.
- *Per Day:* A per-day fee is easier on budgeting for the buyers, and easy for the speakers to estimate a quote for the R&D.

Do You Create the Copies, or Should the Client?

Your fees will reflect whether you create the workbooks and ship them to the event, or the buyer creates them and has them waiting for you.

In a public seminar, you will most often create the workbooks yourself. In a corporate setting, the buyers frequently want to do it as they have copy machines in-house. In associations it can go either way. There are benefits and drawbacks to either.

Clients may want you to send them an original, and they will reproduce it. They can recreate them much cheaper on their copy machines than you can. However this lets your materials get out of your control. We do not recommend this.

In our research we discover that about 55 percent of those we asked prefer to create the workbooks themselves and bring them to the event. This obviously is a great deal of extra work for the presenter: printing, shipping, and temporary warehousing. On the other hand, when your name is on it, you want the highest quality possible rather than a quick and cheap-looking set of papers barely held together by a staple in the corner.

Of course the fee for reproduction of the workbooks may be already added to your total fee. Buyers do prefer it when they are able to buy a simple package with all the benefits included. However, most have a separate educational materials budget.

How to Sell Products Apart from Your Speaking

Some like to call product sales that occur apart from your speaking "passive income." Trust us, there is nothing passive about it! Speakers *must* plan on promoting their products themselves if they want to succeed. We have been fortunate to have major publishers use our work and sell them in places we would not be able to penetrate. But many of the really exciting sales and opportunities occurred because of the promotions we did ourselves for the products.

There are many other ways to market and sell your products. Here are several:

Advance Sales: Include the Products with Your Fee

Some speakers include products as part of their regular fee. This insures a huge product order with every speech they give!

Jeff Slutsky, author of several "Streetfighter" books on sales and marketing, including *Streetfighter Marketing,* includes 150 hardcover books or 300 softbacks with his speech fee of $6,500. This is a nice add-on value that allows the attendees to continue the educational process after the event. If the client has budget problems, Jeff has a tool with which to negotiate. He is able to tell the buyer, "All right, we will deduct the books, and the fee will be just $5,000." The client is able to see the tremendous bargain they will miss by not purchasing the books, which would normally cost them over $10 each. If the client needs more than 150 books, the opportunity is there to sell many more at the quantity discount.

Sell Products Under the Educational Materials Budget

A speaker once called us for an emergency consultation. She had accepted a $1,000 speaking date plus the usual hotel and travel expenses. They had not asked her to furnish workbooks, but she now realized her presentation needed them. She also wanted to include a cassette for each attendee to make her presentation even more effective. The fee was the most allowed in the client's budget for her section of the program. When she checked into how much it would cost to produce these items and found the total was $700, she panicked. What should she do now?

We suggested that she ask if there was an additional budget for educational materials for this program. If so, we told her to ask, "Would you like to make my section of the convention extra special by having an educational workbook and cassette provided for each attendee?" If the answer was yes, then she should continued, "Would you prefer to produce the materials form my original printing, and audio masters, or should I do it all for you and bill you?" I can furnish the package for $20 each.

The client's answer was yes, indeed, they had $2,000 earmarked for educational materials. The client gladly accepted her offer to produce the materials and ship them because it was, for them, a very busy time. The speaker charged $2,000 for her materials. This gave her $1,300 over her own costs for her time in handling the production. The speaker thus netted a $1,000 speaking fee, plus the $1,300 profit from the materials, and was able to deliver a better program. A win-win situation for both speaker and client. The client paid the freight

Convention Registration Gifts

Corporations, professional associations, and seminar companies buy products as registration premiums to increase attendance at their conferences and conventions. Sometimes these gifts are given when the attendees register, sometimes at the door. The clients purchase your products in advance and give them as gifts to each attendee (or those who register before a cut-off date). Depending on the size of the event, this could mean sales of thousands of units.

Negotiate a quantity price for the buyer. This discount should include a good profit for you. Seeing your product in the convention pack will give attendees the feeling of receiving something of great value, because they will see the full retail price listed. But the client will have purchased them from you at a quantity discount. In this case, everybody wins.

Direct Sales to Companies to Use as Premiums, Gifts, and Promotions

Premiums are often used outside of events and meetings. Various premiums often are given away by large companies to purchasers of their product or services. Products purchased for premiums are usually sold in large quantities to these companies and are a wonderful source of profit. Banks might use one of your products as a gift or a premium to their clients for opening a new account; a magazine might use it as a subscription gift promotion. This might even lead to your becoming a paid spokesperson for their company.

Keep your eyes open for advertisements that come in your "junk" mail. These are prime sources of companies that like to work with offering specials. Call their corporate offices and find out who set up their current promotion. Offer your product for their next one!

Set Up a Network of Distributors

Some people love to speak, but are unsure of how to gather the information that will be a proven success with an audience. (See Chapter 5: Become the Expert and Leading Authority, where we tell you how to gather your own information). Consider selling the use of your program to distributors or franchisers who are good speakers but bad researchers. Once your program is proven before many audiences and starts to be in demand in the marketplace, you will be ready to look for distributors. Deepak Chopra, Tom Peters, Peter Senge, Brian Tracy, Denis Waitley, Ken Blanchard, Dale Carnegie and many other famous speakers have done this with great success. Training companies do the same: Performax, Wilson Learning, and Carlson all set up distributors who sell their products and, in some cases, put on seminars for them. This is another way to multiply your gross income and your ability to reach the public.

The best potential distributors for your programs can be found in your seminars. Those who like the subject and are enthusiastic about you personally are the ones to invite to become distributors.

Public Seminar Registration Incentive Give-Aways

Many speakers who hold their own public seminars use their products as an incentive to increase registration.

A speaker who presents seminars for insurance agents offers a free book with each seminar registration. He says the gift book has increased his attendance by more than 100 percent. One speaker gave away a $29.95 book, which cost him $5 wholesale. He increased the retail price of his seminar by $155. He has now registered 6,000 seminar attendees by this method, for a net profit of $900,000 more than he earned without the product as a registration gift at the lower seminar rate.

Advertise Your Products

Advertising in major print media, radio, and television is the most expensive and often the least effective way to sell products. Most speakers use the other methods we discuss in this chapter and in Chapter 7: Marketing Tools for the Speaking Trade.

However, you will find that if you use *targeted* advertising media, you will have a greater return on your investment. For instance, if your material is on sales, then use the many publications on that subject. You would not advertise a product on sales in a flower catalog, unless your material is customized for selling flowers and the catalog is aimed at those who sell flowers, not just those who buy.

Of the large publications, airline magazines carry the majority of management speakers' advertisements, bacuse of the many hours CEOs spend in the air.

Barter for Ad Space

One of the most economical ways to obtain advertising is to trade for it. Certain publications and radio stations trade for articles or training that they wish they could purchase, but don't have the funds. In this case suggest a barter, an advertising exchange: your products or services for an ad(s).

Don't overlook groups for which you are currently speaking. Most meetings have all kinds of pre-, during and post-literature, newsletters, and brochures they produce. It costs them nothing to put an ad in them! If the group itself will not buy your product in bulk before the event, try negotiating an ad in their literature. You might offer to do an additional spouse program for them at no fee in exchange for ads. Once an audience has heard you, they become a prime source of future sales. When the attendees see some of the follow-up materials of the event and see your ad, they will be much more likely to call and order products than through any other source of advertising.

Classified Ads via Bulk E-mail

E-mail is practically free to send. For about $100 you can purchase over 100,000 E-mail addresses. Several companies develop lists of names, and then create a classified ad E-paper. They do the work of sending your ad out via bulk E-mail. This is less expensive and certainly less of a hassle for you. But it is less effective, as is the case with classified ads. These same companies will send just your ad out to a bulk E-mail list for you.

E-mail lists to specific categories of people are still being developed. So if your products are only good for, say, anvil salespeople, you would not do well with the average E-mail currently available. However, if your product is of general interest, a bulk E-mail list might be a great, inexpensive addition to your marketing efforts.

Unlike normal bulk mail which involves no cost to the receiver, those who receive bulk E-mail ads have to pay for receiving them. Normally this only costs them about a penny in computer and access time usage, but it was their penny to spend. If they have not *asked* you to send them something, they might be miffed.

Infomercials and Home Shopping Channels

Infomercials are advertisements imitating news or entertainment shows in length as well as format. Look at the shows that are listed as "paid programming" in your *TV Guide* or newspaper. These are infomercials. The are very expensive to produce, but the profits involved can be equally tremendous. Most 30-minute infomercials cost the same as a 30-second television advertisement.
There are other variable costs, of course, in testing and other miscellaneous items. You need to plan on a hefty investment. On the other hand, in 1995, the 600 infomercials that aired amassed sales totaling $1 billion! Why not your products?

Products Most Appropriate to This Media:
- products in the $20 to $50 range,
- products with mass appeal,
- costs with a four-to-one markup, and
- easily understandable and explained to the average person.

Create Your Own Catalog

When you have a few products of your own, you must then create a catalog to sell them. Since you are going to this expense, you might as well sell other products that complement your own. For instance, if you speak on "quality," you might want to consider selling some of the standard "bibles" of the quality movement by Demming or Crosby. If you are a motivational speaker, you might include works by Norman Vincent Peale, or some of the *Chicken Soup for the Soul* books by Jack Canfield and Mark Victor Hansen. You will see products by Dottie or Lilly Walters in catalogs for presenters. In our own catalog for professional speakers, we carry many products in addition to our own that are of interest to presenters.

Catalogs on the Web

Put your catalog on your website. This is fast becoming a method of sales for all kinds of products of every type. We get calls daily from our catalog on the Web, www.SpeakAndGrowRich.com.

More than 90 percent of businesses currently marketing successfully on-line sell items such as software, books, computer-related materials, and informational products or services. If you have any products that fall into this category, consider putting them on the Web!

You can already allow your prospective customers to see audio and/or video clips on your product on-line.

Bounce-Back Offers

When you ship your products, include a promotion about your other products and services, offering some type of special deal. These are called "bounce-back offers." The offer might read: "As one of our valued buyers, you will receive a 15% discount on any of the items in the enclosed catalog." Or, "With an order of $100 or more from the catalog, we will send you a valuable gift."

Sell Through Other Catalogs and Direct Mail

There are literally thousands of catalogs that sell through the mail directly to the consumer. They are always looking for products to sell.

Every time we have a new product come out, we promote it to every catalog we can think of. Even if the product is produced by a major publisher, we take it upon ourselves to send out the promotions and encourage the catalog company to contact our publisher.

Another important benefit of catalog sales is that your name and products are publicized free. As your name becomes known in your field, you can raise your speaking fees.

Every time you see a catalog, look for products that might be a complement to yours. Seek publications whose audiences have a keen interest in what you have to offer. Call and ask for the person who purchases their products. Ask how those other products have done for them in sales. If they have done well, they will be looking for new products in the same area.

Catalog companies purchase your products at wholesale and resell them at the retail price. They will usually make one of several types of arrangement with you:

- Purchase your products in bulk;
- Purchase your products via drop ship; or
- Sell you space in their catalog.

Let's look at each of these options.

Catalog Bulk Purchases

Larger catalog companies will purchase your products in bulk, warehouse the items themselves, and resell at the retail price. Purchases may be very small, only 5 to 10 items, or huge orders into the thousands. It all depends on the popularity of your products and the size of the catalog's readership.

Drop-Ship Purchases

The term "drop-ship" means that your products are advertised for sale in someone else's catalog, magazine, or direct mailing piece. Rather than warehousing products, the catalog company "drops" the order in the mail to you, and you "ship" it.

Here's how it works: The producers of the catalog or magazine pay for the advertising. They sell your product at full retail, plus a shipping fee. They keep 50 percent (usually) of the retail price and send you (1) the balance, (2) the shipping fee, and (3) a label with the name and address of the buyer. You fill the order.

For a product you produce yourself, like a six-cassette album, your cost will be about $25. Albums retail for about $89.50. The drop-ship catalog makes the sale and keeps $44.75. They send you $44.75 plus the $3 shipping fee. You make about a $19.75 net profit, and you gain a new customer with each sale.

Buy Space in Catalogs

Catalogs are bombarded with products that might be appropriate for their catalogs, so they often must say "no" to requests. However, many will sell you space in their catalogs or in their "special offer" packages. If the catalog has a good target audience for you, then consider it.

Some catalogs include a packet of "special offers" with every package they ship. Usually space in these packets is sold to the distributor of the products. Messages in outgoing customer orders enjoy an extremely high response rate, as people who buy products are an excellent source for additional sales.

Check other catalogs with products that are appropriate to your target market. If they won't carry your product any other way, consider buying space.

How to Sell Products During Events: BOR and Trade Shows

The most effective way to sell your product is to those who hear you in person and are inspired to learn about your ideas and principles. If they see your products available, they will grab them up.

These sorts of sales are made with back-of-room sales and at trade shows. We'll take you step-by-step through these options.

Blockbuster Back of Room Sales

Offering products at a display table at the back of the room usually is one of the most lucrative ways to sell speaker products. Sales at one program can range from a gross of $4,000 on up to $30,000 and more.

There are many tips for boosting your back-of-room sales. Here are some that we find most effective:

Subtly Sell All the Way Through Your Talk

BOR selling is sometimes called "selling products from the platform," a phrase that refers to the time a speaker uses during a program to talk about his or her products. Please note, if the audience feels you "selling from the platform," you are *not* doing a good job! When your program material is good, people will want more. The key is to perfect your presentation skills and speech content to such an extent that the audience likes you and *wants* to take more of you home.

Throughout your speech, make one or two subtle references to your products. For example, do not say, "If you really want an answer to that, you must buy my book." This attitude makes the audience resentful. Instead, use this format: "When I was writing my latest book on _____ (hold up your book), I discovered that _____ (set the book down again)." Or, "In my album (hold it up), I tell the story of _____. It illustrates the point of _____. Here is the story behind the story." Set the album down again. *Then tell them what they want to know!* Audience members will only remember about 10 percent of what you said up there anyway. They will want something to help them remember and revisit your information *if they like you.*

When Lilly does her seminars on "Secrets of Successful Speakers—How You Can Motivate, Captivate and Persuade," she always keeps copies of her books on a table up at the front. When she needs to cite a study or quote something, she casually picks up the book, opens it to the page she has marked just for this purpose, and reads the reference. Lilly, of course, has all of these memorized, but by picking up the book, she reinforces the audience's mind that there is good stuff waiting them for in that book.

Refer to Your BOR Sales Table as "The Autograph Table"

This technique accomplishes several goals. It creates a celebrity image. It suggests that attendees can have something to do after the speech and encourages them to go to the autograph table and purchase products. It also encourages them to stay afterward to speak to you.

Love Your Products

Whenever you pick up your product on the platform, let your body language show that it is valuable. Charles "Tremendous" Jones, a famous motivational speaker, is a master at product sales. He treats each book as though it is a friend of whom he is very fond. He talks to the book, pets it, and hugs it as he shows it to the audience. He proclaims, "I love Napoleon Hill. I want you to have him! You deserve him!"

Location of the Autograph Table Is Key

Locate the autograph table between the exit door, the refreshment area, and the bathroom. Accessibility to heavy traffic areas is vital for the best sales.

Create a Miniature Bookstore in the Back of the Room

Have an enlargement made of your photograph and hire a sign painter to mount it on a self-standing sign for your autograph table. It should say, "(Your Name) In Person!"

Bring a large piece of colorful material to use as a table drape. Felt or knit are best, since these do not wrinkle easily. Stack up your products so they make an attractive display. Store extra supplies under the table out of sight. Bring a cash box, order forms, pens and gifts for volunteers to your program.

Estimate how many products you hope to sell, then ship them to the venue before the event. A second-day carrier will see that they are there before you are. Call and arrange with the convention center or hotel to receive your packages. If you run out of a product at your autograph table, do not sell the last remaining sample. You can take orders and ship the products if you keep at least one set of samples to show. When the engagement is over, the hotel concierge can ship any leftover products back to your office.

Autograph Table Assistants

You must have sales table assistants to make change and handle sales. They will leave you free to sign autographs and talk with people who enjoyed your presentation. Rehearse your helpers in simple sales techniques. Show them how to take credit card orders.

Finding staff can be a challenge. We use these methods:

- Bring a relative or employee.
- Hire temporary helpers.
- Find volunteers among the attendees.

Use the Introducer to Sell Your Product

Let the introducer be your sales assistant. Include simple, short material about your products in your written introduction. Have the introducer wind up with a conclusion. For example, "Thank you so much! Our speaker will be available for questions at the back of the room at the autograph table. He has agreed to make some of his terrific books and albums available for us. The discounts offered are for today only, to this group. There is an order blank on the back of the rating sheets at your seat. Please don't forget to give us your comments on the flip side. Remember, part of every sale goes to _____ (the group's favorite charity). Please turn in your rating sheets with the order form on the back at the autograph table. We are going to have a drawing in 20 minutes from those rating sheets, so stay with us for awhile! Now, let's thank him again!" (While this announcement is being made, take your bows and get to your autograph table before the crowd grabs you! Don't get stuck on the platform. Your presence at the autograph table can double your sales.)

Use Your Rating Sheets as Order Forms

When you use an audience rating sheet, set up the reverse side as an order form. This saves time when attendees come to the table, and the technique helps you follow up after the event with those who are interested in more of your services or products. (See more on rating sheets in Chapter 4: From Free to Shining Fee.)

Prize Drawings

A prize drawing is a great way to increase the visibility of your products and to have the introducer talk about them. It is also an easy way to be sure you get your rating sheets returned. The introducer should explain that there will be a drawing for a free book, randomly selected from the rating sheets they will fill out, then hold up the prize book and mention the order form on the back of the rating sheet.

Build a mailing list that includes the people who fill out your rating sheets. They are prime prospects for notification of new products and other programs.

Offer a "Gift with Purchase"

Everyone loves the idea of getting something extra when they buy. Bernard Hale Zick offers an anthology book as a free gift with the purchase of his power pack of three albums at his seminar's BOR table. Seminars generally have much smaller audiences than conventions, but Barney was averaging sales of 30 packs at $298 per pack, for a gross of $8,940. Then he added a "gift with order" offer. He gave a book away with the purchase of the power pack. This practice has brought his sales up to an average of 68 packs per seminar—more than double his previous rate. His gross from BOR retail products alone now is more than $20,000 per seminar.

Power Packs

A power pack is a package of items the speaker offers to the audience, often at a special price. A power pack typically consists of several albums, books, videos and other items. Most frequently, the power pack is offered at a special discount "for today only," or with a gift with purchase. If you display a $10 item and a $125 item, people will buy the $10 one. Therefore, never put a low-priced item out on the table with a power pack, unless it is the incentive "gift with order."

Sales Must Be Immediately After the Talk

BOR must be done immediately after the presentation. If you encourage them to buy "later," like after lunch, your sales will fall drastically. That magic moment when you have just finished the presentation is the time your products must be available. Make sure there is a 10- to 20-minute break immediately after your talk.

Get to Your Autograph Table

Remember, it is imperative that you get to the autograph table quickly when you finish your program. You court disaster if you do not do so. A speaker at a large convention offered to speak free, because he though he would have massive product sales afterward. He produced a new audio album for the event. But then he made a fatal mistake. The lunch break came right after his talk, so he closed his program by telling the audience that he was as hungry as they were, so he would see them after lunch at the autograph table. The crowd bolted for the door. He evidently thought food was more important than his materials, and so did they. They promptly forgot him when the afternoon session started and went on to hear other speakers. Not one came back to his sales table. His golden time was gone. He packed up his materials and left, angry at the crowd. But the fault was his, not theirs.

Credit Card Status

The ability to take credit cards as payment will dramatically increase your BOR sales. Go to the bank and obtain credit card merchant status.

Trade Shows and Expo Sales

A trade show is a gathering of exhibitors that sell or showcase their products to attendees. Exhibitors usually have their products in booths of varying types.

Many speakers negotiate part of their speaking fee in exchange for a free booth if the client will not allow back-of-room sales.

Trade shows can be a terrific source of sales of your products. Yet, 50 percent of those who try to sell at trade shows don't go back. Here are some tips that will help you be one of the ones to make a profit at trade shows.

Exhibit at Shows Your Buyers Attend

Everyone hosting a trade show will try to get you to spend your money with them by exhibiting at their show. Pick a show that has visitors who can buy what you sell. Trade show coordinators have visitor registration lists from their past shows that will tell you the sort of person who attends. Also check with past exhibitors about their success at past shows, or review show audits.

Create a Focus

If attendees look at your booth and see a huge hodgepodge of many items, they will just walk away. They need to look at your booth and understand with a glance just what you are selling. The name of your company is actually less important than what you are trying to sell. Think "billboard advertising"—five to seven words that deliver your message. Don't make your visitors guess what you're offering.

Be Aggressive

Bring good staff with you who are aggressive in greeting visitors and quickly getting or giving them information. You only have seconds to make an impression with these attendees.

Get Their Information

If prospects seem interested but don't buy, at least get them on your mailing list! We have a big fishbowl for a "drawing." We encourage people to leave their business cards in it. It is more important for you to get their business cards than it is to hand them yours.

Seminars at Trade Shows

Trade shows offer seminars to attendees as a method to increase the value of the show to them, and as a way to give more exposure to those with booths.

Unless you have name recognition, you will not be paid to do one of these seminars. On the other hand, you may want to market your presentation to all of the trade shows that will have potential buyers of your products. This can be very lucrative, a roomful of your prime prospects eager to listen to your message for an hour or more.

Co-op with Others for Trade Show Sales

Buying your own booth at a trade show can be expensive. Look for several others with related, yet noncompeting products and/or services to yours. If you all combine your funds and time, the cost becomes much easier to bear. Also, you can take turns working in the booth.

Becoming Famous: Promotion Strategies with Buyers, Bureaus and the Press

Speaking fees are paid according to how good you are as a speaker, how unique, interesting, and informative your material is, and *how well known you are.*

Celebrity experts are able to command *much* higher fees than the average expert. In fact, the greater your celebrity status, the less effective you need to be as a speaker! Many new speakers don't understand why it works this way. They see a celebrity football player give a weak keynote at a banquet. They think, "Well I'm better than that!" True enough. But people are willing to pay good money to be in the same room with a celebrity. To be fair, the better celebrities are at *speaking,* the more they are able to obtain in speaking fees. In the same vein, once potential clients *recognize your name,* your fees will increase dramatically. To *Speak and Grow Rich,* you must set a simple goal for yourself—generate a celebrity image of yourself as *the* expert in your field.

Most people think promotion is just something to do with advertising. But it is so much more. It is every single thing you do. It begins with your own business cards, stationery, envelopes, and labels, and extends to your personal appearance. Perhaps the best promotion is the aura of excellence you convey in your service to your customers, from the way you answer the telephone to the speed with which you return a phone call, to the personal thank-you notes for every person who helps you or books you. It is also the way you work with other speakers, exchanging ideas and materials. It is joining the associations in your field, and participating in their activities in a positive way. It is also doing everything you can to help the bureaus who obtain bookings for you by handing out their materials at your performances.

In this chapter we will give you tips and ideas to enhance your fame by working with the media and using innovative promotion techniques.

Hansel and Gretel Promotion System

Always leave a "trail" that leads back to your headquarters or to your speakers' bureau. In all your promotion efforts, make sure that nothing goes out that does not lead back to you. For instance, in the articles you write, make sure you work in the name of the town in which your office is located, ". . . now you may think differently about it in your hometown, but at Walters International Speakers' Bureau in Glendora, California, we think . . ." Now we have left a trail for buyers to follow back to us.

Your handouts and workbooks should have your name and phone number clearly on each page (if you were booked through a bureau, make sure to put their name on each page).

Have some of your short essays, poems, posters, or articles printed and decoupaged on plaques. They can be excellent gifts for your clients, meeting planners, television or radio hosts. You may eventually develop these items into commercial products as well. Make sure you produce these on fine-quality paper stock so that people who receive them will want to hang them on their walls. Of course, any item you hand out should say, "A Special Gift from_____, in Albany, New York, 212-444-1212." These become constant positive affirmations for those you give them to, and continuing advertisements for you at the same time.

For example, in an article on "The Speaker Expense Dilemma" which Lilly Walters wrote for a major meeting planner magazine, she included a closing box that said: "To obtain a free copy of the Walters International Speakers' Bureau form for speaker expenses, call Lilly Walters, (626) 335-8069." She received over 495 requests from prospective buyers.

The giveaway was only a piece of paper, but an invaluable piece of information which helped solve a problem for meeting planners. The sheet of paper containing valuable information is the least expensive way to obtain instant response. Begin thinking of a survey you can take, or a series of articles or lists you can compile based on your subject, such as "Ten Rules," "Eight Tips," "Five Little Known Secrets." Make every word valuable to the audience you want to reach.

Scheherazade Promotion System

In case you have forgotten the story, Scheherazade survived a death sentence for a thousand and one nights in Arabia. When the prince discovered his wife cheating, he went on a marrying frenzy, each morning beheading yesterday's bride *du jour*. This went on for some time until our heroine offered to be "next!" As the evening began, she started to tell the prince an interesting story, a story uniquely suited to the prince's background and needs. . . . But by morning she was not quite done. Ah, well, too late, "I suppose it is time to behead me now?" The prince, wanting to know the end of the tale, rescheduled the execution for the following morning. That night she finished the story, and quickly launched into another. Ah! Morning dawns and she is not quite done *again*! What a coincidence! Again the prince postpones the execution for another day, again she finishes the story that night and starts another. This goes on for 1001 nights, by which time the prince has gotten over his misogyny and he and Scheherazade live happily ever after.

In all of your promotional articles and interviews, be sure to drop the Scheherazade hint that you are **the** speaker on the subject, with so much more to tell . . . if only there was time. Be warned, this works only if you give such tremendous information and insights that they are eager to hear more. If your information seems dull or worthless, no one will be interested in hearing more.

Enriching Media Relations

Obtaining free publicity in the media is an effective way to build your fame as an expert and attract paid bookings. However, keep in mind this all-important fact about newspapers, magazines, radio and television stations: *They do not want to promote you.* They are in the business of selling advertisements to people who want promotion.

What they do want is to deliver fascinating, exciting, helpful material to their readers or audiences, so that their circulation and ratings will increase and enable them to profit by charging higher advertising rates. View the media business from their side and you will quickly see that if you help them get such information to their readers, listeners, or viewers, the publicity for you and your topic will naturally follow. You will be identified as a top resource in your field, a celebrity expert.

Let's take a close look at some proven methods for obtaining all sorts of free publicity.

How to Benefit from a Media-Savvy Attitude

As with most everything, working effectively with others in any field starts with your own attitude.

Develop a "You" Attitude

Attract the media's attention by getting the "you" attitude into your public relations, promotions, and advertising. "How **You** Can Overcome . . . says the "you" outright. But a title like "New Method to Obtain . . ." clearly implies the "you."

Study the titles of successful books. You will see that they do not say "I, the author (speaker), am wonderful." The title sets out the benefit: *Seven Habits of Highly Effective People* (the best seller by Stephen Covey) immediately tells us that the author/speaker knows the secrets. The title tantalizes us and implies that in reading the book we will find out what these secrets are and how we can apply them to our careers and businesses. When a media person sees this kind of title in your articles, he will call and ask you, "What are these secrets? We want to do a story about them and how they will help our audience. Can you appear on our show on . . . (date)?"

Know the Media Before You Approach Them

Look at, listen to, or read the media in which you want exposure. Know them before you approach them. Call the producer or editor of the programs or articles pertaining to your topic. If your topic is money, you should not call the beauty editor of a magazine or newspaper, or the host of a beauty show on television or radio, *unless* you can slant your topic effectively to their subject. For example, you could offer articles or interviews on "How to Look Better When You Ask for a Raise" or "How to Borrow More Money at a Lower Rate by Looking Successful."

The Four "Be's" of Beneficial Media Relations

- Be an expert! Keep your name in front of them as the expert in your topic area. Send press releases, notes, updates, via mail, E-mail, and fax, two or three times a year. Not enough to be a pest, but enough to let them know you are out there.

- Be current: Watch the stories that appear in the media. Ask yourself, "How can I tie my expertise in with that and help those people?" Benjamin Franklin's most frequent words in all of his letters to the movers and shakers of his day were, "I observed."

- Be available! If you are not there when they call, or are unable to return their calls within a few hours, they have moved on to the next expert on their list.

- Be nice! So many media people complain that people are hostile to them when they can't use their materials. For heaven's sake, if they close a door on you, don't padlock it on your side by pouting! Just say, "Love to help next time!"

Take a Survey!

Remember the advice we gave you for finding your topic and title: take a survey of people in the field your material is aimed at.

We know of a promotion expert who took a survey of the business owners in her own downtown office building. She wanted to promote her business, but she had a limited amount of money. She decided to use her unlimited skills and ideas instead.

Introducing herself as their business neighbor, she asked the managers, owners, and CEOs, "What bothers you? What hurts as you do business?" The business owners answered, "Being robbed—in our offices, stores, and on the way to the bank."

Once she had identified their greatest problem, the promotion expert thought of an inexpensive way to help them. Her solution was inexpensive, yet worth millions of dollars. She called her printer and had a few thousand stickers made up to be used on buildings, doors and car and truck windows. The stickers said: "No Money on Premises" or "No Money on Board." Her design featured a large "$" sign inside a red circle with a diagonal line through it.

Next she called the media and reported the results of her survey. She titled her information: "Survey Reveals Greatest Fear of Business Owners." In her articles and interviews she offered to give the "No Money" stickers away free to any business that had the problem or fear of being robbed.

Of course, this meant she had to give out her address and the telephone number of her business so that businesses could obtain the free stickers. Her offer was well received because it was a solution to a problem, and offered something free. She was booked for radio, TV, newspaper, and magazine interviews.

She made the free stickers available only if the business owners came to her office in person to pick them up. To sweeten the offer, she also offered them a free "idea session" of ideas to promote their business. These sessions led to so much new business she could hardly handle it all. She spent only $200 on her original order of stickers. If she had paid for air time and publication space with advertising dollars her cost would have been in the thousands.

Often the material you develop in your survey can become a book, an audio or video album, or a CD. There is nothing like talking to the people who are out in the business world to find out what is really going on.

A.K.A.: Dare to Be Unusual

Being the only one of a kind, unusual, rare or notable is often an easy path to enticing the press to come to you.

Image Building Monikers   A moniker (or monicker) is an informal term for a nickname or a signature phrase. It will act as a free advertisement for you that will help people remember both your name and what you do.

Monikers have been used as long as people have had names. Even countries have monikers, "Scotland, the Brave," "America, the Free," and "Ireland, the Emerald Isle." You remember Russia's Queen Catherine the Great or England's King Richard the Lion-Hearted.

Many celebrities have monikers attached to their names. We say, "the Duke," and you think of John Wayne; "the Boss" is Bruce Springsteen. "Old Blue Eyes," or "The Chairman of the Board" both refer to Frank Sinatra.

If your name brings up a picture, perhaps you can use it as your moniker. Example, two speakers we know named Wolf use pictures of wolves, and quotes about wolves, with one of them using "Cry Wolf!" whenever he prints his phone number.

Keep your eye out as you watch television, listen to radio, and read newspapers and magazines. When you hear or see a moniker, write it down. Add it to your moniker idea file. Then suddenly one morning, the perfect moniker for you will jump out of your own expertise and you will know instantly that it is right. Use an intriguing idea about your topic or tie your moniker into your name. Use words that add prestige to your persona.

Print your moniker after your name on your business card, business stationery, everything you create for you career, and use it after you signature.

Look Unusual   Think of ways to look unusual and to help people to remember your name and your topic. Use a special color in your business stationery, business cards or presentation kit. Movie actress Kim Novak became famous for always wearing shades of lavender. Some speakers always wear a hat. There are both women and men who shaved their heads as part of their publicity plan.

Associate with an Unusual Prop   Work with an unusual prop. Gene Harrison told a very funny story about going hunting for raccoon with his college buddies, just like in his younger days! The only one in the story who ends up having a good time is the raccoon. Anyway, Harrison would wonderfully imitate the baying of the dogs in his stories. Before long he used a hunting dog on everything he printed. It became synonymous with Gene Harrison. Some speakers use puppets, monkeys, signs, or other props. Zig Ziglar became famous by using an old-fashioned kitchen hand pump on stage to demonstrate his point of putting some action into your life by priming your pump. Props help your audience enjoy your presentation and remember you.

How to Get in Front of the Press

Our database of media representatives is updated constantly with all contact information: mailing, faxing and E-mail. We use all three to keep current with the press.

If you do not yet have a contact name, direct your communications to the programming director, the news director, or the senior editor. Grab those first few seconds on the phone (or via their eyes on your press releases) and ask, "Would your viewers like to learn how to. . .?" "Would your listeners like to know the answer to. . .?"

Where to Find the Media

There are many ways to help you locate the most appropriate media for you target market:

- Use your phone book. Call the local newspaper, radio, and TV stations.
- Watch the mail, the media, everything that comes to your hand, and ask yourself these two questions:
  a. Is there a possibility here for a story or interview?
  b. How can I be of service to these people?
- Use a public relations firm.
- Use the search engines on the Web or your on-line services. Look in the many directories and phone books there.
- Call the reference librarian at your public library.

Whenever you are searching, check categories under:

- Directory of newsletters
- Trade journals
- Major publications
- Newspapers
- Newswire services
- Television stations
- Radio stations
- Broadcast companies
- Anything to do with your topic
- Anything to do with your target industry

How-to's for Publicity Releases

Publicity releases are short news accounts that should be sent out to the news media when you receive an honor, are elected to an office, have a book published, take a survey, name or make a list of "Ten Best," or launch any other project you want to promote. Copies of the releases and any other mentions they have generated in the media then should be added to your presentation kit.

If you follow the rules, the media will pay closer attention to your news release and work with you:

- Put the source of the release in the upper left-hand corner of your paper. This is the name, address, and phone number of the person to contact for further information. The contact person may be you or someone at your PR service.

- Put the release date, typed in capital letters, slightly below the source information and on the opposite (right-hand) side of the page.

- Sum up the most important thrust of the release in the headline in capital letters.

- If you are sending the release via mail or fax rather than E-mail, use standard 8-1/2 × 11 sheets of paper. Even if you are using fax or E-mail, try to keep this approximate size. Smaller or larger sizes are hard for media people to store. Use only one side of the paper. Keep the length of the release to one page, whenever possible. If you must use more, type "(MORE)" at the bottom. Staple all pages on the top left. On the last page, type "###" or "-30" or "END."

- Your releases should be typed and double spaced. Leave a three-inch margin on the top of the first page and leave margins on each side that are wide enough for editing.

- Dottie's journalism teacher wrote the following poem by Rudyard Kipling on the blackboard the first day Dottie was in her class. It has since helped us in every business enterprise.

    "I keep six honest serving men,
      They taught me all I knew.
    Their names were What and Where and When,
      And How and Why and Who."

Make sure to get all of your "serving men" in the first paragraph of your news release. Put the most important and exciting one at the head of the story.

- Put less important information further down in your release. That makes it easier to "cut," if necessary, for space purposes.
- Use a fine grade of paper. A color other than white may help you stand out in the crowd. But stay in the warm spectrum. (Except for faxing.)
- Don't send out news releases that have a "copy machine" look.
- Avoid highly technical language unless the release is for a technical audience.
- Find out how far in advance each contact wants your information. Send it out when *they* want it.
- Don't pass off nonoriginal material as exclusive.
- Don't try to make an advertisement for yourself out of an article or release. Present fascinating news for readers instead. Make the trail that leads back to you subtle.
- Give a source for additional information (name, address, phone number). Make sure your source knows all the details and does not have to check with someone else for answer if a reporter calls for additional information. This source could be an association or company mentioned in the article, or your office.
- Find a way to make your news noteworthy! Give it a twist that is specific to the audience who will read it. A dog expert working with plumbers might come up with a topic such as "Plumbers Use Dogs to Sniff out Deadly Gas" to catch the attention of a plumbers' publication. Other news media outlets, however, might also find that topic worthy of attention.
- Releases should be the minimum length necessary to present the facts of interest to this audience.
- Keep your news release mailing list up to date. Post changes as you receive them. Media people like to see releases addressed to them rather than to their predecessors.

How to Get Writers to Write About You

You will write many articles yourself, but it is also very desirable to be written about. Here is an easy way to accomplish this.

Bylines are the credit lines given to the authors of articles. This is the person who found the subject, conducted the interview, and wrote the article accepted for publication.

Watch for bylines on articles which have almost any connection to your area of expertise. Call the publications and ask for the writer of those specific stories. The author may be on staff or work on speculation. In either case, when you reach the writer, say how much you enjoyed the article. Never say, "oh, you know, I am the real expert, and I say you made a mistake . . ." Just explain that you have a story you think she might like. The writers' business is looking for interesting people and topics for feature stories. *Briefly* tell the writer about the unique work you do.

Write Your Own Articles

One of the best ways to be seen and have your views heard by potential clients is to write and publish articles related to your topic. These articles not only will keep you in the public eye, but will keep you in front of buyers in the markets you want to reach as well. While it may be a while before you become an international household name, you can start quickly to be a celebrity expert within your defined market by writing articles for that industry's publications.

Once you begin writing articles, be patient for the payoff. Do not, at first, expect to be paid in money for your articles. You will be highly paid in other ways. The value of inquiries from your articles for speaking, training, consulting, and product sales is tremendous.

Note: Give only first-time publication rights for your articles. This means a magazine has permission to print your article once, but the article itself belongs to you. Then you can rework your articles for noncompeting publications, gather them into books or booklets, and reuse and rearrange the text for audio cassettes and video programs.

How to Get Published

Take the most interesting, controversial aspect of your material and write an article highlighting it. Contact the magazines and newspapers who reach the clients for whom you would like to speak.

- *Target their readership:* Call editors and ask for sample issues of their publication and their author's guidelines. Some may charge you for the sample copy. Pay it gladly. You can often use almost the same article for different fields by rearranging and changing the material to fit each publication. Newsletters for dentists, for example, are not in competition with those for doctors, yet they have like needs and would welcome a very similar article.

- *Target their style:* Study the style and length of the articles and the angles from which they are written. That, in addition to their writers' guidelines, will enable you to send a story of the right length and style.

- *Target their timetable:* Address the material to the editor you spoke to, and get your story in promptly, ahead of schedule. You will have a much better chance of having it accepted.

Who Will Want to Publish Your Articles?

In addition to the obvious large publications being published in major magazines and newspapers, you might find a great value in these:

- *Company publications:* When you are asked to speak for any organization, also see if you can write an article on your topic for their company publication or newsletter. (Often they will pay you a fee for this! Make sure to include it on your fee menu!)

- *Trade journals:* As you are booked to speak, ask each clients which trade journals they read. It is often much easier to get started writing for trade journals than for major publications.

- *Small publications and newsletters:* There are special publications for everything you can imagine, from people who jump out of airplanes and parachutes to people who are single parents.

- *Become a columnist:* Paul and Sara Edwards, authors of *Working from Home,* keep their names and products in front of their audience by writing columns for appropriate publications. Your column can appear in anything from the local weekly newspaper to trade publications in your field.

Promotion

Promotion is getting your speaking into the fast lane. This means keeping your name current in the marketplace, using awards, promotional gifts, web directories, Yellow Pages, promotional newsletters, direct mail, and all your speaking engagements as promotion opportunities.

Ways to Keep Your Name Current

There are many creative ways to keep your name in front of buyers. Below are some of the easy ways.

Awards

Follow Suzy Mallery's example. She is president of the Manwatchers' Association. Each year she chooses the "Ten Most Watchable Men" (all of them celebrities) and prepares plaques for them. Then she calls and invites each one to attend a party for the presentation. Of course, she is the one who makes the presentation. Some of the gentlemen who have received her awards include astronomer Carl Sagan and actor Henry "The Fonz" Winkler. She sends out releases about the awards to all the media, which always result in articles in publications all over the world.

Speaking Calendars

Mail your speaking calendar (possibly included as part of a newsletter) to your past and future buyers. Be sure to include your topics on your calendar. We constantly receive calendars from speakers that say things like, "The Smith Group," with booked dates and an address. If only their unique and interesting topics and/or specialty (e.g., "The Cold Call Specialty" or "Expertise on Internet Issues") were listed, then the calendar would serve as a way to cement the name of the speaker with his or her expertise in mind. (Remember: leave a trail they can follow back to you!)

Free Promotional Newsletters

Newsletters are a brilliant way to keep your name in front of buyers. Newsletters can be sent via mail, fax, or E-mail. Our personal favorite format is a one-sided, faxable document with quick, interesting tips that we can use in our business today. This sort of newsletter is more apt to be copied and passed around (which is exactly what you hope will happen).

Your newsletter must be interesting (quick and easy to read), but also include:

- Your name
- Topics
- How to reach you

E-Newsletters

As electronic newsletters (newsletters sent out via E-mail) are almost free to send, immediate, and so each a child can send them, they are gaining momentum fast.

Promotional Gifts

Many speakers we book create unusual gifts to give to speakers' bureaus who book them, or to meeting planners. Your gift should never be embarrassing, crude, personal, or anything that could be construed as a bribe.

If you use gifts, keep them fun, inexpensive and *usable*! Some of the items that have impressed us over the years include:

- Sticky note pads with the speaker's name and address. We got one from the DisneyLand Pacific Hotel, a sticky pad shaped like Mickey Mouse! The first few notes had "opportunity" dates marked on a calendar upon which they offer group discounts.
- Pens with yellow highlighters on them.
- One speaker uses a bag of peanuts that are grown in the state he comes from.
- Another speaker gives a gift bottle of a delightful California wine.
- Nido Qubien gives unusual gingersnap cookies baked in his hometown.

Other Promotion Ideas

Your promotional ideas will only be limited by the time and creativity you give to thinking of them.

- Whenever someone asks you to write a testimonial for their book, or a jacket blurb, or even the forward, do it. Not only will you encourage others, but you will "get your name out there" and be acknowledged as an expert in your field.
- Take a tip from the movie and sports stars. When you are offered the opportunity to publicize a charity event, accept, and give the publicity chair lots of pictures and quotes for them to use in the promotion.
- Shep Hyken professional speaker, told us, "Having a website has landed me three magazine interviews. Somehow three reporters/authors found me via my site. One of the magazines is a large human resource publication."

Direct Mail

Direct mail refers to sending out promotional material to mass-mailing lists you have gathered or rented. Since each speaker's subject and market are different, you will need to experiment with trial runs. At best, direct mail produces about a one percent return. So expect approximately 50 inquiries from a 5000-piece mailing. When you follow up on those fifty leads, you can expect to close about five bookings, provided you had good copy and mailed to the right prospects. We recommend a careful study of the prospect list.

Speaker Card Packs

Several groups offer direct mail advertising card packs of speakers. They are mailed to association, corporation and Chamber of Commerce meeting planners. Each speaker has an ad on one side of the postcard and his or her return address on the back. The meeting planner fills in the card and mails it back to the speaker as an inquiry. When the card pack approach is taken, the important thing to watch for is that the card pack is mailed to appropriate target contacts in your field.

Using Advertising and Directories Effectively

Speakers disagree about the best way to market themselves. Some use only telemarketing; others put ads in newspapers and/or selective directories; some send out blanket direct mail pieces or do fax broadcasting; and now there is marketing on the Internet and bulk E-mailing. Our bureau uses a combination of all these methods. We advertise heavily, attend showcases and events to meet buyers, use selective mail to new and old clients. We are aggressive on the Internet. We do fax broadcasting to our prospective buyers several times a year and we constantly call prospects by phone.

In advertising, repetition is the key to success. Most people do not remember the name of any product or service until they have seen or heard it five times. This is why you will see successful speaker's ads repeated in every speakers' catalog and magazine.

To gain valuable knowledge about advertising, ask speakers in noncompetitive areas about their experience in marketing. You might also arrange joint-venture mailing and marketing with a group of speakers.

List Yourself in Directories That Meeting Planners' Need

All the major associations who cater to those that hire speakers (MSI, ASAE, PCMA, etc.) have directories in which they sell space. For instance, the cost to be listed in ASAE's 1997 *Who's Who in Association Management Directory and Buyer's Guide* is $305 (as of 1997) if you are a member of ASAE and $405 if you are not. It is sent to approximately 25,000 members.

Web Directories and Yellow Pages

Regional as well as national directories of speakers are published and carried on the World Wide Web. Some require membership in their group before a speaker is listed, while others sell listings and display advertising space to any speaker who will pay. Many are free.

Use the major search engines on the Web and look for "directories" or "yellow pages." Also search under your topic area to see if someone is developing a directory of experts in your field.

Advertise in Speakers' Bureau Directories

Often, bureaus publish speaker directories. The bureau pays for publishing and mailing the directory to thousands of meeting planner clients and prospects. Some allow the speaker's advertisement. The speaker's picture and topic are sent directly to the bureau's buyers as part of the directory. A typical directory ad costing $300 reaches 10,000 meeting planner prospects. A speaker could not pay for printing, postage, labor, and "rent" a mailing list to produce such a large mailing for that low price. Bureau directories are an excellent way to advertise, because prospective clients keep them and use them all year.

The address and phone number of the sponsoring bureau alone appears on this type of directory. All bookings go through the bureau.

Team Up to Buy a Joint Ad or Website

Since advertising is often expensive, consider sharing a full-page ad with other speakers in your field. Team up to buy a joint ad or website. For example, we know several humorists who buy full-page ads that show them all together. Since a full page usually costs less than four quarter-page ads, the "team-up" idea works well and saves advertising money. Each one only pays a fourth of the full-page rate.

Another reason to team up is that meeting planners usually want a new humorist for each booking. If they like one of the partners, they are likely to be pleased with the others, as well. However, teaming with others who have noncompetitve topics to yours is an excellent idea also. The planer might hire all of you for the same meeting.

An extra advantage to the teaming arrangement can be shared use of a toll-free, wide-area telephone number (800 number, also known as a WATS line), and sometimes the joint hiring of a staff person to answer phones and send out promotional materials.

List Yourself in Media Directories as an Expert

Several radio and television talent directories are published that will list you and your area of expertise. These directories are often used by radio and television stations when they need someone to interview on a particular topic. Try to be listed in as many categories as is practical. Be sure your title for each is a "grabber." Most have an advertising fee.

Directory of Experts
Authorities and Spokespersons
Broadcast Interview Source
2233 Wisconsin Ave. NW #406
Washington, D.C. 20007
*202 333-4904
Fax: (202) 342-5411
E-mail: Yearkbook@DELPHI.com

Nobel Internet Directories
Lin Doyle
25 Kearny St. #303
San Francisco, CA 94108
(800) 640-5959
E-mail: Lind@Nobelgroup.com

Radio-TV Interview Report
Bradley Communications
312B W. Montgomery Ave.
Box 229, Haverford, PA 19041
(800) 553-8002

How to Trade Your Speaking for Publicity

There are times when it will be beneficial to your career to exchange your speaking fee for advertising space or time. In return for performing, you are able to advertise your services as a speaker or promote your seminars and products in the client's publications or media.

A good example of such an arrangement is the sales trainer who gave a series of sales seminars for radio time representatives. He took his payment out in radio time for himself. Then he made his own commercials and used the radio time he received in trade to promote his public seminars. He thus earned in seminar sales many times the fee he would have earned as a trainer for the radio station. He included a plug for his other speaking and training services in his seminar commercials and was called by businesses to do additional training sessions, as well as conference and convention speeches.

His commercials were so good, the station asked him to do several commercials for other companies for good fees. He now often works in the TV and radio commercial field, and enjoys residual payments.

Attend Trade Shows

There are trade shows of all kinds and sizes aimed at every market. Many trade shows look for professional speakers who will give a presentation aimed at their particular group in exchange for a free booth or display ad in the trade show program or directory. This is a good bargain. You have the opportunity to speak to an ideal audience of prospects and to sell your speaking services and products at a booth. (See more on this in Chapter 9: Speaker Products: Triple Your Income, the section on "How to Sell Products during Events: BOR and Trade Shows.")

Always Use Speaking Engagements as Promotion Opportunities

We stress this point repeatedly in our books and in our *Speak and Grow Rich* seminars for speakers. Whenever you speak, invite people to come and hear you—editors, producers, bureau representatives, potential clients. Inviting people to preview you is excellent promotion.

Find Ways to Stay Connected to Your Clients

Promotion is about finding ways to connect to your customers. This involves getting to know them as people, and just being nice. Remember always that public relations literally means your relationships with other people.

- Actively showing appreciation raises value. Criticism and depreciation lower it. So be delighted with other people's success. Show it. Send appreciative comments. Mean it.

- Send inexpensive gifts that show you know contacts personally:

  1. A travel brochure to a place they said they wished they could go to.

  2. A box of their favorite candy.

  3. A card with a picture of the same type of dog they said they have.

- You can't say "thank you" too many times. When you are on the road, you may think you don't have time for the thank yous that you should send, but you do. There is that endless wait at the airport, or the time on board the flight. Use those times constructively by catching up on your thank-yous via your laptop computer and faxes, or carry big postcards with your picture on them and send personal notes to those who have interviewed you or booked you or helped you.

Find Ways to Say Thank You

Give a promotional gift. Somers White, for example, once called us to ask our bureau for some information. We gladly found what he wanted and sent it to him. The next day, a beautiful wallet and a thank-you note arrived in the mail. It is hard to forget someone who shows this kind of appreciation.

Wally "Famous" Amos, the cookie man, uses a small but very effective gift. His business card has a plastic bag attached that contains two cookies. When we took Wally Amos to dinner, we watched him give one of these little gifts to the restaurant's maitre d', then to the busboy at our table. The people at the next table came over, then the bartender. Before we left, almost the whole restaurant had found us, including the chef! Wally Amos shook hands, greeted everybody, and said, "I want you to have some of my cookies!" Each time he gave out his cookie card. He always carries a box of these small gifts with him. After dinner, we asked him, "Wally, what does it cost to give away these cookie gifts? How many do you hand out per week? Month? Year?" Wally smiled and told us, "You know, I never count them. I just keep planting seeds."

What Goes Around . . .

Develop a "promotion outlook" by looking at every business card with these questions in mind: "How can I help these people? How can these people help me?" or "How can I get these people together with someone who needs them?"

You will find these methods are like casting bread upon the water. You will be rewarded. For example. we once sent a card of congratulations to a client who had been interviewed in a major publication. Our letter was about three sentences. He later phoned us to say we were the only ones who had congratulated him in any way. Then he asked us, "What can I do for you?"

We thought a moment, then replied, "Would you give us the name, address, and phone number of the writer who interviewed you for the article?" We then called the writer and congratulated him on writing the excellent story.

At last count, that writer has written fifteen articles about us, our magazine *Sharing Ideas,* our topic, and our speakers' bureau, all for major publications. Do good deeds, show people appreciation, and be ready to go through the open doorway of opportunity.

Effective promotion takes consistent time and effort. It is not something you do once and stop. Successful speakers continually work on new promotion ideas to grow rich. These ideas and skills are unlimited and they grow and bloom with use, especially when nurtured with the enrichment of those whose lives your work and words will touch.

The Advantages of Working with Speakers' Bureaus and Agents

Once you are receiving solid and consistent fees for your bookings, it is time to consider the advantages of working with those who sell speakers.

Speakers' bureaus are very valuable resources to meeting planners. Instead of needing to call and screen speakers one at a time, the meeting planner has the speakers' bureau's expert counsel, and the availability and fees of hundreds, even thousands, of speakers with one call.

There are actually many kinds of companies and individuals that act as go-betweens for speakers and those looking to buy speakers: agents, management companies, professional meeting planners, production companies, speakers' bureaus, and other speakers. Since the majority of go-betweens really are speakers' bureaus, we tend to lump all of these representatives into a mental category of "speakers' bureau." This limits you in your marketing efforts. We will go into detail about what each type of representative offers, and describe them (by their correct names!). However, often, for simplicity of understanding, we will call anyone who acts as a sales representative for a speakers' *bureau.*

All keep a percentage of the fee paid by the buyer as their recompense for obtaining the booking for you (more on this in a bit).

Who Are the "Representatives" Who Book Speakers?

Many companies make a profit by finding speakers for buyers, and some by finding bookings for speakers. You must appreciate the difference before you begin marketing to them. In our speakers' bureau, we are exasperated when the third new speaker in a day calls and says, "So you get bookings for speakers?"

"No, we are a speakers' bureau; we get speakers for buyers."

"Right. Then you will represent me?"

"Well, a speakers' bureau represents the buyer, but we certainly want to know what your topic is . . ."

"Oh, give me a topic. I can speak on just about anything."

Right.

Speaker after speaker call with no understanding of us, what we do, or what tools and skills he or she needs to make it in this industry. This section will explain just what each type of representative does: agents, management companies, professional meeting planners, production companies, speakers' bureaus, and other speakers who will book you. Keep in mind as you read, that we have painted these descriptions with broad brush strokes. The details of how each individual company operates are unique to those who run them. But these broad illustrations will help you to be one of those speakers that representatives find enjoyable rather than exasperating—especially when you know enough about the industry that you can appreciate the differences each company owner has created.

Exclusive Agents and Management Companies

An agent works for the speaker. Thirty years ago, most celebrity speakers used an agent to handle all of their speech and lecture bookings. Today this type of agency is often referred to as a personal management company. The true agent (personal management) has an exclusive contract with the speaker. In most cases, agents are paid a salary by the speaker or a percentage of the speaker's total speaking income. Obviously, not every speaker can have an agent. The words "agent" and "celebrity" together like ham and eggs. Agents usually do not work for noncelebrities. However, if you become a household name and are able to command speaking fees of $50,000 and above, you will have agents wooing *you*.

The agent represents the speaker in negotiations for speaking engagements. Often, the agent handles the publicity for a speaker and arranges promotional articles, book publishing contracts, and radio and television appearances. Some celebrity speakers have agents who handle all of their business affairs as well.

Some personal management companies work with less well-known speakers. They have a small group of speakers, charging each of them anywhere from $200 to $3,000 a month as a basic fee, plus all expenses of telemarketing and mailings, and a percentage of all bookings. Naturally, these companies promote and sell only the speakers who are paying members of their group.

Most of these exclusive agents give their permission to other types of brokers (see below) to list their speakers in many catalogs. Often the exclusive agent splits the commission with the broker who brings them the business, so it often does not cost the buyer more to use a third party to find out who has these exclusive listings. Most buyers assume that any representative sending them a brochure has exclusive representation of the speakers listed. This is only true for a tiny section of the industry! An exclusive agent usually has only a very small listing of truly "exclusive" speakers. Some exclusive agents force other brokers to add their commission on top of what it would have cost if the buyer had called direct. This practice is called "adding on." It is one of the greatest causes for frustration in the speaking business. (See more later in this chapter under "Commissions, Fees, and Add-ons").

Brokers

Brokering is what many of these representatives do, not necessarily what they are. Like a travel agent, a broker keeps extensive records on where to find speakers. They "broker" with the agents or speakers for the planner. Almost all larger speakers' bureaus have exclusive contracts with some speakers, and broker for the rest of the speakers in their catalogs. A good broker knows the quickest way to locate speakers that are under exclusive contracts with other agents and to assist buyers in finding speakers who are on the open market (speakers who do not have exclusive contracts). This can be a tremendous time-saver for the buyer.

Professional Meeting Planners and Production Companies

Professional planners and production companies offer a huge variety of services: lighting, staging, registration, advertising, hotel negotiations, picking the speaker up at the airport, sound and microphone problems, etc. If they have been in the business for a while, they gain a good understanding of which speakers are in the marketplace and who is effective on the platform. As an add-on value, they often help their customers find speakers and negotiate the contracts.

Planners and production companies tend to add on their commission over the speaker's fee, because they are offering their customers many extra services. Their specialty is not speakers, but they can be a great source of income to speakers.

Speakers' Bureaus (Commercial)

Speakers' bureaus[1] make up the largest segment of those that book speakers. Speakers' bureaus and brokers are much the same. They normally work for the buyer, rather than the speaker. They tend to be experts on speakers available through the open market (those not on exclusive contract with an agent). Traditionally, they receive their commission from the speaker's standard, net fee. In other words, it costs the buyer the same whether they call a bureau or call the speaker direct. For information on Walters International Directory of Speakers' Bureaus phone (626) 335-8069.

Professional Speakers as "Middlepeople"

Some speakers help planners find other professional speakers to fill their needs. A speaker who has worked with a group before and knows what they like may be an excellent source to find other presenters with similar talents. Some speakers form partnerships to help promote each other. They share leads, and sometimes they pay each other a commission. It is vital for the speakers' reputations that they only form this sort of arrangement with other speakers of excellent

---

[1]Public Speakers' bureaus offer speakers to the public usually at no charge. These types of bureaus are usually found at public utilities, schools and universities, political groups, large Fortune 500 types of companies and many other public service types of groups. You may find ways of benefiting from doing no-fee presentations; see Chapter 4: From Free to Shining Fee.

quality (this of course is true of anyone who hopes to be successful in the speaker selling business!) The speakers associated with this sort of group usually have only six or seven speakers for this sort of cartel; rarely more than 20.

Commissions, Fees, and Add-ons

Whoever books a speaker receives a commission, just as a sales representative for a manufacturer is paid for the orders he or she obtains. Think of speakers' bureaus as your "sales reps." In order for this relationship to work, the speaker becomes a product that the bureau can sell for retail. Travel agents work the same way. If it was cheaper to go direct, why would a buyer go to the agent? If you want your sales rep to work for you, you must create fees that have their commission built in.

Over the years, the practice of adding-on has caused problems and created many "war stories" in the speaking industry. For instance, a bureau asks a client, "What's your budget?" After the client answers "$10,000," the bureau then calls the speaker and says, "How much do you want to do this job?" The speaker says "I want to net $5,000." The bureau then calls the client and says, "Okay, you've got your speaker for $10,000." That is "adding on." The speaker gets $5,000, and the bureau keeps the rest. With add-on speakers, agents and bureaus charge the buyer whatever the traffic will bear.

Eventually, however, the buyer will find out that he or she has paid $5,000 more for that speaker than their meeting planner friends have paid. Naturally, the buyer then becomes angry. Many speakers have told us, "Oh, well, what could I do? It's on *their* head." You might be interested to know that the name that gets dragged through the mud is often not the bureau's. It's the speaker's! The speaker is the one in the privileged position of a trusted teacher to the clients. The buyers just don't believe the speaker could have been that naive.

What the speaker can do about this is to set firm fees and stick to them. When a broker of any type calls and says, "What is your fee?," the speaker is able to reply with a real fee, not a "whatever the market will bear" fee. The speaker then says to the broker, "And your commission is _____? Okay, that means I will net _____ and you will get _____. Right?"

Additional Fees and Services
Offered by Representatives

Everyone who books you will expect some sort of payment, a commission, some charge for each booking they obtain for you; some have a registration fee; some have both. The standard of the world for bureaus is 25 percent.

A number of bureaus charge speakers a yearly or monthly fee, which may cover services such as publicity and packaging.

Please beware of companies that say, "Pay our $2,000 membership fee and we will obtain bookings for you!" There is no way a bureau can be credible if they claim they will obtain bookings for you if you pay them a flat fee! It is impossible to guarantee you bookings! On the other hand, if they are offering you a tangible service or product for that fee, you might well have a valuable resource from someone who knows the speaking industry better than you do.

It is very easy to be turned down by representatives if you approach them as a speaker. However, no one turns down a paying customer! See what other "for a fee" services they offer that might benefit you. This may be an excellent way to at least establish a relationship. Note: Do not buy their other services *just* to establish a relationship! Make sure you really want and need the service they are offering.

Some of the other additional services you might need include:

- *Presentation skills or marketing training or consultations:* Here at Walters Speaker Services, we do from two to ten consultations a week, with speakers at all levels.

- *Management services:* Debra Lilly of California is one of several excellent companies that act as your office while you are on the road. Your calls are forwarded to her, and her staff handles your calendar and sends out inquiry information.

- *Directory advertising:* Some bureaus charge a fee for you to be included in their directories. If you are accepted by such a bureau, you will be asked to advertise in this publication (usually $200 to $300). The advertisement works for you all year long and costs less than printing, postage, labor, and the mailing lists you would pay for if you sent out your own materials.

In addition, the fact that the bureau has accepted you for its directory is viewed as an endorsement.

- *Packaging:* A number of bureaus produce matching one-sheets for each of the speakers they represent. They will print these up for the speakers they choose to represent and mail them to their clients. The charge to the speaker for this service and material typically is about $800.

- *Demo tape production:* Some will produce a video tape of your presentation for approximately $5,000 or an audio cassette tape for approximately $1,000 (in addition to the actual costs).

- *Speaker showcases:* Several bureaus and organizations, such as I. G. A. B., produce showcases at which the speaker usually pays a fee to appear on the program. All bookings generated by the event go through the bureau that stages the showcase.

Where Do You Find Representatives?

There are several directories that list speakers' bureaus. The trouble with some of them is that there is no qualification process, so many speakers list themselves as a way for buyers to call them. Here are some you may want to try:

International Directory of Agencies and Bureaus

Walters Speaker Services produces the only complete and updated directory of agents and bureaus which they update constantly. It contains over 500 agents and bureaus around the world, in 18 countries: Bureau name, address, contact names, and usually their phone, fax, E-mail, and specialties. You may purchase this directory for $95 (U.S.), with the added bonus of receiving two years' worth of the largest newsmagazine in the world for professional speakers: *Sharing Ideas for Professional Speakers*. To order call (626) 335-8069, fax (626) 335-6127, or E-mail Dottie@SpeakAndGrowRich.com

National Speakers Association

NSA has a special interest group for speakers' bureaus—the Professional Emphasis Group. Anyone who is interested in becoming a bureau may join, so a good percentage of their membership are learning the ropes. However, a new bureau can be a great contact for a speaker. You may get their directory by simply calling NSA at (602) 968-2552.

ASAE Who's Who in Association Management Directory and Buyer's Guide

This publication has no requirements or proof that these members are actually Speakers' Bureaus. Nonmembers of ASAE can buy *Who's Who* for $160.

The International Group of Agencies and Bureaus

Members of IGAB must prove that they have been in the business of booking speakers for a set period of time before they are allowed to join. They do not make their directory public. (Dottie Walters is the founder of I. G. A. B.)

Meeting Professionals International

MPI has a section in their membership directory called "Entertainers and Speakers." Many of these are speakers and entertainers; some are speakers' bureaus, agents, and production companies. The directory is free to all members. You become a member by finding a qualified meeting professional who is willing to be a member, then you as a speaker can join as a supplier. They started this policy because their membership base was beginning to have too many suppliers and not enough meeting planners. Directories are free to members. Nonmembers may buy the directory for $155. They are located in Dallas, TX; phone 214-702-3000, fax 214-702-3070.

Mailing Lists

You can buy mailing lists from any list broker. They obtain their lists in two ways.

1. They go through every phone book and pull out the businesses listed under certain sections in the yellow pages. You will notice one for speakers' bureaus that has almost 2000 listings. We bought this ourselves, only to discover that it has about 1600 speakers, and only 100 actual bureaus. The cost to us was

$300, and we had the added cost of culling the list down to "real" speakers' bureaus.

2. They call us! We are very proud of the fact that our bureau directory is still the most accurate and largest available.

How to Get Representatives to Book You

If you can make a match with a bureau, you have secured a wonderful business partnership. If you can work up a team of twenty nonexclusive bureaus who will book you just six times a year each, at $2,500 per program, you will net about $225,000 after commissions.

How can you tell which are the "good" bureaus? The answer is obvious. A good bureau is one that gets you bookings, and sees that you get paid for them! Getting them to book you is what this next section is about.

What You Need Before Bureaus Will Consider You

You must develop your own professional business tools and skills. When you are good, have developed fine tools of the trade, and are earning a fee of at least $2,000 per program, you are ready to begin to woo the bureaus.

Speakers who come to our bureau for professional advice usually have many skills, but often they do not have the "packaging" they need to make them look like the experts they really are. Very few bureaus will create your marketing tools for you. It is the speaker's responsibility to create these tools. Without them, you put the bureau in the position of being asked to dig a ditch without a shovel. Bureaus are like manufacturers' sales representatives. They must have attractive catalogs and samples to do a good job of selling your programs.

Because of our high visibility, we have about 200 new speakers contact us each month. We ask all of them the same questions. In fact, we got tired of just repeating the same questions over and over, so we fax or E-mail them the following:

Before You Approach a Speakers' Bureau ...

We get about 200 inquiries, just like yours, every month. The speaking industry is extremely competitive, but not impossibly so if you are willing to learn about how to market yourself. We suggest you do some research into the industry. For instance, you need to have done at least 100 paid dates for fees of at least $2,000 per one-hour program, on topics that can be sold to association, corporate, or college markets, before you approach speakers' bureaus. You also must have the appropriate answers to the following questions:

- What is your main area of expertise?
- What are your specific titles for these topics?
- Which is the major market and industry you are appropriate for? (We do not mean "Associations" or "Corporations.") Be specific.
- Do you have a fee schedule and a menu of services prepared in a bureau-friendly format?
- What else do you offer: seminars, panels, consulting, products?
- Are you a member of a speaker group that shares leads?
- Which other speakers' bureaus have actually booked you?
- What is the average number of leads you give to your present bureaus after each performance?
- Do you have presentation kits prepared: demo tapes (for each topic of a live speech, not a press interview) one-sheets for each topic, and a fee schedule with a menu of services?
- Can you supply references from at least 50 paid speaking engagements?
- Do you have an office set up with: dedicated fax line(s), a system to send your full packages out while you are on the road, and a way to return phone calls within 60 minutes of someone leaving you a message?
- When will you be speaking in my city so that our representative can hear you speak in person?
- Your name: • Address:
- Phone: • Fax: • E-mail:
- Your background industry:

Until you can supply answers to all of the above with the sort of replies that don't rankle bureaus' nerves, we suggest you don't try approaching them!

We have entire areas elsewhere in this book that explain the importance of the questions we asked above on topics and title, targeting your major market, and fee schedules. But let us explain why we ask some of the other questions, and what you might reply:

What Else Do You Offer: Seminars, Panels, Consulting, Products? Bureaus are interested in presenters who offer opportunities from which they can make additional income. You see, whoever books you is entitled to a cut of these other services. When asked this question, a good reply would be, "In fact, last year I paid over $50,000 out in commissions on ancillary sales!"

Are You a Member of a Speaker Group That Shares Leads? All bureaus are very leery of speakers who are members of a speaker group that shares leads. These groups are notorious for sharing leads from bookings that a bureau obtained for them. When you do this, you are handing the lead over to a competitor of the bureau! If you are a member of such a group, qualify your reply, "Yes, but we are very careful never to share leads if the booking was obtained by a bureau." Maybe the bureau will believe you; most won't.

Which Other Speakers' Bureaus Have Actually Booked You? If other speakers' bureaus are booking you now, this is an excellent reference. All bureaus want to know who else in the industry is already working with you. This means bureaus who are getting you paid dates, not just bureaus who said, "Hmm, nice press kit, we'll see what we can do."

When asked, "Which other speakers' bureaus have actually booked you?" reply with the names and have the phone numbers ready to show that you are willing to have this bureau call and find out how well you do.

What Is the Average Number of Leads You Give to Your Present Bureaus After Each Performance? After every presentation, you should obtain leads. The bureaus are most keen to book you if you are diligent about sending these leads to them after each performance. When asked this, a good reply would be, "I average from two to ten leads per presentation. Would you prefer I mail or fax them to you?" (This assumes you do practice this very important business-building strategy!)

Can You Supply References from at Least 50 Paid Speaking Engagements?   Showing a bureau that, indeed, you are a real speaker, by way of a list of paid bookings, is a super way to get them to book you. When asked this, a good reply would be to have letters of reference ready to mail for fax, or a printed client list.

Do You Have an Office Set Up with: Dedicated Fax Line(s), a System to Send Your Full Packages Out While You Are on the Road, and a Way to Return Phone Calls Within 60 Minutes of Someone Leaving You a Message? Bureaus ask this because we know that a sure sign of a beginner is to not have a fax with a separate, dedicated line, and having no one to keep things running while you are away. What good does it do to suggest a speaker, when we can't then find out if he or she will be available for the date? Our customers get angry with our inefficiency, and call another bureau. Before we allow that to happen, we call another speaker who has things set up like a real businessperson.

When asked this, a good reply would be, "My fax is _____. My assistant, Nancy, will be here to help out while I'm on the road. My E-mail is _____. I check it twice a day and will respond immediately.

When Will You Be Speaking in My City So That Our Representative Can Hear You Speak in Person?   Letting a speakers' bureau know when you will be speaking in their home city gives them an opportunity to see you in person and shows them you are the sort of speaker who is currently being booked. When asked this, a good reply would be, "I won't be in your city, but I will fly you to _____, where I will be speaking." Don't offer to fly them if you can't afford it, but if you can, it will show them you are successful in this industry! Most won't take you up on the offer, but they will be impressed.

Your Background Industry   Bureaus ask this because they want to book speakers who have a background that acts as a strong base for the topic they will be presenting. When asked this, a good reply would be two statements. First say which industry you gained your business experience in. Then explain how this ties into your topic today.

Sticky Ethics Issues for Bureaus and Speakers

We find that when the cry of an "ethics" issue arises, it should more rightly be labeled a "communication" issue. Rarely do speakers or bureaus consciously seek the less honorable path. Most often there has been a misunderstanding of expectations.

We find there are four areas that cause the most dispute between speakers and bureaus:

The Touchy Business of Spin-offs and Repeats

A spin-off is a booking that a speaker receives from a company whose representative happens to be in the audience while the speaker presents a program for another client.

Spin-offs are a touchy area when a bureau is involved. Most bureaus feel speakers owe them a commission on spin-offs, even if the prospect calls the speaker directly. Often the speaker does not ask careful questions as to how this potential customer happened to call. A few months later the bureau calls this same customer from a list of attendees at the meeting at which the speaker was originally booked. The bureau finds out the speaker is booked by this customer, and finds out it is a spin-off. Now the bureau is angry with the speaker, and feels the speaker has withheld a duly owed commission. That speaker will never be booked by that bureau agin.

Keep careful records of how your leads come in; then you'll know if it's a spin-off from a bureau booking or not.

Some bureaus want spin-off clients directed through them. They want the speaker to say nothing other than, "Just call my bureau. Here is the number." Some bureaus want the speaker to handle the contract and send them a commission.

If the same client, or another branch of the client company, invites you back for another engagement, it is referred to as a "second time," or "repeat" engagement. Some bureaus expect their full commission on repeat bookings, while others expect only a partial sum.

When you are called directly by the buyer in any situation where a bureau is involved, you should make the client feel comfortable and negotiate in a way that is best for the client. But you should close the deal by saying, "Now that that's all settled, I will call my speakers' bureau to set up our contract."

This makes the clients happy, because you gave them your attention, and your bureau happy because they can again sign a contract with their client. It also gives the bureau that important option of booking other speakers as well for the same meeting. Another aspect is that this transaction tells the bureau you are to be trusted, and that trust certainly makes them think of you when the next call comes in.

When Two Bureaus Work on the Same Booking

If you have several bureaus working with you, record keeping is even more important. Some meeting planners call several bureaus at once. They ask each bureau to make ten suggestions to them according to certain specifications. Often these specs point all the bureaus to the same speaker. If you do not keep careful records of who suggested you for which job, the bureaus start to cross paths. You could have two, three, or four bureaus suggest you for the same job. Then the bureaus fight over who got to the client first.

It seems fair to hold the date for the bureau who called you first. Indeed, that is what we advised speakers to do for years, but we have changed our minds. Sometimes you will lose the date if you do this, because the bureau who called you second (or even third or fourth) is the one the buyer actually likes to work with. So now what? You are holding for bureau one, but bureau two is the one that is going to get the business. A few speakers have told us they "just let the speakers' bureaus fight it out among themselves." Unfortunately, if you do this, both bureaus in question will put you on their "No calls" list. Often speakers end up paying both bureaus a commission to help to avoid hostilities.

As consultants to both speakers' bureaus and speakers, we give two sets of advice. To bureaus we say, "Call the buyer. Ask them which one of the bureaus they want to handle the contract. If the buyer wants the other bureaus to do it then **back off.** If the buyer wants you to handle it, then try to get the other bureau to back off. If they won't, suggest to the other bureau that you split the commission. If that does not work, go back to the buyer and explain that you will assist in a nonpaid capacity to make sure all aspects of using this speaker go smoothly, but the other bureau is insisting they will handle the contract. The buyer is so relieved that the "nice" bureau may gain a new and very loyal client. We know we have.

If the speaker asks for our advice, we tell them, "Pay the double commission!" We know, this feels annoying, frustrating, and unfair (and frankly we agree!) but it's the best suggestion we have. In the long run it will be worth the money you lose to attempt keeping both bureaus happy. We say attempt because no matter what, you, both bureaus, and the buyer are going to be unhappy. It is just that all parties, except you, will be *less* unhappy. Besides, as frustrating as this situation is, it only happens to very busy speakers, and then only once or twice a year.

We understand the very difficult position this puts speakers in. To be fair to speakers, as a compromise, we added this line into our agreement with speakers:

> All future dates with this client are commissionable to Walters International Speakers' Bureau at 25%. If another bureau calls you, you will tell them you are committed to Walters International for this client for this event; you will call us and give us three working days (72 hours) to close this date for you.

Some bureaus don't want to let you know the names of their buyers until the deal is a sure thing. So when another bureau calls you for a date you already have on hold, you don't have any way of knowing if it is for the same client. The only thing you can do is let this second bureau calling know what the problem is and try to get a clear date from the first bureau. Also, nicely inform all bureaus asking you to hold dates that you can't "protect" them if you don't know who the client is, or what the date is they are discussing.

What to Do When a Bureau "Comes in Behind You"

Often, when new meeting planners or buyers call our bureau they say, "See what you can find out for me about Speaker X." We call Speaker X and learn that he has been trying to sell himself to that same client for years. Or, he has already been hired by the client in the past! Does Speaker X owe our bureau a commission if we close this booking? Should the bureau pursue this booking? Do you want the bureau to pursue it for you?

The first time this happened to us, the speaker involved was Nido Qubien. We told Nido not to worry, we would back out of the deal. But Nido insisted that we work on it for him and he wanted to pay the standard commission when we closed it. Lilly was working on this sale and she was very new to the industry at the time. She thought this policy seemed unfair to speakers and, in this case, to Nido. But she realized that he was hoping that we might be the "added touch" that could close the deal. That plus element was worth the price of our commission to him.

Consider the following points when deciding how to handle this situation:

- If a client is still talking to bureaus about other possible speakers, and the contract for you is not signed nor is the deposit paid, *you do not have a firm deal.* It is better to invest part of your fee on a commission to a bureau than to lose all of it to another speaker.

- If the bureau cannot sell you, they will work on selling another speaker to this client. They will either be working for you, or against you.

- By letting the bureau book you, the goodwill you create is bound to get you more bookings. Beginning speakers do not realize that bureaus have many choices of good speakers. All things being equal concerning several speakers' ability and content, the speaker that helps increase the bureau's business is the one the bureau will call the next time.

What if the bureau does not already have a relationship with the buyer, but is trying to solicit a new potential client? This buyer mentions to this new bureau that they are just now thinking about Speaker X. The bureau says to Client XYZ, "No problem, I'll handle that for you."

The bureau calls Speaker X and says, "Client XYZ wants me to handle this contract." The confused speaker (who has been on the phone every day to XYZ) says, "Okay," thinking the buyer must want this bureau involved for some reason. Sometimes the buyer wasn't even interested in the bureau helping to get Speaker X. But the bureau saw the situation as a method of making a few fast dollars at the speaker's expense. Luckily, this does not happen often, but it does happen.

The only way to know for sure which situation you are dealing with is to ask the client. However, we do *not* suggest you do this! You put the buyers in such an awkward position, they may decide to not use you at all!

If you doubt the bureau's honesty or it is the first time you have worked with them, you might want to exercise some caution. We do suggest you proceed with the booking in the hopes of keeping everyone happy and making a new bureau friend. But, politely and respectfully inform the bureau that you need your portion of the fee to be made payable to you on or before the day of the presentation. This is not an unreasonable request.

When Buyers Lose Track of How They Heard About the Speaker

When you work with many speakers' bureaus and buyers, a system for accurate lead tracking is essential if you wish to maintain and build strong relationships with those who obtain bookings for you. (See Chapter 4: From Free to Shining Fee.)

If the lead has occurred because of something done by a speakers' bureau, you should collect the information, then turn the contract writing over to the bureau that made the solicitation with this client.

If the lead did not occur because of a bureau, you still need to know how it originated. Then you can begin to get an idea of which method of advertising or promotion is bringing in the best results.

Lead tracking means that you:

- Must keep scrupulous records of incoming calls and be sure to ask, "How did you hear about me?" Then carefully record and process the answer.
- Develop a retrieval system so you can quickly access data.

Unfortunately, some speakers still do not keep records on how their business originates. We know how tempting it is to just work an inquiry without finding out how it originated, but that is a very shortsighted approach. One speaker who wanted our bureau to book him told us, "I can't be bothered asking people how they heard about me." He never could understand why we could not be bothered to work with him.

Trouble occurs like this: The bureau calls you to send your package to a large company. This company holds committee meetings on whom to hire, so nothing comes immediately out of these efforts. It may take years of transitional date shuffling and restructuring of their company and event objectives. Often the meeting planner is fired, transferred, or promoted. A new meeting planner takes over. In the meanwhile, your promotional package was sent up the line to the CEO, or the CEO's secretary, then back down the line to a VP, whom neither you nor the bureau even knew was going to be involved. Finally, someone with enough authority decides to hire you, but calls you directly, having no clue how the promotional package arrived in their office in the first place. When you receive that phone call, how do you remember how you initially got the lead, perhaps a year or more earlier? Often, you don't. Sometimes not only has the date of the event changed, but the buyer or even the company name has changed. But you can bet the bureau that recommended you is going to remember, and be none too happy that you didn't.

Each time a call comes into your office, ask the inquirer first, "How did you hear about me?" We hear you thinking, "Shouldn't the bureau be on top of this and *know* that the buyer is coming around to a decision about now?" Yes, but look at the bigger picture. Think of future bookings from the speakers' bureau in question. The bureau will be thrilled if you call them with a sale they were not expecting. You'll find them suggesting you much more often because you have proven that golden opportunities lie in suggesting you to their clients.

A Sample Agreement Between Speaker and Speakers' Bureau

Once a speakers' bureau or agent is willing to represent you, you will be asked to sign an agreement or contract. Below is an example of the agreement we ask speakers to sign. The signing occurs only after we have seen them perform (at least via video), after they have provided us with all of their tools of the trade, after we have checked their references, and after we feel they are suitable for our clients. All bureaus and agents have their own contracts. We don't suggest ours is anything other than what we ourselves like.

Figure 11:1. Sample Bureau Speaker's Agreement

Sample Walters International Speakers' Bureau Speaker's Agreement

Billing, Fees, and Terms

1. Walters International Speakers' Bureau (referred to as WI) will receive 25% commission, paid from your standard fee on all engagements, product sales, consulting, recording rights, and other services booked for you. The gross fees you give us to quote must be the same as the ones you quote when other clients call you direct. We will not add our commission to the top of your standard fee.

2. You will honor fees we have quoted for you if you have agreed verbally by phone. You agree not to raise your fee for that particular client, for that date.

3. WI will issue the contract and handle negotiations with all clients.

4. WI sends the booking contract to the client. The client pays 25% down to WI to secure your hold on the date. This is referred to as the "holding deposit." The 25% is also our commission. The 75% balance is paid to you directly by the client on the day of the presentation. You agree to send a bill to the client for expenses, ahead of the date, if possible, and no later than a week after the performance. (See Chapter 4: Free to Shining Fee, for new ideas on travel expenses.)

5. We will send a reminder of your speaking date and the terms of the contract to the client 10 days before the program. We will send a copy to you.

6. You agree to provide us with your current fee menu for each type of presentation you offer. If you offer a discount for additional programs at the same event, or a discount if a minimum purchase of products is included in the contract, you agree to indicate how these discounts apply so that we may negotiate on your behalf. You agree to notify us at once of any changes, and to honor all commitments to clients made before the changes are received at our office.

Expenses

7. You agree to make your own travel arrangements, unless the client wishes to do so themselves. (We will notify you of the client's wishes.) You agree to submit vouches and bills for reimbursement.

8. You agree to inform us of your travel requirements before we suggest you to a client, so that we may include them in the contract. (Many clients will not allow first-class air.)

9. You agree that all travel expenses shall be prorated with other clients on the same speaking trip, whenever the prorating will offer an advantage to both buyers involved.

10. You agree to travel and food expenses for one person only, unless approved by WI and the client before the contract is issued.

11. You agree that you will not charge any personal or outside business long-distance phone calls or liquor to the client.

12. If you charge our client for anything other than coach air, airport taxi, and two moderately priced meals (if needed), such as any other expenses or handout materials, you agree to advise WI before we send out our booking contracts. These items must be included in the contract. Out 25% commission is not charged for any transportation or meal expenses.

13. You agree to let us know immediately if you do not receive your check from the client as specified. WI will follow up and assist with the collection process. If there is any problem on the collection of your fee because the client goes out of business, you will receive 75% of any amount (including the deposit) WI has received. This does not apply to a client who refuses to pay because of Clause #32 in this contract.

14. If the booking date is canceled, and WI has already collected a deposit, we will send you 50% of what we have collected for holding the date.

Promotional Materials, Correspondence, and Follow-Up

15. You agree to furnish us with one set of the following items: Professional demo tape before a live audience, professionally produced; a full audio program of your work; your professional presentation kit, brochure, photos, testimonial letters, fee schedule, and reprints of appropriate articles you have written. You also agree to have many sets of these same materials ready to send to prospective clients as we request them for bookings, all prepared in pro-bureau fashion.

16. We will call you to clear a booking date and confirm the fee on each prospective client and/or engagement. You then discuss any negotiation of multiple fees, products, etc. with us. You will give us approval to proceed with this client on your behalf. We send you written confirmation of our conversation, with the prospective client's name, address and phone.

17. We will often ask you to send your presentation-promotional package to the client from your office. You will provide your materials with our address and contact information such as your brochures and demonstration tapes.

18. You agree to send your package of materials to our client the day we call you. If you are away on the road, you agree to make arrangements for someone else to send your package out promptly.

19. You agree to send our client a personal letter in your package, stating you have been requested by WI to send your material. You will ask them to call Lilly Walters at Walters International Speakers' Bureau, (818) 335-8069, if they have any questions.

20. You agree to copy us on all correspondence and inform us of your communications with our client at all times.

21. You specifically agree not to call our clients or prospective clients without checking with us first. We call our clients frequently to follow up for you.

22. Our policy is to have you speak to our client directly as soon as it is appropriate, but only upon our specific request. Sometimes we need your assistance to help us "close" the booking. However, clients often use our bureau because they don't want to talk with multiple speakers "up front." We always do what makes the client most comfortable. We expect your full cooperation.

23. Clients often want an immediate answer on availability and contract terms. You agree to maintain an answering service or other means of reaching you promptly. You agree to return our call on the day we place it.

24. You agree to send out your materials to our client on the day we call you. Delay can mean we both lose the booking. (We are competing with other bureaus and their speakers.)

25. If the client decides you are not the speaker they want for this engagement, we will notify you by fax, so that you can take our temporary hold off your calender.

26. If our client decides that they want you, we will call you immediately with the confirmation of the booking. We will send a contract to the buyer and copy you when it is returned to us. We guarantee full disclosure to you.

27. If the client decides to book you, you will send a photo and bio to them and a short description of the talk you are planning for them, or any other information the client requests.

General Etiquette

28. You agree that you will not give out the name of our client or information about their future needs to any other speakers or bureaus.

29. If you receive a letter of recommendation from one of our clients, you are not to use it in any promotional material to other bureaus or speakers.

30. If a prospective client calls you direct, we ask that you always answer their questions regarding your relationship with us. You may discuss your fees with them. This is appropriate because we will never quote different fees than those you quote yourself.

31. Once you or your office have given your commitment verbally to WI by phone to hold a date for a client, we will negotiate on your behalf. You will not release this date for other buyers, bureaus, agents, your own personal business or for any other reason without checking with us first.

32. You will engage in no vulgar language, dirty jokes, off-color or inappropriate material, drinking or other unprofessional behavior, either on or off the platform, as designated by the client. If you persist in such behavior or use material that the client specifically asks you not to use, you understand that you will forfeit your fee and expenses for the engagement, if so requested by the buyer.

33. You will charge no incidentals to the client's master account: e.g., alcohol, massages, long distance phone calls.

34. You agree to keep in touch with WI, letting us know your whereabouts at all times, and will send us your updated literature and any fee changes.

35. If more than one bureau calls you for the same client and date, you agree that the first bureau to call you on the date is the one you work

with for that booking. You agree to tell the second bureau you are already pledged with WI for that same client.

36. You agree to keep careful records of how your inquiries originate. You will call WI immediately when you receive an inquiry from any of our clients.

Repeat, Spin-off, and Future Business

37. All business and inquiries at any future date from clients booked for you by WI will be referred to our Bureau. Refer all arrangements and negotiations to us. You agree not to engage in separate contracts with our clients, for any speaking, consulting, training, or product sales.

38. On every incoming call to your office, you agree to specifically ask, "Where did you hear about me?" If the client says, "The Walters Bureau recommended you," you will ask all the pertinent information about the booking, then turn that client and the information over to WI. There is no time limit.

39. You agree to keep careful records of the source of your booking. If WI is in any way connected to a booking, you agree to call WI and have us handle the contract. If the caller says, "I heard you at a speech you did," you will research your records to find how that date was booked for you. If it was a booking made by WI, you agree to refer this new spin-off lead back to WI. WI will handle the contracts on all spin-offs from any bookings we obtain for you.

Product Sales and Referrals

40. Any product sales at the performance must be cleared and arranged with the client first. If we arrange for a quantity purchase of your products as part of the contract, we require a 10% commission on the gross of products sold.

41. Referrals: If you have a lead you cannot handle, or a date you are unable to make (with clients other than the ones we book you with), we appreciate your turning the lead over to us. We keep careful records of these leads and will send you 10% of the bureau commission on the first booking.

42. We appreciate your being an ongoing subscriber to *Sharing Ideas* Newsmagazine. We will feature you in our publication. *Sharing Ideas* is mailed to our bureau clients. It helps us to suggest you. We appreciate your enthusiastic support, in the same spirit that we give it to you.

43. Walters International, Royal Publishing, and all of its employees are not responsible for any injury you incur while on an assignment or in any way associated with an assignment you are performing for a client booking we obtain for you.

Most Important of All

44. You agree that we will work together as a three-way team. We want our clients to feel that WI is an extension of your office and of theirs. We serve them and you. We need your help. Please back us up with everything you do. Let the client know they receive the very best for themselves by using both of us. Our job is to make your booking go smoothly and successfully, so that this client will use you again, and use our services again. Thank you for your support.

Failure to perform any of these requirements, points 1 thru 44, will mean that Walters International Speakers' Bureau must eliminate you from our rolls.

Once your professional speaking efforts are put into motion and settle into a solid, productive, upward path, speaker's agents and speakers' bureaus can help you get your career into high gear.

As long as you practice the right attitudes and take the honest approach to the speaking profession, many friends, buyers and bureaus will continue to book business for you. As your bookings increase, so will your income and visibility. Your success will generate even more speaking engagements and opportunities to enrich the lives of hundreds more with your message.

Setting Up Your Business Headquarters

One of the enduring images of success in business is to have your own office and staff of employees. Some popular speakers do, in fact, have large office facilities and a number of workers on their payrolls. Yet, many speakers are able to easily handle their business from a spare room or corner of their own homes with the assistance of their spouse and/or a part-time staff person. A good rule is to hire people to do tasks at which you are no good (or just plain don't like).

If you plan to stay at your present job until your speaking business gets off the ground, then setting up an office at home is a great way to start. Consider, as other successful speakers have, converting a spare room, basement, a guest house, or the garage into an office. Such an office has many advantages.

- more time with family,
- far less expense,
- a spouse or older child often becomes part of the team,
- no need for nursery schools,
- ability to work at odd times without leaving home, and
- eliminates commuting, parking fees, office rent, and other overhead costs.

Speakers are a "commodity," and that commodity is often on the road. Buyers complain about this lack of accessibility to a speaker more than any other issue. The answer? The "virtual office," a computer and modem that travel with you, so wherever you are, there is your office—or a link to it.

The Speaking Road Warrior's Virtual Office

Smart speakers have developed a system for working away from home, because proper time management is essential to continued success. A speaker may be away from the office for one day, sometimes two, or a week or more before returning home.

Speakers who are unable or unwilling to work away from their offices often have stretches of time on the road with nothing to do, while back at the office the pile of work and research to be done escalates. The solitude of travel can be a wonderfully productive time, if you are prepared with tools to use the time to advantage.

How to Be Accessible from the Road

How easy is it to find you? Yes, you think you are easy to locate all the time—after all, you always know where you are. What did you think of those few times your clients mentioned that you were a bit difficult to locate? Did you intellectually dismiss it as just plain silly on their part? Pay attention. Make it easy for them to buy. The information age is giving way to the "access age" which offers all kinds of ways to keep you accessible to your clients.

The world no longer waits for you to return to your home office to answer requests. When a bureau or meeting planner inquires about your availability for a program, a fast answer is needed. If you cannot be reached, you have lost the opportunity for that business. We once tried to reach a speaker for three days, leaving messages on his machine. No response. Our client was waiting. This speaker lost a $5,000 engagement simply because we could not reach him. His lack of a professional response forced us to find another speaker for our client. We called another speaker and reached his answering machine at his office in New York. In less than two hours he had returned our call, even though he was on a tour in London! That is professionalism. Responding to every telephone message promptly, which means within three hours, is the way to jump ahead of your competition. If they can't find you easily, they will use a speaker they can find.

Laptops and the Road Warrior

Most successful speakers have a laptop computer with a fax modem and E-mail. Several times every day they walk over to a phone, plug in, and check their E-mail. They are able to do this from anyplace with a phone: hotel rooms, airports, or even on break in their meeting rooms. Once they have checked their E-mail they log off without replying to it. Now they compose a reply at their leisure, or even during the next break in the seminar.

You may have a message from home letting you know a client needs the outline for the presentation you are presenting for them in a few weeks. No problem. All the information lives in the laptop. Click, click, click. It's E-mailed on their desktop *now*. Another client has left a message on your voice mail, wanting to know your availability for a workshop next year. You check dates, type a few words of reply, then click to the fax this time, (we're pretending this client does not have E-mail), and the fax goes off. Once all the messages have been answered, you log back on, hit the "send" button, and zoom! Everything is delivered for the price of a local phone call to wherever your clients are at that moment.

During waits in airports, or in hotel rooms at night, the laptop comes out again with manuscripts for the books and articles you are working on.

Out-of-Office Work for Speakers Who Are Techno-Challenged

For those of you who are still *technology resisters*, and don't have a ten-year-old in your life who can teach you how to use the technology you need, we understand. Until you can borrow or rent a child, you will need to do your work on the road the old way.

Make a plan for out-of-office work. Plan your calendar months in advance, noting which speeches and articles you can write while on the road. Be sure to pack a folder with the information you will need to accomplish these goals, along with whatever supplies you need to write your material.

1. Use simple, lined legal pads, pencils, and 3 × 5 cards.
2. Rent a typewriter from the hotel.
3. Use a small audio cassette record for dictation, and utilize the hotel's secretarial service to transcribe the tape.

When we interviewed Steve Allen for our *Sharing Ideas for Professional Speakers,* he told us he keeps a number of small audio recording machines around him at all times. Each has a cassette in it labeled for a different project he is working on. It is then easy to travel with one machine and keep one in the office to work on different projects.

You can dictate onto a cassette while on the road, then mail the cassette or carry it back to your office to be transcribed into business letters or speeches.

Be sure to take along a folder of office stationery and your address book, your personalized postcards printed with your picture, and some stamps.

Make arrangements for your mail to catch up with you if you will be gone for a long period. Or, have someone at your office read your mail to you daily over the phone. Be prepared to give instructions for an appropriate reply.

Another method of getting your work to your office for completion is to use a public fax machine. Most hotels have fax machines available.

A Properly Equipped Office Space for Your Home Team

Your office should have real space for storage of files, products, office equipment, and communication equipment. This section will focus on the "real office."

Five Tips on Locating a Home Office

1. The size of your office depends on the scope of what you plan to handle in-house rather than jobbing it out.
2. Do not set up your home office in a hall where there is traffic, near the kitchen with its loud noises, or in the living room, where you will disturb your family—and they will disturb you.

3. Choose a quiet, brightly lit place to work. If you do not have a spare bedroom or den to convert into an office, try starting with a corner of a bedroom where you can shut the door, a partitioned-off section of your garage, or a portion of your basement or attic. Quiet is all important.

4. If possible, choose a room with an outside door and a separate bathroom, so your staff and delivery people can come and go without disturbing the family. Cutting a door to the outside of an existing room is inexpensive compared to adding a whole new room to your home.

5. If need be, consider converting an appropriate section of your home to accommodate this type of office. Who says you must do your "living" in the living room, or the den could not be an office? Take a careful look at the space in your home.

Team Up with Other Speakers

If it is not convenient for you to set up a home office, you can consider teaming up with other speakers to rent office space. New office complexes frequently offer their tenants answering services, copy and facsimile machines, and the use of conference rooms.

Testing Answering Services

If live operators will be answering your calls, be sure to call in and listen carefully to how they answer the phone. If the incoming caller always gets "Hellohold," do not use that answering service.

Technology and the Speaker's Office

Once you master a computer, you will never go back to a slower, old-fashioned typewriter. We finally dragged Dottie (kicking and fighting) into the computer age. She was still using her old Underwood typewriter! She would not even use an electric typewriter; she claimed her old "friend" was faster. She liked whacking those hard old manual keys. She spent at least eight hours a day on that Underwood doing rough drafts of all her correspondence and manuscripts, then her secretary would retype them into the computer! Lilly finally talked Dottie into using a computer. Now Dottie spends 8 to 12 hours on her old Macintosh computer. (She has kept that Underwood in the cabinet in her office, *just in case!* "We may have a power shut down! she insisted.) But her staff is able to turn her documents around in a fraction of the time.

Would you try to do business today without understanding the use of the telephone or copy machine? Of course not! Neither is it acceptable for you to think you are "high-tech" because you finally added a fax to your answering machine.

Introductory computer courses are available from many sources. Check with the nearest community college or your local computer store. Most offer cheap, if not free, computer training. But you will find, as most of us have, that the best way to learn is to just buy a computer and start working.

How Techno-Wild Should You Go?

If you still have not stepped into this compelling technological world, you will not understand this point at all. You have not become *infected* with the strange techno-nerd affliction we all get once we buy our first computer. We find an insatiable need to own *stuff!* We must have the 2.0GB mega-ram 603 microprocessor at 132 Mhz thingy. We have no idea what any of that means, except it does stuff *faster! Better!*

We do suggest that you find ways to be at least as advanced as those to whom you are trying to sell yourself. If most of your prospective buyers use laptop computers, you must learn to use a laptop. If they all use E-mail, then you must learn how to use E-mail.

But you really do not need *every* gizmo the day it is released on the market. One speaker told us he makes the decision to buy new equipment by simply asking himself, "How long would it take and how much would it cost for me to do this task with a pencil?" An honest answer to this question might save you thousands every year.

There are as many possibilities as the mind can imagine in high-tech gizmos. Even if we included them all here today, by the time this book was in your hands tomorrow, they would be passé and outmoded. We feel those listed below are the minimum required to be successful in the speaking industry *today:*

- A computer for your staff with a fax modem.
- A laptop computer with a fax modem for you.

- Word processing software.
- A scanner.
- A dedicated fax machine for incoming faxes.
- E-mail system.
- On-line access (Internet access and services).
- A business communication system: enough telephone lines, voice mail answering system, and a pager or cellular phone.

Set Up a Business Communication System

If you are in the speaking business, you need to be on your phone a lot. If you have only one line, this means your fax is then unusable. If the fax is in use on the one phone line, you are unusable! If your computer is getting your E-mail, you and your fax are both unusable! If business is good, the phones are busy, then what? Your customers get busy signals, are left on hold, or leave messages you don't answer for days. Buyers and bureaus want answers now.

We immediately know we are not dealing with a professional speaker when the speaker has call waiting, or when we are told "Oh, just phone first if you want to send a fax so I can turn it on. If I am not home, just keep phoning me all day until I get home." Your fax must always be on, 24 hours a day. Remember, the other side of the globe is awake while you are asleep. Keep your fax door open to business at all times.

How Many Phone Lines Should You Have in Your Home Office?

You will need at least three phone lines, but you should consider five.

- Two for your incoming and outgoing calls with a call rotating feature and voice mail.
- One separate, dedicated line for incoming faxes.
- One line for the fax/modem on your computer to get E-mail and send outgoing faxes.
- One for your family. (Install a separate unlisted line for family use only. Do not give this number to your clients.)

Promotional Materials and Correspondence

Once you set up your office, you will find that it will quickly fill up with supplies, promotional materials, presentation kits, research files, and machinery such as answering machines, computers and printers. If you keep your supplies and materials organized, you will be able to handle more business efficiently and effectively.

Speakers with the real drive to succeed write books, articles and press releases that enhance their expert image and increase their bookings and fees. Without a scanner and the appropriate disk storage space, these projects take up considerable office space. Not only do you need to store the originals, but you must keep many copies of these materials to send out in your presentation kits to buyers and speakers' bureaus. If you write as much as you should, it will soon become almost impossible to keep all your materials straight without office preplanning.

Staff! Who Will Hold the Horses?

Once your speaking and consulting career gets underway, you will discover quickly that you cannot do everything yourself. The efficiency and success of your business, therefore, will depend on having access to dependable, affordable assistants.

Family as Part of Your Business Team

The majority of professional speakers must have at least one part- or full-time office person running things while they are on the road. We have noted an interesting cycle:

1. In the early days of the speaker's career, family members are the easiest and most economical assistants to employ in this capacity. Many speakers start on a shoestring in their homes and hire family member as staff.

2. As the speaker become more successful, they often move to an office in a fancy building, hire staff, and incur very large overhead. Now, in addition to being on the road to speak, they are also away from home when they are in town.

3. After a few years of being on the road and driving back and forth to the office, they buy a larger home, streamline the business to its most productive areas, and move their office back home again. Often, they again call on family members to run the office and thus gain income formerly paid to outsiders.

Your family is very interested in your career, so they often make the best partners you can find. We have always included our family in our businesses. Talk shop with them, ask for their opinions, and work with them as part of the team. Three generations of the Walters family are now working in our business.

Rewarding Your Family Staff

When spouses, family, and staff are *included* in goals, plans and rewards, they will be fervent in their support rather than resentful toward your business. Success in any business is no accident, so form your own team of staff and family.

Commission incentives for your family team are a big motivator! If you are willing to pay an outsider, then show the same respect to every member of your family when you expect them to do the same task. Don't bring your family in and expect them to work for free. Your family members will soon refuse to work with you, and the work you do get out of them will be sullen and inferior. Teach them the value of results and rewards. If you ask them to do a task that you would have needed to pay an employee $10 an hour for, how can you justify not paying them the same? On the other hand, do not pay them for substandard work. Expect them to perform better, longer, and harder than the rest of your team, just as you expect more from yourself.

Hiring Staff Outside Your Family

Before you bring in a staff person, create a list of qualifications and skills that you require, and a list of other skills that would be beneficial but not necessarily required. For instance, bookkeeping skills might be mandatory, and graphic skills a nice plus, but not necessary. Or sales skills might be at the top of your list, and slow typing skills acceptable. Think of what the perfect person in your business might be. Take the time to create a qualifications checklist before you hire someone.

Once you have a good idea of what you need, decide if you would be better served by using alternatives to traditional staff.

Alternatives to the Traditional Office Staff

There are at least several alternatives if you decide that you do not want, or cannot afford, a full-time office staff.

If you are currently employed and plan to do paid speaking on a part-time basis, here is an idea. Ask a secretary in your present business to consider doing work for you in the evenings and weekends at home. This person should know your wants, habits and dislikes and be well-suited to assist you by doing such tasks as picking up your messages from your answering service, going to the post office to pick up and drop off mail, process mail and orders for you, and make routine phone calls.

Also consider the Remote Office Management Companies we talked about earlier in this chapter, in the section "The Speaking Road Warrior's Virtual Office."

As your career develops, your office support needs will be sporadic. If you can set up a system to pay your assistants by the job instead of by the hour, you will do better than having a helper sitting in your office full-time with work that is only part-time.

Outside Services

Try using professional outside vendors and service companies for secretarial, copying, mailing, answering service, facsimile (fax) delivery, collating and bookkeeping needs.

Some secretarial services will send out a speaker's press kit and other promotional materials. They will keep your letterhead stationery on hand so that you can dictate letters to them over the phone, by fax, or by audio cassette. In this way, you can keep your business moving ahead while you are on the road.

By using outside services, you do more than eliminate the hassle of having to keep many employee payroll records. Withholding taxes, vacations, sick leave, and unemployment benefits will also be eliminated.

Hiring an Inside Sales and Marketing Person

One of the first people you may want to add to your growing staff is an inside marketing person who is good at selling your speaker services and products. You may want to use some of the following techniques:

- Be sure to put the words "telephone" and "sales" in your ad copy. There is no use hiring someone who dislikes either one.
- Hire your marketer from his or her phone personality. Put your phone number in the ad and have respondents call you. Listen to their voice projection and their telephone personalities. Consider having them call a private line with an answering device. Your message should give simple instructions about leaving their resumes on the voice message machine. You want to know how their personalities sound, and if they can follow instructions.

Once you narrow down your candidates from their phone charisma, you will be ready for in-person interviews:

- Observe how prospects move when you meet them. One way is to arrange the situation so that they must walk a distance toward you while you are seated at a desk. Watch the walk. If they drag along, slouch, or have no bounce—look out! Another way to judge by movement is to have candidates come in one at a time. Get up and move the interview chair a few feet away after each applicant leaves. Then ask the new applicant to "Please, pull up a chair and sit down." You will be astounded by the results. You will hear various responses:

    "No, I like it where it is." (This one will argue with you about everything.)

    "Move it where?" (This one does not listen.)

    "I would be glad to," with a smile. Hire this one!

    The applicant's reply will give you an instant view of the cooperativeness, pleasantness, attention, and concentration of the person.

- Ask candidates when they want to start. If they say "Right now," or "Thursday morning," hire them. Someone who whines and says, "Well, I *guess,* I could *try* to get stuff arranged for *maybe* Thursday . . ." will drive you crazy with a lack of drive and constant excuses. This candidate will continue to give you excuses for not producing, or showing up for work.

Training Your Marketing Person

We strongly suggest you give your marketing person a copy of this book. In addition:

- Have the new worker sit by you while you make the calls for the first day. Next, sit by him or her and listen for at least two days more. Praise every good thing that is done.
- Show the new marketing person how to keep records of calls made and bookings closed.
- Pay a good salary, but not a high one. Pay high commissions with bonuses and perks.
- Ask the marketing person about personal weekly goals. Put those goals on the wall, then reward the achievement of those goals. Help other employees set their sights higher each time they achieve their marks. Increase the commission percentage as the goal goes higher.

Remember the advice given by Knute Rockne when he was asked for his formula to bring out the best in his team members. He responded, "Some players need a pat on the back. Some need a kick a bit further down. I give each team player what they need to get them going."

Phone Tips, Tricks, and Professionalism

Teach your team to answer your phone with the right words and a warm, smiling, positive tone. For example, "Thank you for calling the Walters office. How may I help you?"

You and your company are judged by how well your phone is answered. A grumpy teenager with a mouth full of peanut butter who mumbles, "No, dunno where she is. Call back." (Slam!) does not project a good business image.

Hold a staff training conference and discuss methods of answering the phone and taking messages. Whoever answers your phone should enhance your image as a successful, highly paid professional speaker.

Set Up Your Office for Quick Response

- Have message pads, client inquiry sheets, and pens ready by every telephone.

- Answer your phone on the first ring to let callers know you are ready and able to help them.

Teach everyone what to say and how to say it.

- Do not let anyone answer your phone with "Hellohold." No one likes to be ignored or put on hold.

- It is most important that the person answering your phone project a caring, friendly attitude.

- Teach your team to take messages. Never ask someone if they would mind calling back later. Trust us—they mind! *Take a message.* Teach your people to take complete messages with all the information you will need to solve problems and give service when you return that call.

- Teach your staff to close with, "Thank you for calling us!" and mean it.

- Teach your staff the words that convey concern to every customer: "She very much wants to speak to you about this. She will call you back as soon as possible."

- Teach them to say, "I will find out for you!" instead of "I don't know."

- Have them convey the sound of success on the phone by moderating their voice tone. Clients interpret a bored and uninterested voice as saying, "We don't care about you." Train staff to say, "Thank you for calling us!" by matching the sound of each note as they go up the musical scale from middle C to G. Let them hear the difference between the tones of "hellos" that go up the scale (positive) or down (negative). Bringing the voice up at the end of a sentence works well, too, because it makes the listener lean forward, eager to hear more.

- Hang a mirror by the phone. A mirror shows how you sound to your clients. Your voice actually changes when you smile, so you will sound much better when you have a pleasant expression. A mirror with the word "smile" written on it will remind you and your people that the telephone is the front door to your business.

Create the Right Environment

- Use a headset, the kind that are lightweight and leave your hands free to take notes, keyboard data into the computer, or look through the files. Headsets enable you and your team to keep your head upright in a normal position so that you project a more vibrant, outgoing, "professional speaker" image. Your hands can work a computer at full speed while you listen with a headset.

- Use a long telephone cord. It enables you to stand up, walk around your desk, step over to your filing cabinet, pick up a file, etc. We like standing up when calling, and do this as a habit. The long cord enables us to move around, grab material, and keep our circulation moving. You can even open the door for a delivery person while you talk, or you can do a couple of wall push-ups. A long cord enables you to sound full of life, excitement and dynamism because you feel physically better than if you have been sitting all day while you talk on the phone. A long cord is an investment well worth its low price.

Business Goals for Your Entire Team

Set your speaking goals. Goals are dreams with a deadline. Put them up where everyone in your office can see them and make every bit of work you do propel you toward them. When you reach those goals, aim for new ones immediately. Put up the new goals like an athlete raising the height of the jump bar.

We have seen instances where the actions of family or staff members almost sabotaged a business, because they felt left out. Lavish praise and rewards on your staff. The day you achieve your goal, reward them. Then set up a new and higher goal.

ò▲

Curtain Up!

We suspect that before you read this book you may have thought professional paid speaking meant you stood in front of an audience and delivered a 45-minute speech. We hope *Speak and Grow Rich* has opened your eyes to the myriad opportunities that paid speaking offers throughout the world.

You are about to step into a dance with your audiences, your customers, and the great minds of the ages. As you take each step, *Speak and Grow Rich* will act as your instruction manual and your source of information and inspiration.

We wish you the very best with your speaking career. Never stop learning and growing. If we may assist you as you *Speak and Grow Rich,* be your mentors as we are to thousands of other speakers, just contact us at P.O. Box 1120, Glendora, California 91740.

Glossary

Ad hominem: When you direct your argument to your audience's personal feelings, emotions, or prejudices rather than their intellect or reason.

Agenda: A list of things to be done; especially, a program of business at a meeting. "Agenda" is plural of the Latin gerund *agendum,* and it is used today in the sense of "a plan or list of matters to be acted upon." Agenda is a singular noun; its plural is usually agendas: The meeting's agenda will be printed in the program.

Agent: Representative of speakers. Usually the speaker has an "exclusive" agreement with one agent which may include a guaranteed number of dates per year. The guarantee usually applies only to celebrity speakers. Speakers are clients. Agents often are in charge of publicity. Bureaus broker with them for dates with their exclusive celebrity client speakers. Speakers in the $10,000 and above range have agents.

Apron: The part of a theater stage in front of the curtain.

Audience participation: When the speaker has the audience do something other than listen to a lecture, e.g., discussions or games. Some will argue that when audience members are actively listening, they are participating.

Audience response system: Typically, attendees sit in front of a big screen, and have keypads, one-way video, two-way audio, and record responses to a presentation.

Autograph table: Many speakers call the table on which they sell their products at the back of the room the Autograph Table.

Autoresponder: See Mailbot.

A/V booth, A/V area: Area of the meeting where the audiovisual is controlled (see Sound Booth and Tech Booth).

A/V: Abbreviation for "Audiovisual."   Refers to all the audio and visual requirements of an event, e.g., overhead projectors, tape recorders, video players, microphone needs, etc. This term came into usage in 1935–40 (see Sound Booth and Tech Booth).

Back-of-Room sales: Selling books and other products at the back of the room, usually immediately after the speech. Sometimes referred to as BOR sales.

Billing: The order in which the names of speakers or entertainers are listed in a program, brochure, advertisement, playbill, etc. and the position in such a listing.

Bio: Short for biography. See Biographical sheet.

Biographical sheet: Usually referred to as the bio, curriculum vitae, CV, or vitae. Lists speaker's credits and a brief history of career. For speakers and presenters this is not a job resume. Length can be one paragraph, usually not longer than one double-spaced page.

Blocking: 1. The way you present yourself, your props, your lighting, and your equipment. 2. The path of action you take to move from one spot to another on stage. If done well, it gives the greatest clarity of movement for the communication.

Bounce-back: An offer included with an order.

Breakout session(s), breakout: The break-out of the main group into smaller groups. A session at a convention or meeting where attendees are divided into several concurrent sessions to hear special material on differing special interest topics.

Broadcast classroom: A speech or lecture that is broadcast to other students. The old Romper Room TV shows were broadcast sessions. Today this usually refers to a live presentation in a distance learning situation.

Bureau (speakers):   See Speakers' bureau.

Business television: Communication network used for in-house communication. A network could be extended to include others, possibly prospects or customers. This is live or prerecorded television delivered via satellite or phone lines for private business use. It offers companies a fast, powerful, and impactful way of disseminating corporate news, product information, and training programs to staff and customers.

Buyer: The person or group who signs the contract and pays for the speaker. Usually a meeting planner, employed by an association or corporation. Referred to as the client by bureaus, as the buyer by agents.

Byline: The line at the head of a news story or article in a newspaper, magazine, etc., giving the name of the writer. This is a U.S. term from the 1920s from the world of graphics in journalism.

Camera-ready: A piece of material that is of a quality ready to be photographed for reproduction by a printing press, copy machine, or camera.

Presenters are often asked to develop handouts or workbooks to supplement their talks and are often asked to supply an "original" (the master image from which identical copies are produced) for event coordinators. Most coordinators request this master original to be camera-ready so they will not need the piece typeset.

Canned: For speakers, this has come to mean a standard speech or presentation. The myth is that if a speech is "canned," the audience is left feeling they were listening to the same old thing, like a recording. This only happens when speakers lose their enthusiasm for that same old speech and it shows to the audience.

Chestnuts: Stories, jokes or songs that have been overused and are stale.

Classroom style seating: When the seating for the audience is set up with tables in front of seats.

Client: Whomever is paying for the service. A company or association are clients when they buy the speaker. A speaker may be the client of an agent who is paid to manage him or her.

Community service speakers' bureau: A speakers' bureau that sends presenters into a community of industry, usually at little or no cost, to speak on topics that promote the sponsoring company or on public awareness issues.

Concluder: In a speech, the final remarks made to finish the presentation. A concluder could be used by the speaker to close a presentation, but it also refers to the remarks the MC or announcer makes to conclude that particular session.

Concurrent (sessions): Concurrent or breakout session. (See Breakout.)

Consultant: Person who gives professional or technical advice. Speakers often consult with clients to prepare customized material for programs or workbooks for an added fee. An example might be an expert who sits in on telephone complaint calls in order to prepare material for workshops to train employees in handling problem customers. The term came into usage in the late 1600s.

Cooperatives: A group of speakers, with varying ideas of expertise, who team up to share leads and marketing expenses.

Cordless: Short for cordless microphone; wireless mike. A cordless could be handheld or a lavaliere. (See Lavaliere.)

Curriculum vitae: Also called just plain vitae or CV. A brief biographical resume of the presenter's career and training. This term is most commonly used by the academic community. (See Biographical sheet.)

Curtain speech: A talk given in front of the curtain at the conclusion of an event, most often thought of as coming from the theatrical world.

Curtain: The concluding line of speech, or the concluding speech, line, or scene of an entire event.

CV: See Curriculum vitae and Biographical sheet.

Dais: A raised platform, as at the front of a room, that the speaker presents from. Also called platform, podium, riser, or stage from the Latin *discus*—table.

Date clear: Formal permission to clear a date that is being tentatively held for a booking.

Demo: Audio or visual demonstration tapes. Used to promote speakers' services or speeches to buyers.

Direct-broadcast satellite (DBS) television: DBS refers to the high-power satellite broadcasting that can be directly received by consumers with small antennas.

Direct mail sales: When products are sold directly to the consumer via the mail.

Distance learning: The United States Distance Learning Association defines distance learning as "The delivery of education or training through electronically mediated instruction, including satellite, video, audiographic, computer, multimedia technology and other forms of learning at a distance." The term Distance Learning is often interchanged with Distance Education, sometimes referred to as Distributed Education, possibly because of the several medias used.

Downstage: At or toward the front of the stage.

Electronic whiteboard: A computerized version of a clear drawing or writing space, but in desktop videoconferencing, it appears on everyone's screen.

Emcee: Informal way of saying the Master of Ceremonies at a banquet, often spelled MC. (Also see Introducer, Master of Ceremonies, MC, and Toastmaster.)

Emoticon: On the Internet, emoticons are drawings composed of text characters that allow for a show of emotion (hence the name emoticon). Here are just a few (tilt your head to the left to see the effect):
:) is a smile, ;) is a wink, >:-) is a devil, 0:-) is an angel.

Exclusive: The speaker signs an agreement with an agent to handle all of his or her speaking engagements. Bureaus broker with the Exclusive Agent to obtain the speaker for their client. The bureau and the agent split the commission. Sometimes done on a regional or market basis. (See Partial exclusive.)

Experimental exercise: Audience participation exercise in which the lessons learned are derived from experience used to convey the lesson. (See Audience participation.)

Extemporaneous: Prepared with regard to content but not read or memorized word for word. From the Latin *ex*—out plus *itempus, temporis*—time.

Firm: An engagement that is definitely confirmed.

Flip chart: A chart with pieces of paper, usually set on an easel. Used by the speaker to clarify points. (See Easel.)

Flyer: A one-sheet piece of printed advertising, letter or legal size. Often produced to promote the presenter's program, products, or services.

Footpace: A raised platform in a room, as for a lecturer; a dais.

Forum: 1. An assembly for discussion of any variety of topics. 2. Electronic forums are online discussion groups. They're the electronic equivalent of the office water cooler. This word comes from the public marketplace of an ancient Roman city, where popular assemblies met and most legal and political business was transacted.

General assembly (session):   A gathering of all attendees at a meeting or convention; usually implies a session other than a meal function. A general assembly often, but certainly not always, follows a meal session, in the same room, because everyone is already sitting in that location.

Glossy: Short for a glossy photograph. Usually refers to a black-and-white promotional photograph of the presenter. Also called a black-and-white or B&W.

Green room: Room backstage in a theater, broadcasting studio, or the like, where speakers can relax when they are not on-stage, on-camera, etc.

Gross fee: The total fee the buyer is charged for a booking, including agents' fees, excluding expenses.

Handheld: Short for a handheld microphone. A handheld may come in a corded or cordless version.

Handout: Informative or educational material given to the audience at the speaker's presentation. Often in flyer form. Term refers to anything that is handed out to the audience.

Hands-free mike: Microphone that attaches to a speaker's clothing.

Head table: Table at the front of the room. Reserved for the key people at a meeting.

Heart story: A story that touches the heart, spirit, or soul of the listener. They are usually thought of as those vignettes that bring a tear to the eye.

Heightening: Intensifying the audience's or the presenter's awareness, sensitivity, or understanding of a subject. Presenters heighten themselves when their presentation creates a greater enthusiasm and/or a great dimension through their connection to the audience. The audience is heightened if the connection is made and understanding and enlightenment dawn in their minds.

Honorarium: Payment given to a speaker. Usually refers to politicians and others in industries that forbid a set fee for speaking.

House (the): Slang expression for the building in which you are speaking, or for the number of attendees in the building.

House lights: The lights that illuminate the audience rather than the stage.

Hypermedia: A computer-based information retrieval system that enables you to gain (or provide) access to texts, audio and video recordings, photographs, and computer graphics related to any subject that another user has made available.

IDL: Interactive Distance Learning.

Inforbot: See Mailbot.

Improvisation: To compose and perform or deliver a speech (or music, verse, drama, etc.) without previous thought or preparation. From the Latin *in*—not and *provire*—to foresee.

Infomercial: A commercial television program or relatively long commercial segment offering consumer information, such as educational or instructional material, related to the sponsor's product or service.

In-house: When the audience is composed of only employees of the same company.

Instant demo: A new experimental method of having the speaker's demo played for prospective buyers by calling an 800 toll-free telephone line.

Interactive broadcasts: A message sent from one to many that has the ability for those receiving to send it back. At a receiving site there is some way for the viewers to respond to the instructor (phone or keypad).

Interactive television network: *Larry King Live* is an interactive television show. Interactive television network in the business setting means a closed, in-house setting.

Internet (the): The world's largest computer network. A global network of networks or inter-network, therefore "Internet." The "Net" evolved in the U.S. from a military research program in the late 1960s, but today the government has almost no role in its operation; the Net is unregulated and extends far beyond America's boundaries. The Net's underlying technologies have given it flexibility, openness, and enormous capacity for growth. As a social network the Internet supports a large community—tens of millions of people throughout the world. On AOL, you too can use your computer to interact with others around the world. And you can search the Net for information on just about every subject.

Internet provider: The company you buy your Internet access from.

Internet server: The machine(s) that your Internet provider uses.

Introducer: The person who introduces the speaker and usually leads the audience into a look at the speaker's history. Also see Emcee, Master of Ceremonies, MC, and Toastmaster. From the Latin *intro*—within and *ducere*—to lead.

I.P.A.: The International Platform Association. A U.S.-based association for public speakers.

ISP: Internet Service Provider.

Keynote: Originally meant the fundamental point of a speech, today refers to the main speech at a meeting. One of the featured spots at an event, such as a meal function or to open or close an event, to the entire convention in the main room. Often presented by the celebrity speaker. Sets the tone of the convention, and carries out the theme.

Kiosks (interactive): A small structure, often open on one or more sides, used as a newsstand or booth, or a cylindrical structure on which advertisements are posted. An automatic teller machine at your back is a type of *interactive kiosk*. Any similar structure used as a booth where attendees, perhaps at a trade show, would go and gather information, might be called a kiosk. If it is interactive, it would usually be electronic and have a method for the viewer to gather information in various forms: text only or multimedia. *Multimedia kiosks* are often designed and constructed for trade shows and marketing displays. Customized features may include: touch-screen monitors with video, audio and text interaction; CD-ROM capabilities; and custom card scanning devices for automated mailing of selected documents such as sales and marketing brochures.

Lavaliere: A hands free microphone that attaches to your lapel or part of your clothing, as opposed to a stationary or hand-held mike. Can be on a cord or cordless. Originally a lavaliere was a pendant, from the French *la vallière*—a round or oval ornament worn on a chain around the neck, named after Louise de La Vallière, 1644–1710, mistress of Louis XIV.

Lectern: Small desk or stand with sloping top from which you present a lecture (see Lecture). Sometimes it has a stationary or hand-held mike attached, a shelf underneath, and a light. Sometimes called (many will argue incorrectly) the podium.

Lecture: A discourse given before an audience. The archaic meaning of the word "lecture" is "the act of reading aloud." From the Latin *agere*—to read.

Lyceium: 1. A hall where public speeches, concerts, etc., are presented. 2. An organization sponsoring public programs and entertainment. The word comes from the Greek *Lukeion,* a grove near Athens in which Aristotle taught school (335–323 B.C.).

Mailbot: Infobot (aka autoresponder). The Mailbot is a variation on the E-mail concept of transmission of unlimited text-based information to anybody with an Internet connection. Also known as Inforbot.

Master: Of or pertaining to a master from which copies are made. In photography, a master film (also called a copy negative); in recording, an audio or video tape or disk from which duplicates may be made; in printing, the camera-ready piece used to make other copies from, for handouts, workbooks, overheads, etc.

Master of Ceremonies: The person who acts as a moderator and connects the separate sessions at a meeting together. Also see Emcee, Introducer, MC, and Toastmaster.

Materials: The things you use in your presentations: handouts, products, giveaways, workbooks.

MC: Pronounced MC as it is written, it is an abbreviation of Master of Ceremonies. Sometimes spelled emcee. Also see Emcee, Introducer, Master of Ceremonies, and Toastmaster.

Media: 1. All the ways of communicating with the public, as radio and television, newspapers and magazines. 2. An area or form of artistic expression, or the materials used by the artist or speaker. The media a speaker uses would be the "tools" he or she uses, such as overheads or videos. Dianna Booher, business communications expert, says, ". . . or, used more loosely when referring to speakers, 'media' may refer to pantomime, magic, drama or any other means of conveying a message or feeling other than words." Media is the plural form of medium; it was first used in reference to newspapers two centuries ago and meant "an intervening agency, means or instrument."

Meeting planner: Person in charge of all planning for the meeting—logistics, meals, hotel arrangements, roomsets, travel, and often hiring of the speakers. Often called simply the "planner."

Menu: Fee schedule listing all programs and prices offered by a speaker.

Module: A self-contained section of a presentation.

Moniker or Monicker: An informal term for a name, signature or nickname. (Probable blend of monogram and marker.)

MPI: Meeting Professionals International. An association for those involved in all aspects of the meeting professions.

MPINet: The online forum of MPI located on CompuServe.

Multicasting: A computer term, meaning taking data and sending it out in one long stream in such a way that many people (users) can "grab" it. For example, if you scream down a hallway, in a multicast situation, everyone who opens a door in that hallway would get the data (in this analogy the "scream"). This allows trainers to send the message/data just once. A speech to a live audience could be considered multicasting. Giving the speech to each person separately would not.

Multimedia: The combined use of several media, as sound and full-motion video in computer applications. A speaker may use overheads, videos, and live music in a multimedia presentation.

Multimedia authoring: A tool that allows you to create multimedia training systems.

NSA: National Speakers Association (of the United States).

On-site: Where an event is held. Also refers to an event where meeting planners preview a hotel or venue as a prospective meeting location.

Overhead projector: A projector of images from transparent pieces of film onto a screen.

P.A.: The public address system. The loudspeaker equipment that amplifies sound to the audience.

Padding: Extraneous material added to written work, such as a speech, to make it longer.

Panel: A group of speakers and others are often presented to discuss a subject. Audiences are encouraged to participate in a question and answer period. Speakers may be paid, or offer this service free as an inducement to close the contract for the main event.

Partial exclusive: When an agent or bureau has an exclusive contract with the speaker for a select area. Example: Only the college market, or only Texas, etc.

Photo-quality: See Camera-ready.

Pit: The main floor of the auditorium of a theater, especially the rear part; also, the audience sitting in this section.

Plagiarism: An act of artistic or literary theft. This word goes back to the Latin word *plagiarus,* meaning kidnapping—especially in keeping and stealing of a child, not the act of holding children for ransom. So when you used someone else' words or thoughts as your own, you kidnap them.

Planner: See Meeting planner.

Platform: The raised area or dais on which speakers stand while they address an audience.

Plenary (session): A general session, that is fully or completely attended by everyone at a meeting, in comparison to the breakout sessions where we "break" them into groups and several meetings are going on at the same time.

Plug: An advertisement, not in the form of a formal ad; usually a mention, either given verbally from the platform or written in a publication, to help promote a product or service.

PMT: Acronym for "photo mechanical transfer." (See Camera-ready.)

Podium: Often a riser or risers; a small stage; also called a dais, platform or riser. This word comes from the same root as pedal and podiatrist (the Greek word *podion*—diminutive of *pous, podos*) meaning foot. So the podium is the place you step on. But common usage is wearing away at the correct translation of this word. Although not all new dictionaries have given in to those who insist on calling the lectern a podium, sometimes podium will be used to refer to the lectern.

Power pack: A set of speaker materials, such as three audio cassette albums plus a book, sold as a set. May be any combination of materials. Usually offered at a special sale price to an audience.

PR: Abbreviation of public relations—promotion, publicity, advertising— all the tools of keeping a speaker in the public's eye.

Premium(s): A prize or an award. Something offered free or at a reduced price as an inducement to buy something else.

Press kit: A promotional package that includes the speaker's letters of recommendation, audio and/or visual tapes, bio, articles written by and about the speaker, and other promotional materials. The name originates from the promotional packages that were originally sent to the press— newspapers, media, etc.—to help promote someone.

Pro bono speech: A speech done without compensation for the public good. (Latin *pro bono (publico)*, for the (public) good, *pro,* for and *bono,* ablative of *bonum,* the good.)

Product(s): Items the speaker has available for sale; usually books, audio cassettes, videos, workbooks, posters, etc.

Production company: A vendor that helps produce a meeting or event. A production company might handle the taping, lighting, sound, and, on occasion, even bring in the speakers and entertainers.

Professional speaker: A public speaker who is paid a fee for performances.

Projector: An apparatus for sending a picture onto a screen: overhead projector, slide projector, film projector.

Promotional package: See Press kit.

Prompter: An electronic display of a magnified written text so that it is visible to the presenter on a clear screen but is invisible to the audience.

Prorate: A verb, meaning to divide, distribute, or assess proportionately. Speakers often prorate their expenses between clients on a tour.

Public domain: Material and things on which the copyright or patent has expired or that never had any such protection. This is material anyone can use and not give credit.

Public seminar: A public seminar is open to the public, rather than open only to a specific group. Tickets are sold to individuals, rather than the costs being paid by one overall group.

Public service bureau: See Community service bureau.

Public speaker: Someone who speaks in public.

Q & A: The question and answer session of a presentation.

Real time: In the duplication process of audio and video tapes, a tape can be duplicated at a high-speed rate. Sometimes, especially in editing, the tapes are worked with at real time, the same time they were recorded in, not a high or slow speed.

Referral: When someone suggests you to other buyers.

Repeat engagement or booking: When a speaker does a second booking for the same client.

Risers: Short portable platforms used to raise an area in the front of the room so that the presentation may be more easily seen by the audience. A portable stage, dais or podium. Also called dais, platform, podium, or stage.

Road show: Originally this meant a show presented by a troupe of theatrical performers on tour. Today some speakers use this as slang for a tour of repeated speeches and accompanying performances or events.

Role-play: An audience participation exercise in which the audience or presenter pretend to have the attitudes, actions and dialog of another, usually in a make-believe situation. This sort of exercise is used in an effort to heighten understanding of differing points of view or social interaction.

Rostrum: The dais or stage area used by a speaker. The platform for speakers in the Forum of ancient Rome was decorated with the bows of ships captured in war. Guess what these bows were called? You got it! "Rostrums." Rostrum came to mean any platform for speakers in ancient Rome.

Satellite TV: Business television that is delivered via satellite rather than phone.

Seasoning the presentation: Things that increase the enjoyment, zest, or impact of a presentation.

Second time (booking): A booking with a client you have spoken for before, also called a repeat engagement or booking.

Seminar: Classroom-type lecture. One hour to many days. Usually an educational session. At a convention, the breakout or concurrent sessions are often referred to as seminars. Usually thought of as having more lecture formats than a workshop.

Seminar leader: Teacher. Sessions can be two hours to several days. Teacher is an expert who instructs seminar attendees in depth.

Set piece: A speech or part of a speech planned beforehand and carried out according to a prescribed pattern or formula.

Shared whiteboard: Usually refers to an electronic whiteboard that is accessible to several users, at remote locations, at the same time. When one user draws or writes something, it appears on everyone else's computer screen.

Sight line(s): Any of the lines of sight between the audience and the stage/presentation area. When a presenter is offstage, he or she is out of the sight line, in a place where the audience can't see the speaker.

Signature story: A story that is credited to a specific person, that is as unique as his or her own signature. These sorts of stories are not public domain. It is considered very bad form to used someone else's signature story, especially without crediting the owner.

Site: The location of the meeting, sometimes called the venue.

Slick: See Camera-ready.

Snail mail: Mail that does not travel electronically, e.g. mail sent by postal service or a next-day carrier.

Sound booth: The area where the controls for the sound are kept, referred to as a booth regardless of how it is set up. Often it will be set up on a dais in a corner of the room, and will be combined with the tech booth. May also be referred to as the A/V booth or A/V area. (See Tech booth.)

Sound; sound system: The audio sound amplification systems for speakers.

Speakers' bureau: A booking or sales company that provides speakers and humorists for meeting planners. They usually represent speakers on a nonexclusive basis.

Special event broadcast: Business television that is used for a special meeting. This implies a network set up just for one event.

Special events company: Brings in all kinds of special effects and theatrical acts. May contract to put on an entire convention, or parts of it. Sometimes also hires speakers.

Spin-off(s): A speaking engagement that occurs because of another speaking engagement, either from referrals or from someone in the audience that day.

Spokesperson: A person who speaks for, in the name of, or in behalf of another, a company, or an association.

Stage left: The side of the stage that is left of center as the presenter faces the audience. Also called left stage.

Stage lights: The lights that illuminate the stage area.

Stage right: The side of the stage that is right of center as the presenter faces the audience. Also called right stage.

Symposium: Today means a meeting for discussion of a particular subject, or a collection of comments or opinions brought together; perhaps a series of brief essays or articles on the same subject, as in a magazine.

Tailoring: The speaker's adjustment of the material to the particular needs of the audience.

Tech booth: The area of the meeting from which the sound, lights, and technical equipment are controlled. Referred to as a booth regardless of how it is set up. Often it will be set up on a dais in a corner of the room. The sound booth is often part of the tech booth. (See Sound booth.)

Tech crew: The people who operate the sound, lights, and technical equipment.

Technical writer: Speaker who prepares scripts, workbooks, audios, videos, and articles for a client on contract. Fee varies according to complexity and time involved.

Teleconferences: A conference held among people in different locations by means of telecommunications equipment, such as closed-circuit television or phone lines.

Telecourse: A course of televised lectures. Often used in academia.

Teleprompter: See Prompter.

Testimonial: Usually a written letter of recommendation from a former buyer or colleague who is familiar with your work.

Theatre style seating: When the seating for the audience is set up in rows, much like in a theatre, with no tables.

Toastmaster/mistress: A person who, at public dinners, announces the toasts, calls upon the various speakers, etc. Also see, Emcee, Introducer, and Master of Ceremonies.

Toastmasters International: One of the largest personal development associations in the world to assist in building confidence in public communication skills.

Trade-out: An exchange or barter of services and/or products for all or part of a speaker's fee.

Transcript: To copy or recopy in handwriting, typewriting, or electrical recording, a presentation or program of any type. From the Latin *trans*—over and *scribere*—to write.

Two-step seminar: One free seminar at which attendees are encouraged to buy a second seminar or set of products.

Upstage: The part of the stage farthest away from the audience. (See Downstage.)

URL: Universal resource locator. Your website address.

Velox: A brand name for a film paper. (See Camera-ready.)

Venue: Site of the meeting or event, often a hotel, conference, convention center, college or restaurant. Originally used to mean the place where the action was. Middle English used venue to mean attach, probably because they took it from the Latin *venir*—to come.

Videoconference: A teleconference conducted via television video/audio system. Includes two-way audio and two-way video, as compared to business TV, which normally has only one-way video, and two-way audio.

Vitae: See Curriculum vitae and Biographical sheet.

Web: See World Wide Web.

Web browser: A software program that allows you to navigate your way around the Internet. The "windows" of the Internet.

Wings: Sides of the stage in an auditorium, out of sight of the audience.

Wireless: A wireless mike without a cord. Works by radio waves through the PA system.

Workshop (session):   Educational, classroom-type session, usually with handouts or workbooks. Rarely less than one hour, could be as long as many days. Usually considered to use more audience participation and experiential exercises and project assignments than a seminar.

World Wide Web: World Wide Web is officially described as a "wide-area hypermedia information retrieval initiative aiming to give universal access to a large universe of documents."

Index